D0585003

TANGO JULIET FOXTROT

TANGO JULIET FOXTROT

HOW DID IT ALL GO WRONG FOR BRITISH POLICING?

IAIN DONNELLY

Biteback Publishing

First published in Great Britain in 2021 by
Biteback Publishing Ltd, London
Copyright © Iain Donnelly 2021

ISBN 978-1-78590-716-6

10 9 8 7 6 5 4 3 2 1

A CIP catalogue record for this book is available from the British Library.

Set in Minion Pro

Printed and bound in Great Britain by
CPI Group (UK) Ltd, Croydon CR0 4YY

This book is dedicated to the men and women of the British police service past and present. I'm very proud to have been a member of your family.

CONTENTS

Introduction   ix

Chapter 1   TV cops vs real-life cops   1
Chapter 2   What am I going to do with my life?   11
Chapter 3   Familiarisation   19
Chapter 4   Selection   25
Chapter 5   Training school   31
Chapter 6   Street duties training   45
Chapter 7   First relief   63
Chapter 8   Clapham   77
Chapter 9   The model police officer   83
Chapter 10 Institutionally racist?   101
Chapter 11 Inner-city violence and deprivation   113
Chapter 12 Special Branch   127
Chapter 13 Terrorism   145
Chapter 14 Sent to Coventry   165
Chapter 15 Staff officer   187
Chapter 16 Stechford   195
Chapter 17 PPU   207

Chapter 18 Sexual exploitation   219

Chapter 19 CTU   229

Chapter 20 CSE project   241

Chapter 21 Chief inspector   253

Chapter 22 Operational superintendent   269

Chapter 23 Last twelve months   285

Chapter 24 Can we turn it around?   295

Chapter 25 Do I think that the job is actually fucked?   319

Appendix   The UK police service – how does it work?   333

Acknowledgements   343

INTRODUCTION

I am no longer a police officer.

But every single day memories about some of the things that I did over the course of a long career in policing pass through my mind. Running breathless through suburban back gardens, vaulting over garden fences and demolishing some of them in the process whilst chasing a burglar. Rolling around on the pavement with a violent criminal who's trying to escape, desperately trying to get to my radio to call for help. Sat in the back of my surveillance van in central London, stripped to my underwear on a boiling hot summer's day with sweat pouring down my face. Patiently watching a doorway through the viewfinder of my camera before snapping the image of some terrorists meeting in public for the first time. Crying with laughter at the results of a complex, well-planned and cruel practical joke played on a colleague who was sent on a wild goose chase to the other side of London to pick up a non-existent prize of £500. Removing the soiled clothes from a dead child in a mortuary and taking them to a high-street launderette, before delivering them back to his heartbroken parents.

Can you imagine having a job where every day you cannot wait to start work and where every day is completely different? A job where you, and the teams that you are part of, change thousands of people's lives for the better and you all have incredible fun in the process? Can you imagine having a job where you meet every type of person, from every single part of this rich, diverse, vibrant nation, and offer them the hand of friendship? A job where you can encounter the deep sadness, joy, fear and excitement of life in the course of a single day?

I had that job for thirty years, between 1989 and 2019. However, somehow, something went very badly wrong somewhere along the way.

It's very hard to pinpoint when I thought, for the first of many times, that everything was going wrong in British policing. I don't know exactly when this realisation occurred, but what I do know for certain is that those tragicomic events began to become so frequent that what had previously felt like isolated moments of pathos quite quickly became the new normal.

Was it in 1998 when the expression 'added value' entered the lexicon of ambitious but clueless senior managers? Such a manager had told me to leave his office after failing to make a decision about a highly time-sensitive piece of terrorist intelligence because I hadn't 'added enough value'. This was my first memorable encounter with one of a new breed of senior police manager who could tell you everything about how to get through a promotion process but hardly anything about doing the actual job or catching bad people.

Was it when the Metropolitan Police Service, where I was serving at the time, was branded 'institutionally racist' by Sir

William Macpherson in 1999? After hearing about the Macpherson Report's findings we all sat looking at each other aghast with a sinking realisation of what this would mean for an entire generation of police officers who had overwhelmingly acted and behaved impeccably to everyone, regardless of their colour, race, sexuality or social standing.

Perhaps it was in 2004 when, as a uniformed sergeant, I listened to a pair of senior officers berating one of my sergeant colleagues for failing to find a plausible alternative explanation for what was obviously a domestic burglary in order to hit the 'reducing burglary' monthly target?

Was it in 2009 when my best mate in the police finally decided to throw in the towel after a particularly pompous corporate chief inspector said to him, 'We need to get buy-in on the forward-looking piece'? My very capable and experienced friend told that chief inspector that he had 'no fucking clue' what he was talking about and resigned shortly after in complete exasperation. By the way, that nonsensical expression was quickly included in a hilarious Gilbert and Sullivan-style mini operetta penned by a talented but equally frustrated detective sergeant.

Maybe it was in 2010 when Theresa May delivered crippling cuts to police budgets and made it crystal clear that she was going to 'sort out' the police? To be fair, whilst this was awful, the rot had well and truly set in by this stage, and May, in her own unique, soulless and robotic way, was simply delivering the *coup de grâce*.

I don't know exactly when I realised it had all gone wrong, but on Friday 29 March 2019 at 5 p.m., I took my work mobile phone out of my pocket and switched it off before walking out of police headquarters for the last time as a serving police officer. I had completed my contracted thirty years of service and very soon the organisation would class me as a 'police pensioner'.

In this book I will take you through my incredibly varied career from the start right to the very end. Perhaps then you will form your own judgements as to what went wrong, because it's you, and people like you, that I joined the police to help. It's you that I care about. I also care deeply about my police colleagues past and present (well, maybe not all of them, but most of them), and I'm writing this for them as well as for you.

Over a period of thirty years, I was a uniformed constable, a detective constable on counter-terrorism investigations, a photographer on a counter-terrorism surveillance team, a uniformed sergeant, a detective sergeant in a criminal investigation department, a uniformed inspector, a detective inspector in child abuse investigations, a detective inspector in counter-terrorism, a detective chief inspector in an intelligence department, an operational superintendent and a superintendent running a national data analytics project. Phew!

I started my career typing reports in triplicate using carbon paper and old typewriters and I ended it running a predictive analytics project that used artificial intelligence, supercomputers and cloud storage to analyse 500 million lines of data relating to millions of individuals in seconds.

I want to try to explain what it's really like to be in the police service. And not the telly drama police with their completely improbable storylines involving detectives who single-handedly sort everything out in forty-five minutes; nor, for that matter, the police in fly-on-the-wall TV shows who self-consciously ham it up for the benefit of the cameras.

I also want to write about what it's *been* like to be in the police over the past thirty years. How has the job changed? When and why did those changes happen? What was it like to live through this tumultuous period in the history of British policing?

But, perhaps more than anything else, I want to try to understand how the British police service, that I joined thirty years ago and that I love so much, came to be so horribly damaged within what feels like quite a short period of time. Neighbourhood policing is now almost non-existent because of the loss of tens of thousands of police officers, police staff and the closure of hundreds of police stations. Detection rates for crime solved by police have plummeted and are now at an all-time low. The charge and prosecution rate for total recorded crime in England and Wales sat at a relatively stable and respectable rate of around 16 per cent in the years leading up to 2015. This figure has steadily fallen year on year to a rather dismal and embarrassing rate of 7 per cent in 2019/20. The statistics for fraud are even worse. In 2018/19, there were 227,667 victims of fraud living in the three largest force areas in England: London, the West Midlands and Greater Manchester. Only 2,164 of these (or 0.95 per cent) resulted in any sort of prosecution. This means that, today, any member of the British public that is unfortunate enough to become a victim will have little expectation that the police will catch or charge the criminal who was responsible, and for criminals there has never been a better time to commit crime in the UK.

The number of murders in England and Wales rose by 35 per cent between 2013 and 2017. Hospital admissions for assault with a sharp object in England and Wales rose by 41 per cent from 2014 to 2019 and offences involving firearms increased by 42 per cent from 2013 to 2019. This increase in murder is despite the huge improvements in emergency medical care that is now routinely delivered by highly trained paramedics at the scene and the A&E doctors who learned so much about keeping people alive from colleagues returning from the Iraq and Afghanistan conflicts in this period. God only knows how many murders we would have had if those paramedics and doctors were ill-equipped and badly trained.

From 2015 to 2019, the cuts to police numbers *really* began to bite. Drug-related violence was identified as the single biggest cause of the rise in homicides, increasing from 232 in 2009 to 319 in 2018. Coincidence? I don't think so. This was the period in which I and my colleagues in the West Midlands, London and Manchester were all running around as if our hair was on fire as we didn't have enough people and resources to do our jobs properly.

Ten or fifteen years ago, a victim of burglary would have received a rapid response from uniformed officers, who would have conducted an initial investigation, taken statements and preserved forensic evidence on the scene. This would have been followed up that day by a visit from a forensic scene investigator, who would have retrieved forensic evidence, followed by a more comprehensive investigation conducted by a detective. In those days, we solved and prosecuted about 13 per cent of domestic burglaries. Today, it is common for a serious offence like burglary to be recorded over the phone, for there to be no attendance by police and, therefore, for no proper investigation to be carried out.

Chief constables and Home Office civil servants will argue that the volume of 'traditional' property crimes like burglary and car theft have fallen in the past ten years and that technology has changed crime and offending in that time. That is true. However, what they won't admit is that the police are now just as unlikely to solve 'old' types of crime, such as burglary, as they are to solve the 'new' crimes committed on the internet.

In 2019, Boris Johnson realised that they'd screwed up badly and he made a commitment to recruit 20,000 new officers. However, with retirements and an increasing flood of resignations, over 50,000 new officers need to be recruited just to get back to pre-2010 levels. Flooding the service with rookies in the next three years will create its own headaches and trying to solve the problem in this way feels rather like Boris trying to put the toothpaste back in the tube after Theresa May already squeezed it out.

There has also been a corresponding collapse in the criminal justice system, which is generally evidenced by a dramatic reduction in cases coming to court. This was bad before the Covid-19 crisis, but now, in 2021, due to a massive backlog in cases, it is unlikely that even a fairly simple case will see the inside of a court for several years after a defendant is charged. This then further reduces the likelihood of a conviction because victims get fed up waiting and withdraw their cooperation, witnesses forget what happened and suspects walk free.

The final straw for me, and what propelled me to write this book, was the shameful sight of police officers running away from protesters, many of whom were just kids, in Whitehall during the Black Lives Matter protests in June 2020. The police service were then routinely lambasted by the media and politicians for either intervening or failing to intervene after the chaotic implementation of constantly changing Covid-19 restrictions.

How did we get to this very unhappy situation?

When I joined the police in 1989, I was confident that the organisation I worked for and wider society would support me in my role. The law-abiding public trusted the police to exercise considerable discretion in deciding how to respond to calls for service. We told time-wasters to stop wasting our time, and we prioritised those who needed our help most. Crucially, there were enough of us to confront and control lawlessness on the streets and provide a visible presence to reassure the public.

Thirty years later, I left a fearful, enfeebled service that had been decimated by a combination of government cuts and twenty years of political meddling. The police are now often too busy trying to sort out pathetic squabbles on social media to deal with serious criminality. Furthermore, officers now have almost no expectation whatsoever of being supported by the courts, the media, the government or, for that matter, their own organisation if they make an honest mistake.

Today, it's much more likely for members of the public to stand and film a police officer struggling with someone in the street and then upload the footage to YouTube rather than do the more courageous and decent thing of trying to help them.

There is also something of a chasm between front-line police officers and many of their senior 'leaders'. There are hundreds of examples of really fantastic senior police officers nationally but, generally speaking, front-line officers don't trust many of their own leaders. They despise a lot of them as being 'weak and woke', vying to outdo one another with virtue-signalling Twitter posts promoting their latest gimmicky initiative, pandering to people who hate the police and putting their own career prospects before the best interests of the public, the organisation or their own people. Uniformed officers and investigators will often roll their eyes behind the backs of senior managers who talk in riddles about 'customer journeys', 'future visioning', the latest 'statement of strategic intent' or 'multi-stakeholder partnership engagement'. The police officers under their command would much rather hear about how they plan to catch and convict more violent criminals and drug dealers.

When I joined the Metropolitan Police in London in 1989, I soon became familiar with the often-repeated refrain from officers that 'the job's fucked'. That expression, always shortened in conversation simply to 'TJF', has been in constant usage since I joined and is often used by British police officers in a similar way to 'FUBAR' (the US military expression for 'fucked up beyond all repair') or 'SNAFU' ('situation normal: all fucked up').

TJF would generally be said contemptuously by an officer ordered to do something pointless that didn't make any sense. Alternatively, an officer might say it in response to some new policy announcement that would tie everyone up even further in red tape. A policy in all likelihood dreamt up by someone at HQ who wanted to make a name for themself and get promoted, or perhaps someone from the small army of bean counters at the Home Office.

Many years ago, early in my service, I met a very elderly gent who, to my delight, told me some fascinating stories about how he had served for thirty years in the police in London and had retired in the 1950s, after serving throughout the Blitz. Quick as a flash, he asked me, 'Is the job still fucked?' I laughingly confirmed that yes, it was.

The point here is that British police officers have been using the expression 'TJF' for a very, very long time. Therefore, it's tempting, particularly for certain disreputable politicians or senior officers, who are in a state of institutional denial, to argue that everything's fine. However, only the most deluded, disingenuous or wilfully blind commentator could try to claim that the British police service is in a good place. It's not. It's in a terrible mess after more than twenty years of political meddling from parties on both sides of the political divide.

In this book, I will describe what it was like to work through the years when police officers were able to use a lot of discretion to protect the public and focus on fighting crime, albeit in a way that was arguably lacking in accountability and transparency. Then I will talk about the cash-rich years of policing under New Labour when policing did well financially but became tied up with all sorts of Home Office performance measurements that resulted in a culture of trying to hit a variety of bizarre targets that had almost nothing to do with keeping the public safe.

I will finally describe the painful and horrible years when Theresa May was Home Secretary and then Prime Minister and the impact of losing 20,000 officers and 23,000 support staff on the police's ability to protect the public. I will consider whether the British police service has now gone beyond a tipping point from which it may be difficult or impossible to recover. There is now a definite sense that the British public no longer knows what to expect from their police, and the police no longer understand what anyone expects of them.

Society has changed beyond recognition in the past thirty years and attitudes to all sorts of things have changed for the better. It would therefore be silly to suppose that the police could or should be exempt from any of those changes. The UK's police service is an infinitely more professional, inclusive, tolerant and enlightened organisation today than it was in 1989. Still, clearly, something has gone badly wrong. So, in this book, I will consider whether the job is *actually* fucked and, if it is, how and why did that happen?

I need to make it very clear that the views that I express in this book are my own opinions; however, these opinions are shared by pretty much everyone I know well who has worked in policing, past and present. Those who have left policing are generally very relieved indeed to have gone, and those who still serve feel unable to speak out and powerless to change anything. I accept that this book will make for uncomfortable reading for some – particularly those ex-chief constables who conspired in all this, caved into political pressure and then presided over an increasingly dysfunctional organisation.

I am not a political person and I have no affiliation whatsoever to any political party. I am rather boringly centrist on pretty much every political issue. Growing up in the madness of Northern Ireland in the 1970s and 1980s was quite enough to put me off politics for life. I have tried to be as even-handed as possible in this regard. Both Labour and Conservative politicians created this mess and, on that basis, this book will make the argument for keeping politicians and clueless civil servants well away from public protection. I will also make the argument that we need to start listening to what the majority of the public want the police to do. Not a tiny, vociferous subset of the public – i.e. self-appointed 'community leaders', left-wing activists and the chattering classes in north London dinner parties. I mean the *actual British public*.

Some will accuse me of looking back at a bygone era of policing through rose-tinted spectacles. Certainly, I am nostalgic about those days when I first joined the police, but there were many things that badly needed to change when I first joined. Nonetheless, in those days, unlike today, at least British police officers knew what they were actually expected to do.

When I started writing *TJF* I had no real intention of it becoming a book; however, once I started writing, the words began pouring out of me in a way that took me by surprise, and I quickly realised that there was more to this than just leaving a legacy. So, having now had nearly two years to reflect on the previous thirty, here are the reasons I have written this book.

Firstly, in keeping with my original intentions, I wanted to write it for my four kids: to educate them, hopefully inspire them and ensure that they never fall into the trap of lazily stereotyping police officers or unfairly criticising them without being in possession of all the facts.

I then quickly realised that writing was becoming a cathartic process; helping me make sense of some of the craziness of the past thirty years: the different jobs that I had done, what those jobs had taught me, the great memories of the mostly wonderful colleagues and managers and the bad memories of the truly terrible ones. I wanted to record my memories of the fun, the fuck-ups and the fear.

Furthermore, I discovered that I was holding inside me a great deal of what psychologists might describe as 'unprocessed trauma'. I had never really had time to think about it properly. I had dealt with so much death, much of it violent or gory, and all of it sad and tragic. Coming back to the police station and finding tiny pieces of human tissue caught in the laces of my boots and blood splattered all over my trousers. Memories of horrible road traffic accidents, suicides, murders, industrial accidents and, worst of all, the many dead children from when I was working on child protection. Sitting with a mother and father as they cuddled and talked to the body of their dead child, having to gently explain that the doctors needed to take the child away to obtain tissue samples and evidential swabs. Watching babies being dissected and cut apart by pathologists until they no longer even looked like a baby; more like a raw chicken being cut apart and prepared for the pot. Helping a doctor to undress a dead ten-year-old child who had committed suicide by hanging. The crunching sound of walking through millions of dead flies that had completed their entire life cycle, having fed on the decomposing body of an old man who had died alone in his flat. Desperately trying to keep someone alive using CPR and having to give up after realising it wasn't working. And other memories that are just too disturbing to be shared with you in this book. I wish that those protestors who get out their black marker pens and scribble 'ACAB' on their pathetic, shitty little cardboard placards would have a think about *that* side of policing.

When writing, I also realised how angry and frustrated I had

felt for years about the scandalously unjust way that UK policing has been treated by politicians and many parts of the media,
which has undermined public confidence and the morale of
police officers and put the British public in a very great deal
more danger as a result. Trashing the police is completely perverse, self-defeating behaviour, rather like ripping all the smoke
alarms out of your house, discarding the fire extinguisher and
then letting the kids run around with lit sparklers in the middle
of the night. It's never going to end well.

Over the past ten years or so, all this reckless damage has resulted in the completely unnecessary and avoidable murders of
dozens of children and young men up and down the country
who have been the victims of knife crime. Many of them would
almost certainly still be around today, growing up, sorting themselves out, maybe raising a family, but their names are now forgotten by everyone apart from their own families and friends.
The police service has become unable to function effectively in
inner-city communities and no longer works with young people
in schools building strong, trusted relationships with their
teachers, social workers and their families. We no longer have
enough people to identify the young people who are going off
the rails and help them to access support services. We no longer
have eyes and ears in the community to gather intelligence on
knife crime and gang membership, nip things in the bud and
disrupt serious criminality before it spills over into fatal stabbings and shootings or the exploitation of children by County
Lines gangs.

Through a combination of arrogance, incompetence and reckless indifference, a small number of politicians and their advisors

have created a public safety crisis in the UK. This may become something of a national security crisis over time, with a significant loss of experience and talent leaving the service and no longer moving up into the units responsible for investigating terrorism and the most serious types of crime. I spent thirty years being trained and equipped to manage critical threats to public safety and national security, so I know what I'm talking about in this regard. The brutal truth is that this government has probably done more to undermine public safety in England and Wales than any hostile foreign power, terrorist organisation or organised crime group could ever dream of. Who needs Russia, North Korea and Al-Qaeda when our politicians are responsible for our safety?

Finally, through writing this book I was confronted with the stark truth, reinforced over the past four years of working as a voluntary hospice chaplain, that life is not a dress rehearsal. I have sat and talked with hundreds of terminally ill people of all ages during that time who have described their sadness and sense of loss in the face of their own mortality. Many of them talked about their regrets but I never spoke to anyone who regretted not making enough money or wished that they'd spent more time at work. Many of them regretted not following their dreams or putting up with situations that were damaging to their happiness or to their mental or physical health. They regretted broken relationships and wished that they had swallowed their pride and reached out to people who they cared about. It would have been much easier for me to just walk away from policing and get on with the rest of my life when I retired. However, I want to try to speak for police officers in the UK because it feels like very, very few people are doing that, and I don't want to have the regret of not having done so one day.

If I try, and nothing changes, then at least I can look myself in the mirror and say that I tried. I didn't join the police for an easy life, so why should police retirement be any different?

CHAPTER 1

TV COPS VS REAL-LIFE COPS

B efore I take you on the journey through my thirty-year career, I first need to debunk a few TV myths. This is mainly a cathartic process for me, but if you find it helpful too then all the better.

There is a relentless focus on policing in the British news media. Police officers are portrayed as heroes when they tackle terrorists or save sick children from runaway trains on a Monday and then as villains when they're caught up in some sort of high-profile, controversial incident on a Wednesday. This will be a recurring theme in the book, but there is also an endless fascination with the British police in TV dramas, films, fly-on-the-wall documentaries and sitcoms. This media obsession inevitably shapes public perceptions of real police officers for better and for worse.

I'm not a fan of any of the police dramas broadcast in recent years. Most of them are nonsense but thankfully fairly harmless nonsense most of the time. However, some of them are harm*ful* nonsense and the worst offender, *Line of Duty*, is sadly one of the most popular. It's fair to say that the degree to which the British public loves *Line of Duty* is only surpassed by the degree to which most British police officers hate it. But why do the police hate it?

- It's inaccurate in so many ways – far too many ways to mention.
- The plots are nonsensical and fantastical.
- The characters patronise each other as if their colleagues had all joined the police earlier that day.
- Death by three-letter acronym – most people in the police don't understand or use any of them.

However, the thing that makes police officers really annoyed is that such shows portray a dystopian version of British policing that is completely riddled with corruption. Inevitably, this will lead many viewers to believe that it must bear at least *some* relation to reality. Sorry, but no, it doesn't. Have there been instances of genuine corruption in the British police? Yes, there have. However, thankfully those instances have been extremely rare, and as the saying goes, 'nobody hates a bent copper more than a good copper', and most coppers are good people. Therefore, when such programmes come on most of us just roll our eyes and change the channel. As my author friend and ex-colleague Dominic Adler recently commented, 'It sticks in my craw when the series is lauded for its hard-hitting realism simply because the characters say "CHIS" a lot. As far as real policing goes, *Line of Duty* might as well be *Game of Thrones* with warrant cards and stab vests.'

A medical equivalent to *Line of Duty* would be a TV drama

that suggests that most doctors are sexual deviants and predatory paedophiles who just can't wait to get their grubby hands all over patients and install spy cameras in the toilets. Doctors wouldn't be happy about that characterisation one little bit and that's exactly how police officers feel about *Line of Duty*.

I'm really sorry if you love *Line of Duty* but the police advisors really should hang their heads in shame. However, I suspect that the scriptwriters completely ignore what the police advisors tell them and insist on characters doing and saying ridiculous things.

So, in the spirit of helping you understand more about *real* policing, here are my top twenty TV police drama irritations that conspire to make watching any of them quite a tense experience for my wife if I'm in the room. At best I sit rolling my eyes, and at worst I end up shouting at the TV.

The following points are explicitly directed at TV scriptwriters, directors and producers who have been making these basic errors for so long now that I suspect that they have become unquestioned facts in the minds of the general public.

1. Uniformed officers standing at attention either inside or outside a room where a suspect is being interviewed. I have *never, ever* seen a uniformed officer stood at attention, like a spare prick at a wedding, outside or inside a police interview room. In case anyone hadn't noticed, the police service in the UK has barely got enough officers to deal with a burglary any more, never mind stand around outside interview rooms for no reason. Yet, scriptwriters and TV producers seem to have decided, unquestioningly, that uniformed constables have

absolutely nothing better to do than stand mute, sentinel-like and useless outside an interview room.

2. Uniformed officers wearing their hats inside the police station. Police officers do not wear their hats inside the police station. Why would you do that? The police station is their territory, their sanctuary. They can relax, chill out, take the piss out of each other and take their hats off, because they're hot, sweaty and pretty uncomfortable. Indeed, to my considerable irritation, I very rarely see real police officers wearing their hats *outside* the police station these days, never mind *inside*.

3. Blue lights left flashing on a stationary police car. This is even more annoying when it's parked on the gravel drive of a wisteria-clad house in the Cotswolds responding to yet another middle-class pretend murder in the village. Blue lights on a police car are only ever used to facilitate progress through moving traffic when responding to an urgent call or to warn of an accident ahead or a dangerous obstruction in the road. Once you get to where you're going, you switch them off. Otherwise, you will get a flat battery and your colleagues will quite rightly take the piss out of you.

4. Senior officers pompously addressing junior officers as 'constable'. Senior officers generally refer to junior officers by their first name, e.g. Paul or Sarah. There are only three categories of people who ever use that expression when addressing uniformed police officers. Firstly, government ministers at the gates of Downing Street or upper-class twits trying to avoid getting arrested for drink-driving by name-dropping that they were 'speaking to the chief constable earlier that

day'. Secondly, certain pompous barristers in court who are psychologically and procedurally stuck somewhere between 1850 and 1911. Finally, left-wing students at demonstrations who think they're absolutely hilarious. In this last category, they tend to pronounce it 'cuntstable', with the emphasis on the first syllable.

5. Senior officers interviewing suspects in custody. Senior officers (including senior detectives) *never* interview suspects in custody. That would be done by a detective constable or a detective sergeant – i.e. someone who knows what they're doing. I had many skills as a superintendent, drawn from a long and varied career; however, I knew my limitations, so, unlike Adrian Dunbar in *Line of Duty*, I would never have wanted to sit on the opposite side of a desk and interview a suspect.

6. Senior uniformed officers directing serious crime investigations. Uniformed officers do not direct crime investigations. Detectives run investigations, generally detective inspectors or detective chief inspectors; however, the lion's share of the work is done by detective sergeants and detective constables, all of whom wear plain clothes. Uniformed officers mostly work in the community, managing day-to-day policing services to the public or in corporate departments. I have nothing against uniformed officers as I was one myself at many ranks. However, they do not investigate serious crime.

7. Several uniformed officers of various ranks (often a couple of police constables (PCs), a sergeant and a completely random chief superintendent thrown in for good measure) following the detective around like extras from *The Walking Dead*,

sitting in meetings but never saying anything or contributing anything. See point 1 above regarding the loss of 20,000 officers.

8. Suspects in interviews crumbling under pressure and confessing their guilt. Suspects almost never tell the police what they have done or admit that they are guilty. Ninety-nine times out of a hundred, on legal advice, they answer 'no comment' to every single question asked of them, apart from confirming their name and date of birth. Sometimes, amusingly, they even answer 'no comment' to that until their solicitor advises them that they can answer that question.

9. Surveillance officers sticking out like sore thumbs and making it completely obvious to anyone in a 200-yard radius that they're a surveillance officer. Surveillance officers are highly trained to blend into pretty much any environment. They do not wear dangly radio earpieces, speak into hand-held radios or sit in cars in broad daylight watching someone through binoculars or photographing them with a long-lens camera. In reality, it is extremely difficult to spot a good surveillance team unless you have been trained as a surveillance operative yourself.

10. Characters following a suspect in a car on their own, driving directly behind them for miles until they eventually gain the crucial evidence that they need. It is almost impossible to successfully follow someone driving a car without a full surveillance team of at least ten people. You certainly couldn't do it on your own because you'd get stuck at the very first set of traffic lights. If you need to follow someone on your own your best bet is probably a helicopter, if you have one handy.

11. Corrupt officers everywhere you look. Corrupt officers are thankfully extremely rare and anti-corruption units identify and weed them out pretty quickly – unlike in *Line of Duty* where pretty much everyone is corrupt.

12. Actors wearing police helmets that are far too big for them, which makes them look like complete idiots.

13. Actors wearing police caps at a jaunty angle, which also makes them look like complete idiots.

14. Actors wearing police helmets with the chin strap fastened. Doubly annoying if combined with point 1 above. Chin straps are generally only fastened in a situation where the helmet is likely to get knocked off – e.g. in a volatile crowd-control situation/pub fight/football match when it's starting to get a bit 'lively'.

15. The pathologist getting involved in the criminal investigation – e.g. BBC's *Silent Witness*. The pathologist is a doctor who conducts post-mortems on behalf of the coroner to establish a cause of death. If it's a crime or a potential crime they will be a highly trained forensic pathologist; however, the role remains the same. That is all. They do not get involved in the criminal investigation in any way.

16. The coroner getting involved in the criminal investigation. The coroner is a legal entity, who represents the state, and their role is to establish the facts surrounding how a person came to die regardless of whether the death resulted from a crime, an accident or an unexpected medical emergency. They don't roll their sleeves up, jump in their car and start investigating what happened.

17. A prosecuting lawyer or barrister (or God forbid Judge John

Deed) getting involved in the criminal investigation. The role of a lawyer is to assess whether there is enough evidence to have a realistic prospect of a conviction at court and then to present the evidence during the court process. That is it. My mother-in-law becomes very frustrated that Judge John Deed seems to get it all sorted out pretty quickly, so why on earth can the police not manage to do the same? To be fair, I suspect that her thinking is somewhat clouded by the fact that she has the hots for Judge John Deed.

18. Scriptwriters completely ignoring all of the most basic legislation – e.g. the Police and Criminal Evidence Act, which has been in use since 1984 and dictates every aspect of what the police can do and how they are allowed to do it. Every dramatic representation of a police investigation that I have seen in TV dramas would get thrown out of court on the first day. In truth, it would never get to court in the first place because of the cavalier approach to the rules of evidence taken by TV scriptwriters.

19. Crime scene investigators examining and photographing a crime scene, correctly wearing their white forensic suits, paper bootees and face masks, followed by the senior detective wandering in wearing his suit and tie, with (probably) dog shit all over his shoes, who starts picking things up. A crime scene manager decides who enters a crime scene and anyone who they permit enters and leaves via a pre-defined route wearing a forensic suit. They touch nothing whilst they are in there, and there are no exceptions regardless of rank. Forensic examiners are highly trained to do a challenging and unpleasant job. They don't need any 'help', and senior

investigators rarely enter the crime scene because they are too busy trying to identify, locate and arrest the culprit.

20. Cops shouting, 'Oi, you! Come here!' when they see the person they're looking for in the street, alerting said person and giving them a head start. They then run away, resulting in a totally unnecessary chase on foot, by car or both. If a police officer is looking for someone who is wanted for questioning and sees them in the street, they discreetly and nonchalantly get as close as they can, so as not to alert them, and then they take them firmly by the arm to stop them running away. It's much easier but admittedly less dramatic than huffing and puffing around the streets, across rooftops, over garden fences and jumping between railway carriages.

The question for me is this: to what extent do these TV misrepresentations of policing influence the public perception of and trust in real police officers and investigators? I don't honestly know how much, but I suspect it is quite a lot. I suspect that either it creates unrealistic expectations when the police haven't solved a given crime inside forty-five minutes or it makes people believe that all police officers are bent like in *Line of Duty*. On the other hand, maybe I and every other police officer in the country just need to switch our brains off and chill out.

CHAPTER 2

WHAT AM I GOING TO DO WITH MY LIFE?

My introduction to uniformed life in a disciplined service was not an encouraging one and was certainly not something that set the scene for a long and generally enjoyable career in the British police service.

Like many undergraduates anticipating the end of student life, when considering my post-university career options all of the 'typical' professions bored me to death. I dipped my toe in the 'milk round' – the process whereby the big corporates visit university campuses and try to woo graduates with the promise of 'structured career paths, company cars and an "exciting" working environment'. But frankly the idea of spending my life working for a company that churned out breakfast cereals or car tyres made me want to throw myself under a bus. No, business life definitely was not for me!

I was, and still am, an outdoor type and someone who thrives on uncertainty. I don't enjoy routine and I'm never happier than when I'm out in the fresh air, ideally being a bit lost and having no idea when I'm going to get home or how I'm going to get there. Therefore, the army seemed a good choice and, after doing a bit of homework, I decided I wanted to be a British Army officer, ideally in an infantry regiment. In the army I could get my outdoor fix and, in the best traditions of the British officer class, I could get every other poor bastard under my command lost outdoors too.

And so it was that I found myself suited and booted one morning, walking to the Army careers office in Birmingham city centre to have an interview with a colonel from the Irish Guards, which was my regiment of choice.

Arriving promptly at 8.45 a.m. for my interview at 9, I introduced myself to a burly, ginger-haired uniformed sergeant on the reception desk. He seemed an amiable sort of chap and he apologetically advised me that the colonel hadn't arrived yet and that he wouldn't be there until 10 a.m. He was then joined by an equally burly sergeant, who had overheard the exchange, who also suggested that I was too early and needed to come back later that morning. The ginger-haired one suggested that I go and get myself a cup of coffee and come back at 9.45 a.m., at which point the colonel would have arrived and I could have my interview.

Therefore, I did as he suggested and wandered off to what was then, back in the 1980s, the thoroughly depressing Pallasades Shopping Centre, and what is now the swanky Grand Central. I bought a newspaper and sat down with a cup of coffee to pass the time.

Before telling the next part of the story it's important to point out that throughout the course of my life my timekeeping has generally been spot on. Lateness in others has always been one of my bugbears and, in the vast majority of occasions, if I say I will be somewhere at a particular time, I will definitely be there. There are other personal shortcomings that I am very aware of, but bad timekeeping is not one of them.

Finishing my coffee, I started wandering back towards the army careers office in New Street and walked through the door at exactly 9.45 a.m. as directed. The same burly, ginger-haired sergeant was on the desk and the exchange went something like this:

'Hello, has the colonel arrived yet?'

'Sorry, what do you mean?'

'The colonel… for my interview… you said he hadn't arrived yet… and that I should go and have coffee and come back in an hour.'

'Sorry, mate, I have no idea what you're on about.'

Feeling thoroughly confused by this point, I said, 'I came here for my interview at 8.45 with Colonel Jones and you told me to go away and have a coffee because he wasn't here yet.'

The ginger sergeant then called behind him into an office and the second sergeant emerged.

'This bloke says he came here at 8.45 for an interview. Do you know anything about that?' the ginger sergeant said.

'No, never seen him before. What did you say your name was, mate?' enquired the second sergeant.

Feeling completely baffled and starting to get annoyed, I said, 'I told you both what my name was earlier. It is Iain Donnelly!'

'Iain Donnelly?' said the ginger sergeant. 'You should have

been here an hour ago for your interview! The colonel's upstairs and he's been waiting for you for over an hour and he's not best pleased!'

By this time my head was properly spinning. I stood there in front of these two clowns in my new suit and the penny suddenly dropped that they had completely stitched me up.

Quickly climbing the stairs, I then knocked on the door of the interview room. A gruff voice from within bade me enter and I walked in to find a middle-aged senior officer sat behind a desk. He didn't look happy.

I introduced myself and said, 'Listen, Colonel, before we start can I just apologise for being late. In actual fact I was here at 8.45 but the sergeants downstairs told me that you weren't here yet and that I should go and have a cup of coffee and come back in an hour. However, when I walked in again five minutes ago, they said that they'd never seen me before and denied telling me to go away and come back in an hour. That's why I'm late.'

The colonel began to look as confused as I had been feeling and asked me if I was sure about all this. I insisted that I was completely sure.

He picked up the phone on the desk, dialled a number and then said, 'Sergeant, can you please come up to the office?'

After a few seconds, and with a growing sense of dread, I heard the sound of heavy boots climbing the stairs from below, followed by a knock on the door. The colonel called the sergeant into the office, and he stood at attention in front of the desk.

'Mr Donnelly, can you repeat to Sergeant Harris what you have just told me?'

I then repeated word for word what had happened.

'Sergeant, is this true?' the colonel asked.

'Sir, this man walked into the office downstairs ten minutes ago and, as God is my witness, prior to that I'd never set eyes on him before. He then made up a cock-and-bull story about coming here earlier today.'

'Well, Mr Donnelly,' said the colonel, 'what have you got to say to that?'

'That's not true and he knows it!' I blurted out angrily.

'Mr Donnelly, are you trying to suggest that one of my longest-serving NCOs is a liar?'

I looked at the sergeant square in the eye. He glared back at me defiantly.

'Yes, I am.'

The colonel was now looking thoroughly irritated by the whole thing. 'Sergeant, you can go now,' he said. 'This is most irregular and frankly I don't know what to make of it.'

At this, the sergeant spun on his heel and left the room, leaving me alone again with the colonel.

He told me to take a seat and suggested that we get on with the interview. But, of course, by this time I was fuming. My head was spinning and I was so angry that my voice was actually shaking. I could feel my eyes beginning to burn and was suddenly terrified that I would start blubbing.

Pulling myself together, I answered the first couple of questions as if in a daze. Then, on a sudden impulse, I stood up and said, 'I'm sorry, I don't think I want to be in the army after all. I can't believe what has just happened and to be honest, if that's what I can expect in the future then I'm not interested.'

The colonel made a half-hearted attempt to persuade me to

carry on with the interview but I think he could see that my head was gone and I was never going to be able to give a fair account of myself.

I walked out of the room and down the stairs. Both sergeants were standing behind the desk smirking at me. I said to them, almost in tears of rage, 'What a pair of arseholes you both are, you bastards!'

At this the ginger sergeant's face darkened, 'What did you call me?' he shouted. I called them both bastards again as I walked out onto the street. At this point the ginger sergeant literally vaulted over the counter and came after me at a run.

At the time I was strong but skinny, weighing about eleven stone dripping wet. My potential assailant was the same height but about fifteen stone of solid muscle. I therefore made the sensible decision to make a tactical withdrawal, legging it away from him up New Street in my suit and slippy leather-soled shoes.

Being a runner, I pulled away from him fairly easily after about fifty yards despite my slippy shoes. He stopped running and watched my escape. At a safe distance, I turned around and, standing in the middle of New Street in Birmingham in broad daylight, I gave him the middle finger. I could see him laughing as he turned and walked back towards the army recruiting office.

Sometimes I tell people that I had the shortest career in British military history, but in truth I never even got off the starting blocks. I can laugh about that incident now, but at the time and for a long time afterwards I was really pissed off about it. It was outrageous that those idiots had stitched me up like that, and many times afterwards I asked myself why they did what they did. Could it have been because my surname is Donnelly and because I came from Northern Ireland? After all, this was 1988 and the height of the Troubles. Could it be because they had served in Northern Ireland and perhaps they had some bad experiences out there and didn't want someone like me in their beloved regiment? Who knows really? It's probably more likely that they were simply a pair of tossers who fancied livening up a dull Monday morning at my expense.

Either way, it was back to the career drawing board.

Once I had licked my wounds and moved on from this unpleasant episode, I began to consider other options. My brother had joined the Metropolitan Police in London a couple of years earlier and I found the stories that he told about life on the beat amusing and interesting. It struck me as an unpredictable job, which appealed, and also a career where you could actually make a positive difference to the lives of other people. My grandfather had been a police officer in the Royal Irish Constabulary, which had preceded the Royal Ulster Constabulary, so clearly policing was in the family DNA.

It all seemed to make sense, so I sent off for an application form, which I promptly filled in and duly waited for a response.

CHAPTER 3

FAMILIARISATION

B ack in those days, there were two ways of joining the police. You could apply in the normal way or you could apply to the Graduate Entry Scheme.

The Graduate Entry Scheme allowed undergraduates or graduates to apply to the police and follow a fast-track process. The scheme would more or less guarantee that you would rise to the rank of chief inspector within approximately five to seven years of joining. You still needed to sit and pass the sergeants' and inspectors' exams along the way; however, you could progress your career much faster and, in many ways, the scheme was a bit like a military officer selection process.

For the vast majority of people wanting to be police officers, the other process was to apply to be a police constable and to progress your career, if you wanted to, in your own time.

The common denominator was that everyone, regardless of how they joined, would spend a minimum of two years on the beat in uniform as a police constable. This was and is seen as a necessary period without which it is almost impossible to understand what front-line policing involves.

I toyed with the idea of joining under the Graduate Entry Scheme. I found out that there was a familiarisation course lasting about three days which would allow you to gain an insight into the organisation and decide if it was for you. Therefore, I applied to do this familiarisation course and they gave me a date to come down to London.

On the allotted day, I arrived in London and met a few other people on the same course. They put us into pairs and my buddy, whose name was Paddy, seemed a decent sort. He was a burly rugby player type and the way he spoke suggested that his family had a few quid and that he probably had a private school education.

The general idea was that the Met would spend several days showing us around various departments of the force, which would presumably help us to decide whether the police was for us or not. I can't remember all that much about some of the duller sessions we had over those few days. Many of them were delivered by rather earnest sergeants and inspectors on the scheme and tended to focus on policing areas that didn't exactly inspire me. It was a bit like wanting to join the Parachute Regiment to jump out of planes but then being taken to see the finance department that procured the bloody parachutes. However, there were a couple of sessions that I remember very well.

One of the visits was to a local criminal investigation department (CID) office where we would have the opportunity to speak to a senior detective. We were taken to Golders Green in north London and shown into a fairly typical Victorian police station. It was a lovely old building that had stood the test of time and was a rabbit warren of corridors, staircases, tiled floors and leaded windows. I can remember being taken with Paddy up several staircases and along corridors past offices full of cigarette smoke and the tap-tapping of typewriters. Our guide showed us into the detective chief inspector's (DCI's) office.

We walked in and were offered a chair in front of the DCI who was sitting behind a desk. He was in his forties and had jet-black hair which was brushed back with hair lacquer. He had a sharp, hooked nose, a flinty gaze and a Mediterranean complexion. There were large maps of Golders Green and the surrounding geographies on the walls with dozens of pins in different colours dotted or clustered around the maps, presumably representing various types of crimes in different locations.

I could see immediately that he was looking at us with an expression of mild distaste, which he was attempting to hide but not trying very hard to do so. We asked him a few questions about life in the CID and he answered them as briefly as he could to the point where it soon became quite oppressive in the room. I listened to my voice and I cringed inwardly at the stupidity of some of the questions I was asking him. His demeanour and monotone delivery made us both feel pretty uncomfortable.

At one point a plain-clothed detective popped his head around the door and apologetically asked him for a minute. He addressed him as 'Guvnor'.

He got up and left us alone for a couple of minutes. Paddy looked at me, grinning nervously. 'This bloke bloody hates us… do you reckon?' he whispered. I nodded in agreement, and we sat there waiting for him to come back.

He returned a moment later and sat back down on the other side of the desk, looking at us coldly.

Plucking up courage, I asked him what he thought of the Graduate Entry Scheme. He pursed his lips and wrinkled his nose as if a horrible smell had just wafted into the room.

'It's not how I would choose to do things,' he said. 'There are a few decent people on the scheme, but mostly they're all useless and they'll never be police officers as long as they've got a hole in their arse.'

And with that, our interview with the DCI was over. He apologised and told us he had things to attend to, and someone escorted us back to the front office to await our chaperone.

I reflected on the meeting when we left. In a weird sort of way, I had found it both fascinating and alluring. Here was a guy who operated in a completely different world that I had never experienced and didn't understand one tiny bit. He was obviously deeply suspicious of 'academic' types and had little time for 'bright young things' who leap-frogged everyone else, and who did not have to climb the greasy career pole that he and people like him had had to climb.

I had a second memorable experience on the last evening of the course. We had been at an event in a school hall or somewhere like that. It had involved members of the public in some consultative capacity with the police. I can remember it was a bad-tempered meeting, and the inspector who was fielding questions from members of the public had begun to look somewhat flustered.

After the event, they had arranged for a vehicle from the local police station to pick us up and take us to Euston Station where we would get a train back up to Birmingham.

As we left, we could see the police car parked with its engine running in the street. Our chaperone spoke to the driver briefly and opened the door to let us in. I can remember this encounter as if it was yesterday. Both the driver and the navigator were in their early thirties. Both were thick-set and were wearing short-sleeved white uniform shirts. I could see that they both had tattoos on their arms.

The car was a Rover SD1. At that time it was the fastest response car in use by the Metropolitan Police. We both climbed into the back seat. Against the low background rumble of the 3.5 litre V8 engine ticking over in that quiet, suburban street, I could hear periodic transmissions coming from the radio set in the car. I strained to listen to the short snatches of dialogue from different crews responding to the Scotland Yard operator. It all sounded thrilling as I caught phrases like '...suspects decamping...', '...armed robbery in progress...', '...violent male threatening officers with a knife...'. The voices of the radio operator at Scotland Yard and the police officers out on patrol around London sounded very calm and very professional in stark contrast to the nature of the incidents that they were responding to, which sounded pretty alarming. There were lots of acronyms and language used that meant nothing to me – I was desperate to understand it all. It's worth pointing out here that, whilst the technology has changed beyond recognition, the way that police officers are deployed to urgent jobs and the language used is more or less the same now as it was thirty years ago. It worked well then, and it still works well now.

The driver of the car turned round to us and asked us what we had been doing. I told him that we were thinking about joining the police and that we were on a familiarisation course that had just finished.

I can remember he had a broad Cockney accent, and he looked as if he could handle himself in a fight. This was my first encounter with front-line officers as opposed to handpicked corporate types who could be trusted to stay 'on message'.

He gave my explanation a moment's thought and then said, 'Why the fuck do you wanna join this job? This is a fucking shit job.'

And with that pithy observation, he gunned the big Rover and set off at an alarming speed through the London traffic. I can remember sitting in the back of the car on that warm summer night, watching everything going past in a blur, the sound of the big V8 engine roaring away and the disembodied voices bubbling out of the radio as we made our way extremely and unnecessarily rapidly towards Euston.

We got out of the car at the station and stood grinning and laughing at each other like a pair of big kids. We laughed at the exhilaration and what felt like the borderline insanity of the drive to the station.

From that moment on, I was in no doubt whatsoever what job I wanted to do.

CHAPTER 4

SELECTION

So, having decided that the police service was indeed for me, I sent off for an application form, which I promptly filled in and duly waited for a response.

I decided to apply to be a constable rather than via the Graduate Entry Scheme. Everything that I had seen and heard suggested that being on the scheme would put up lots of barriers with my colleagues. I didn't want them looking at me with suspicion, thinking that I was some career butterfly who had no interest in learning how to do the job properly, flitting around various departments for two minutes before moving on to the next posting. The Graduate Entry Scheme continued under different guises for many years. The criteria for admission changed from time to time; however, the basic premise that someone could accelerate their career up to the rank of chief inspector remained. At the risk of generalising, in my experience, the good people on that scheme were in the minority. Many of them lacked a degree of common sense, which is absolutely essential in policing, and they tended to gravitate towards non-operational corporate roles in headquarters. Some of them would find themselves parachuted into senior detective roles for their 'development', but that generally didn't end well for anyone.

After a period of time, I received an invitation to attend an exam, an interview and a medical in London.

This process took place over two days and we were put up in a grotty, cheap hotel somewhere near Paddington. I was sharing a room with a big skinny lad from the north-east of England. We all went for a few beers in a local pub on the first evening and the next day we attended Paddington Green Police Station for our physical tests, dental checks and medical.

My memory of the exact chronology of the two days is a little hazy. However, we first had to do a fitness test in a gym, which involved a bit of running, jumping and lifting, which was a piece of cake for me. I was as fit as a fiddle and a keen runner and rock climber at that time, although I do remember a few people getting binned at that stage who couldn't do one press-up!

After lunch, the next stage involved a dental check and a medical. The dental examination was a fairly straightforward affair. This is more than can be said for the medical, which to this day remains a source of amusement and profound mystery to everyone I know who had to go through it.

The entire process that I have described so far was something of a conveyor belt involving dozens of male and female candidates. The medical examination was carried out in a room with red and green lights above the door. Red indicated that an examination was in progress and green indicated that it was safe to enter.

They put us into groups of about ten and instructed us to go into small changing cubicles, remove our clothing and put on dressing gowns. We then had to take a seat in a row of chairs by the medical room to await our turn. I remember smiling at the motley collection of dressing gowns worn by the candidates. Some of the lads looked like Ebenezer Scrooge in their nightshirts, whilst others were resplendent in various bold highland tartan affairs. Some of the girls had obviously borrowed their granny's floral bathrobe, and others looked like they were glamorous extras on a James Bond set, showing lots of cleavage and thigh. I've since heard stories, which I'm entirely confident are true, of especially pretty girls who were slightly too short to reach the height requirement being told to keep their heels on whilst being measured.

Eventually, it was my turn. The light changed to green and I heard my name being called. I got up and walked through the doorway.

In front of me, there was a desk in the centre of the room with a middle-aged man in old-fashioned pince-nez spectacles sat behind it. On either side of him were two women, one in her thirties and the other much younger, in her early twenties. I assumed that the chap was a doctor and that the others were administrators of some sort. However, I never really knew, as none of them ever introduced themselves to me.

The 'doctor' checked that I was indeed Iain Donnelly and asked my date of birth. He then rather gruffly told me to hang my dressing gown on a hook on the wall and step onto two black footprints painted on the floor, facing him in front of the desk. I took off my dressing gown and did as he asked. At this point he glanced up at me from his documentation and with an irritated look said, 'Mr Donnelly, please remove your underwear. You were advised outside to remove everything.'

I had somehow misunderstood the instructions, so I took my pants off, put them on the floor and returned naked to place my feet on the black footprints on the floor about shoulder-width apart.

Standing naked in front of three complete strangers, two of whom being attractive young women, was obviously not something that I did every day.

The doctor then asked me if I had ever taken drugs, to which I said that I had not. Immediately I thought, 'Oh God… do I look like a bloody drug addict?' He then told me to stretch out my arms to show him the backs of my hands. I did this. He then told me to turn my hands over to show him my palms, which I did.

He then told me to turn around, spread my legs and touch my toes. I was utterly bemused by this, but I did as he asked, bending over and displaying my (hopefully) clean arsehole and balls to my audience of three, who, to my slight disappointment, failed to give me a round of applause. I briefly considered putting one hand on my backside and looking coquettishly back over my shoulder at them but I decided that probably wasn't a great idea.

The doctor then said, 'Thank you, Mr Donnelly, that is all, you may go now.' I put my dressing gown back on and left the room feeling completely baffled by the whole experience.

I returned to my cubicle to get dressed and then, with a sinking feeling, realised that in my haste to leave I had left my underpants in the room. I weighed up my options to decide which was the least humiliating solution. Should I just put my trousers back on and go commando? That was the easiest option, but there was a risk that if I did this a member of staff might confront me, waving my pants in my face and asking, 'Have you got no pants on? Why on earth didn't you ask someone to get them for you? Idiot!' The other option was to admit that I had left my pants in there and suffer the humiliation of having to retrieve them.

I decided on the latter option and told one of the staff what I had done, apologising profusely. She looked at me like I was the biggest idiot she'd ever met and, rolling her eyes, told me that she'd get them when the light next went to green. A few minutes later, she came back and almost threw my pants in my face.

This was the end of day one, and I returned gratefully to the crappy hotel in Paddington where, to my surprise, I found my Geordie roommate packing his bag to go home. I asked him what had happened, to which he replied, 'I failed the dental check.'

'Really? How on earth did that happen?' I asked him.

'They don't accept people with false teeth,' he said sadly.

'Have you got a false tooth then?' I asked him, seeing his disappointment.

'No, not just one... I've got a full set of dentures.'

I was amazed. This lad was no older than me, in his early twenties, and I genuinely thought that the only people with dentures were old people like my grandparents.

'They told me that it's too dangerous and that I could choke if they came out in a fight,' he explained.

I didn't want to say to him that if that happened everyone would probably be too busy laughing at him to continue fighting, so we said our goodbyes and off he went.

The next day I returned to Paddington Green, where we had to do a test of verbal and numerical reasoning, followed by an essay on something or other. I remember there were several subjects to choose from, some of which had titles like 'Should we arm the police?' and 'Were the miners justified in striking in 1984?' Presumably, this was a devilishly cunning way of identifying and weeding out the gun nuts and rabid Bolsheviks from the pool of applicants. An ex-colleague, seeking to avoid controversy, chose a title about the rights and wrongs of the annual seal cull. He began his essay with, 'The annual seal cull is a cull of seals that takes place every year.' It deteriorated factually from that point on. I'm not sure why they were interested in our views on the annual seal cull. Perhaps they were watching to see if anyone became too enthusiastic and started writing about baby seals being bludgeoned to death. Spot the psychopath.

Finally, I sat an interview. I can't remember that much about it, but I vaguely recall being interviewed by a rather serious uniformed chief inspector and an attractive, slightly flirtatious female sergeant. It was more of a chat really, and I got the feeling that it went pretty well.

I returned to my flat in Birmingham, and a few days later I received a letter telling me that I had passed the selection and that I would be offered a place to train to be a police officer in the Metropolitan Police.

CHAPTER 5

TRAINING SCHOOL

Back in 1989, all recruits to the Metropolitan Police began their twenty weeks of residential training at Hendon Police Training School in large cohorts of about 120 recruits. At any one time, there would have been about three cohorts training at Hendon simultaneously, overlapping by about six weeks.

My cohort was 'Green' intake, and in front of us by about six weeks were 'Blue' intake; in front of them by six weeks were 'Yellow' intake. After our first six weeks, we rejoiced at no longer being the clueless newbies when 'Purple' intake started. It's fair to say that Hendon was something of a conveyor belt, churning out a fresh batch of recruits every six weeks.

It's a measure of how things have changed that from about 2010 almost none of the forces in the UK were allowed to recruit for budgetary reasons, which led to police training schools closing and the dire state of policing that resulted.

They split each cohort into different classes of about twenty recruits. My class was 'E class' and our sister class that we did certain things with (e.g. drill and physical training) was 'F class'. Every class had three instructors. There was one sergeant and two PCs. The sergeants were addressed as 'Sarge' and they told us to address the PCs as 'Staff'.

The first few days at Hendon came as a bit of a shock to almost everyone. Only those who had previously served in the armed forces found the regime familiar.

It was an unambiguously disciplined environment where we marched everywhere as a class, were inspected on parade in the mornings as an intake and the instructors did not tolerate infringements in discipline or standards.

On the very first day, our intake gathered in the main auditorium, still dressed in our civvy clothing for our first welcome briefing. They gave us a long list of 'do's and don'ts' which boiled down to something like, 'Very soon you will cease to be private citizens. You will belong to Her Majesty, the Queen and the commissioner of the Metropolitan Police and you will do exactly what he tells you to do.'

We were then told that a very senior officer would soon join us to take our affirmation (oath). A rather shouty sergeant advised that when he called us to attention we should get up and stand smartly at attention until the senior officer told us to sit back down. He practised with us a few times and once he was satisfied that we no longer looked like we were doing a Mexican wave at a football match, we waited for the senior officer's arrival.

After a couple of minutes, we heard the door of the auditorium swing open, and immediately the sergeant bawled, 'Green intake… attennnnn…shun!' More or less as one, we jumped to our feet. I remember looking around and feeling oddly moved by the sight of this motley crew of civilians trying their best to stand at attention, all suddenly looking quite serious even though we were still wearing what we had arrived in. Some of us were in business attire and others were in jeans, jumpers and sweatshirts. It suddenly struck me that we were just about to become part of something much bigger and so much more important than ourselves.

A senior officer, who I later found out was an assistant commissioner, strode down to the front of the auditorium to address us and told us we could sit down.

This particular officer, and what he said, made a huge impression on me that day and this stayed with me for the rest of my career. He was an impressive-looking character in his fifties with short silver hair, ramrod-straight posture and an immaculate uniform with lots of medal ribbons and silver braid. He welcomed us into the family of the Metropolitan Police Service, the greatest and the oldest police force in the world, where we would very soon become crown servants of Her Majesty the Queen. He told us that we would form an unbreakable bond and find lifelong fellowship with those officers who had served in the past, the present and the future. He told us lots of other things, but I particularly remember him saying that from this point on we would need to be the people who kept a calm head when everyone else was losing theirs, and that we would sometimes need to do things that terrified us. He described how we were about to set out on a journey that was unlike any other and would be doing things and seeing things that we could not yet even imagine.

There was complete silence in that auditorium as he spoke, and it made the hairs stand up on the back of my neck. Every word of what he said that day came true for me.

We then took our affirmation together, line-by-line repeating after him:

I, do solemnly and sincerely declare and affirm that I will well and truly serve Our Sovereign Lady the Queen in the office of constable, without favour or affection, malice or ill will; and that I will, to the best of my power, cause the peace to be kept and preserved, and prevent all offences against the persons and properties of Her Majesty's subjects; and that while I continue to hold the said office I will, to the best of my skill and knowledge, discharge all the duties thereof faithfully according to law.

And that was it. We had been committed to the 'Thin Blue Line' and to a career preserving the Queen's peace. Everyone left that room buzzing, and we felt about 10ft tall as we went off to get measured up for our uniforms.

The training school stores were staffed by comical, world-weary but kindly veterans who'd seen it all a thousand times before. With a single glance they knew exactly what waist size, leg length, collar and chest measurement you were. However, there were a few odd-shaped recruits who found themselves on the wrong end of comments from the police tailors, who teased them about how their arms were too long or how their head was too big for their body. Some of my classmates were big, strapping lads in their thirties, whilst others had only turned nineteen and had barely started shaving, so we were a mixed bunch.

We all giggled at each other when trying on helmets that were far too small that made us look like Stan Laurel, or ones that were far too big that made us look like we had buckets on our heads.

Police uniforms have changed beyond recognition in the past thirty years. A uniformed police officer really looked quite something back then. The old uniforms with the smart tunics, silver buttons, whistle chains and iconic British police helmets inspired confidence. They had an air of authority that the modern uniform doesn't with its hi-vis jackets, one-size-fits-no-one combat-style trousers and, in some forces, bloody baseball caps, which make officers look like gormless fourteen-year-olds.

However, the old uniforms were pretty impractical for the rough and tumble of policing. Not only that; we had no protective equipment or means of defending ourselves whatsoever. Today, officers all wear bullet- and knife-proof body armour, carry retractable steel batons and incapacitant spray. We had no armour and a rather pathetic wooden truncheon which was stored in a pocket down the side of your trouser leg and was next to useless in a fight. They issued our female colleagues with wooden truncheons which were comically small and some of the guys used to hit each other with them as hard as possible, just for a laugh, to demonstrate how pointless they were.

British police uniforms have strayed too far away from that traditional look that was once the envy of the world. I would love to see more of a compromise between tradition and practicality, starting with getting rid of those horrible hi-vis jackets. As well as looking awful, have you ever tried sneaking up on someone in the dark in a hi-vis jacket? It doesn't work.

When we got back to our rooms, most of us put everything on and stood staring at ourselves in the mirror in excitement and disbelief. Our instructors gave us a lesson on how to iron the long-sleeved white shirts properly, how to put pin-sharp creases in the trousers and how to iron creases into the front of the arms of the dark-blue serge woollen tunics. We also had to learn how to 'bull' our boots with black shoe polish and droplets of water to make them shine like glass. Every class had recruits who were ex-army and they showed the rest of us how to do it. They also earned themselves a few extra quid or a beer by bulling other recruits' boots for them. To our considerable amusement, we even had to iron sharp creases into the front and back of our white training shorts, which we wore with light-blue cotton vest tops. We also had to wear these horrendous-looking white socks and white rubber plimsolls, which needed to be regularly re-whitened with liquid shoe whitener. Stood in a line we looked like something out of a 1930s Pathé News film, and we hammered it up accordingly.

'I say, Johnny! Bet you can't wait to give those Huns a good bashing, eh?'

'Yes, old chap… do you think we'll be leaving dear old Blighty awfully soon?' Etc. etc.

Once we had our uniforms sorted it was time to be taught drill and how to march by the drill instructor, who was an ex-NCO in a Guards regiment. Each class, together with their sister class, was put through their paces over and over on the drill square until the majority of us got the hang of it. Again, this was where the ex-military recruits came into their own and, in my class, we had Vince who had, until very recently, been a Grenadier Guard. He was incredibly patient with the slow learners and between him and our class captain, who was also ex-army, they whipped us into shape in the late afternoons and evenings after classes finished.

Every morning was a frenzy of polishing, ironing and checking each other over for the tiniest piece of fluff or dust on our uniforms before the parade. We used to wrap our hands in sticky parcel tape and dab every inch of ourselves and each other to keep our uniforms immaculate. We knew that if just one person let us down, the whole class would be punished with extra duties until we got it right as a team. I can remember one of my classmates almost crying with frustration when someone accidentally stepped on his toe, badly scuffing the polished shine about five minutes before morning parade started. Vince told him to take the boot off and he then quickly and expertly rebuffed it just in time.

It was this spirit of selflessness and teamwork, combined with a strong sense of individual responsibility, that bound us closely as a class and as an intake and underlined the strong sense that we were part of something much bigger and more important than ourselves.

We also had loads of laughs, and that is my overriding memory of training school. We mercilessly took the piss out of each other and the instructors (when they weren't in the room), and we played childish and stupid jokes on each other. A cadet would come back to his room to find everything – bed, wardrobe, desk, chair – all turned upside down and balanced precariously in a huge, wobbly pile in the middle of his room.

The swimming pool was always good for a laugh. Twice a week we would all have to get changed into our swimming costumes and briefly shower in freezing cold water before standing in a line, in number order, at attention by the side of the pool, waiting for the physical training instructor to join us. It was absolutely forbidden to get in the pool until the instructor told us to get in, and I do not doubt that they enjoyed keeping us there shivering for as long as possible.

The Olympic-sized pool was like a mill pond, and on one occasion someone got pulled from behind and toppled backwards into the pool, causing a huge tidal wave. He climbed out spluttering and coughing and got back in line just before the instructor walked out of his office. I remember the instructor going mad, seeing the huge ripples in the pool and shouting, 'Who's been in the pool? Who's been in my pool?' He stalked up and down the line of recruits, glaring at everyone until he got to the guy who was stood dripping like a drowned rat.

'Did you get in my pool?'

'Yes, Staff.'

'Why did you get in my pool before I told you to get in?'

'I forgot, Staff.'

'Forgot what?'

'I forgot that I wasn't allowed in the pool.'

He then turned to the recruit standing beside him.

'Why did you not stop him from getting in my pool?'

'I'm sorry, Staff, I don't know.'

By this time, of course, we were all trying to stifle giggles, and it was actually a relief when we were all ordered to get down and do press-ups as a punishment for 'letting him' get in the pool.

The classroom sessions and learning felt relentless because there was a lot to learn. Having a university degree didn't help at all because it was all rote learning, and everyone had to know reams and reams of criminal legislation word-perfectly: acts, sections, subsections and definitions of burglary, theft, deception, assaults, criminal damage, road traffic offences and so on. There were tests at the end of every week which determined whether we would be allowed to progress to the next stage of training. Cadets who failed were offered support, but if they didn't make the grade they got either back-classed (i.e. sent back six weeks) or binned. If someone suffered an injury or experienced family problems they were offered the opportunity to go back six weeks to join the next intake. I can remember how upsetting it was for those who got back-classed as they had to leave the group that had become such a close-knit unit.

The learning from the classroom lessons and exams was reinforced with lots of role-playing practicals where we had to take it in turns to play the 'shopkeeper/victim/witness/assailant/bus driver' with a classmate playing the part of the police officer. Everyone would stand around watching and then the instructor would debrief the whole thing and we would discuss our rationale and the nuances of our thinking and decision-making. These role-play exercises usually became a great source of entertainment. Afterwards, we would take the piss out of one another if we had put in an abysmal performance or made a completely ridiculous decision.

There was lots of physical training too, together with lessons in self-defence and restraint techniques. They taught us how to restrain people with wrist locks, arm locks, how to make someone comply by using pressure points and generally how to make people do what you wanted with the minimum amount of fuss. We would work in pairs in the gym, doing the routines over and over again until we all got it right. Many of these basic police holds and locks had been in use for decades and they are still taught today. In thirty years of regular refresher training, I learned lots of different self-defence techniques. Sometimes we would be taught the latest fads from the USA or Israel, but to be honest, when I needed them, I always returned to the simple but very effective stuff that I was taught right at the start at Hendon.

I particularly enjoyed the running, and we had to regularly repeat the initial entry requirement to run 1.5 miles in twelve minutes as well as lots of push-ups and sit-ups. At that stage in my life, I was pretty fit and usually managed to do the run in under eight minutes.

The current police fitness test has been criticised for being too easy and, to be fair, my observations of many new officers in the past ten or fifteen years would support that view. Many relatively young officers are very out of shape. There is also no real incentive to maintain a healthy weight or fitness, and I have never known or even heard of an officer losing their job as a result of poor fitness or being overweight. In the 1990s the police also did away with the height restriction, which until that time was 5ft 8in. for men.

In my, likely unpopular, opinion, the abolishment of the height restriction, together with the relaxing of the fitness requirements to the point where fitness barely matters, has resulted in the recruitment of many police officers who do not exactly command respect from the public. The reality is that front-line policing can be quite a brutal and physical job, and you rely on your colleagues to be able to look after you and to be able to look after themselves. If you find yourself crewed with someone who can do neither, that is not a good situation to be in when confronted by a large, angry person at 2 a.m. during a domestic incident.

I accept that the height restriction will not be reimposed, and the Greek police had a finding against them in the EU courts as recently as 2017 for trying to impose a height minimum on candidates. However, it would be reassuring to know that the officer sent to help you when you dial 999 isn't going to be bent double, clutching their sides, coughing, wheezing and sweating profusely after running fifty yards in pursuit of a criminal on a hot day.

My twenty weeks at Hendon flew by, and we all began to get excited about finishing and finally getting our first operational posting. But first we had our passing out ceremony to prepare for. On this day we would officially become police officers, receive our warrant cards and be joined by proud family and friends to see us on the parade square. We also had the small matter of the final exam to sit and pass, so our days, evenings and weekends were filled with relentless studying, marching practice and preparations for the big day.

In our last week, my class all sat and passed the final exam, much to our relief. Passing was far from being a 'done deal' and quite a few people failed it in other classes. After clambering over each other at the notice board we then found out where our postings would be.

This first posting was crucial to everyone, and we had all given several preferences of where we wanted to go. I had asked to go to 'L district' in south London because I knew it was hectic and I wanted to be right in the thick of things. We all yearned for action, so imagine my dismay when not only did I not get my first choice but I didn't get my second choice either. The Met had posted me to 'Z district', which was a semi-rural area right on the outskirts of London. I was to be posted to Sutton, which is a largish borough between Croydon and Epsom. I had never heard of it, but I knew that Z district was pretty quiet compared to the inner-city boroughs like Lambeth, Hackney and Camden.

I was distraught and went to see my teaching staff to see if I could get my posting changed. The staff apologetically told me that the decision was pretty much set in stone unless I could find someone to swap with me. They told me not to worry because if I didn't like it at the end of my two-year probation I could ask to move. They might as well have told me I could move in eighteen years, and I returned to my room very unhappy, hearing mates chattering excitedly about where they were going. It seemed like everyone else had more or less got the posting they had asked for, and it felt very unfair to me. I asked around to see if anyone wanted a swap, but I knew what the answer would be and, sure enough, no one wanted to go to Z district. I decided to try to put it to the back of my mind and focus on preparing for the passing out parade.

The big day in June 1989 arrived. We made sure that we had ironed everything and that our boots were spotless and polished. We were to be inspected by the commissioner, the much-loved Sir Peter Imbert, and we would march with the band of the Royal Marines, so it all felt very grand and important. Our families started to arrive and there were lots of tears, hugs and the inevitable photographs. It was nice seeing the families of classmates we had got to know so well. Some of them had kids and they'd really struggled emotionally with the separation for so many weeks. In those days, the Met was unique in British policing in that people joined not only from all over the UK but from many Commonwealth countries too. During my time I never got tired of listening to all the regional and international accents of my colleagues and their families – many of whom had travelled a long way for this passing out ceremony. My parents were there, of course, and for them this was the second time they had experienced this event.

It was a very emotional day, and at the end of an intense five months we all said our goodbyes, wishing each other luck and promising to stay in touch.

I find it sad that police recruits no longer have the amazing bonding experience of attending a training school together. It was so much fun, and we learned how to operate as a team and how to look after each other. During those twenty weeks I formed incredibly strong friendships that would last my entire career.

CHAPTER 6

STREET DUTIES TRAINING

A rriving on your first day at your first divisional operational police station is a pretty terrifying experience. Additionally, nothing can prepare you for walking out onto a busy street in broad daylight in full police uniform for the first time.

There were about six of us who arrived from training school and we soon found out that half of us, including me, would be posted to Sutton and Wallington and the other half would be posted to Epsom and Banstead. We all had to complete a ten-week phase of continuous training which was called 'street duties instruction' and involved us being chaperoned at all times by experienced officers for the first few weeks. We would then be allowed to patrol unsupervised on foot in pairs.

The other operational officers treated us literally as if we were invisible and it was apparent that we were the equivalent of pond life in the pecking order. It was depressing that we had gone from being at the top of one tree at training school to the bottom of another one on division. However, the street duties instructors were a good bunch and treated us with patience combined with a great deal of piss-taking at our cluelessness.

The first week involved very little police work as such. It was more about getting used to being out and about, mixing with the public, learning the basics of radio communications and getting to know the geography of the division. This is always the hardest thing about arriving at a new division, even for experienced officers, because your safety and the safety of your colleagues depends on you knowing exactly where you are at all times if you need help in a hurry. Therefore, you have to learn the names of the main thoroughfares and the streets running off them quite quickly. You also have to get into the habit of remembering the name of the street that you have just turned into and the street duties instructors would regularly test this by asking us every twenty minutes or so which road we were currently in and which road we had just left.

Effective radio communications were vital, and we had to get used to having a conversation with a member of the public whilst simultaneously listening to radio commentary from others, which on a busy late shift was more or less continuous. In particular, we had to get used to listening out for our own call sign, which was our collar number. After a few months, this became completely second nature, and it has always amazed me how the human brain can pick out a tiny scrap of information in the midst of lots of background noise, whilst multi-tasking or having a conversation with a member of the public. We learned the importance of keeping our radio transmissions accurate, brief and easy to understand. Our initial efforts were pretty poor, and we all incurred the wrath of experienced officers and control room operators when we messed up the phonetic alphabet or failed to respond to our call signs.

We had to learn the call signs of all the vehicles in the division and, in time, also the collar numbers of all our colleagues. The vehicles were given call signs depending on what they were there to do. Every division had its own rapid response car which was called the 'area car'. These were driven by advanced drivers who were highly trained to navigate the busy London roads at high speed to attend the most urgent calls. They were also authorised to pursue stolen vehicles or vehicles refusing to stop and probably therefore involved in crime. I had already had a small taste of the considerable skills of the area car driver at the end of my familiarisation course many months before. The area car was also crewed by a PC 'operator' whose job it was to navigate, operate the in-car radio and do most of the paperwork along the way. The operator posting lasted for a month at a time and was a highlight for a trainee PC. It was also an opportunity to really screw everything up, as area car drivers could be extremely demanding taskmasters.

The Sutton area car had the call sign 'Zulu 4' and the other surrounding stations and divisions had their own area cars prefixed by the letter Z. Then there were incident response vehicles (IRVs), the drivers of which were allowed to drive fast using blue lights and two-tone sirens but were not permitted to pursue. Arguably one of the most important vehicles in the divisional fleet was the van which had the call sign 'Zulu Tango 2' (ZT2). The vans were essential for carrying violent detainees who could not be placed in a car because of their aggressive behaviour. They were also used to transport half the occupants of the canteen who had run into the yard, leaving their food half-eaten, to go to help a colleague calling for urgent assistance. I can remember many times when six or eight officers would pile into the back of ZT2 as the driver was wheel-spinning out of the station yard, frequently with one or more officers falling out the back doors which hadn't been closed properly, much to everyone's amusement. I don't think I heard the terms 'health and safety' or 'risk assessment' for at least the first five or six years of my police service and we generally adopted a pretty reckless approach to our own and each other's safety.

Finally, there were the 'Panda cars' which were driven by officers who were not authorised to use blue lights or two-tones and were used for non-emergency calls. In practice, at this time, what you were allowed to do as per regulations was given little heed. In reality, if an officer was calling for assistance or if you were going to a call relating to suspects being chased on foot, many of these regulations were conveniently ignored. If you had a prang you usually had to explain how it happened to a hard-faced traffic sergeant who had had his sense of humour surgically removed. As a result, there was the ever-present danger of at best being banned from driving a police car and at worst being prosecuted for dangerous driving. This all stopped in the mid-1990s with the introduction of in-car recording black boxes, which could be used after an accident and would show exactly what speed the car had been doing, when the brakes were applied, the level of acceleration and so on. After this point, irresponsible driving came (mostly) to an end.

Each division formed part of a larger district. Thus, Sutton was part of Z district, which comprised a big chunk of south London from Wimbledon in the north, across to Croydon in the east and Epsom in the south. Sutton was pretty much in the middle of the district. The district to the north and west of Z district was V district and this included places like Wimbledon, Kingston upon Thames and Mitcham.

I soon realised that whilst Sutton didn't have the same inner-city grit and high levels of crime as some of the divisions that I had hankered after, it did have a lot going on and it was not the worst place to learn the basics of policing. It also had a diverse demographic in a relatively compact area. It had several large council estates, leafy suburban enclaves, wealthy pockets of London's 'stockbroker belt', a bustling high street with lots of shops, pubs and semi-rural villages towards Epsom. It also had many fast arterial routes in and out of London towards the M25. These roads were frequently used by criminal gangs travelling out into the wealthier parts of Surrey to commit high-value burglaries and armed robberies using high-powered stolen cars, so Zulu 4 used to get involved in a lot of high-speed pursuits, sometimes travelling down into Hampshire or Sussex, all monitored above by the Met helicopter ('India 99').

In the first few weeks we were taught how to deal with relatively trivial issues. For example, we spent a lot of time dealing with minor traffic infringements. The thinking was that handling such infringements taught you how to deal with members of the public in a context where you were enforcing the law but where it didn't matter too much if you got it wrong or messed up. The easiest offences to spot and deal with, and thus the best ones for fledgeling probationary police officers, were committed around pedestrian crossings – either traffic-light controlled or zebra crossings – for example, parking on the zigzags on the approach to a crossing or failing to stop for a pedestrian using a zebra crossing are easy offences to enforce.

Therefore, we were shown how to 'hide' behind bus shelters and lamp posts to watch the crossings, and when we spotted an offence we would have to smartly step out into the road and motion the driver towards the side of the road to stop. We would then have to speak to the driver, advise them that they had committed an offence and do the necessary paperwork. Most of the time, the people we dealt with were apologetic and embarrassed, which made the whole exercise fairly painless. However, inevitably we would often deal with people who 'failed the attitude test'.

The 'attitude test' was something we very quickly learned to be a key component of Met policing jargon. The test was failed most commonly by two types of people. Firstly, by individuals who already had a criminal record and had had previous brushes with the law. Their response to us stopping them, or dealing with them for anything, was met with four-letter words, the waving of arms, raised voices and generally a fair bit of drama. This can be quite intimidating for inexperienced officers, many of whom come from very law-abiding backgrounds and wouldn't dream of speaking to a police officer in such a way. Most police officers learn to be quite thick-skinned, or they jack the job in because they can't deal with confrontation. Personally, after the initial shock of having this behaviour directed towards me, I learned to detach myself emotionally from it completely. Weirdly, I often found it entertaining to watch someone lose their shit, and the more agitated they became, the more polite I would be. Sometimes this was hard, however, particularly if I was feeling tired or emotional about something going on outside work and some 'scrote' had said something really nasty to me. Police officers get told some really unpleasant things pretty regularly. 'I hope you die painfully of cancer' is a popular one. Another common one is, 'I'm going to find out where you live and rape your wife/girlfriend/mother when you're at work.' Charming.

One of the best pieces of advice that I was given during my street duties training was from my PC instructor Bob, who told me never to swear at people and never to get involved in an argument or to raise your voice. By doing these things, Bob explained, you have immediately lost and you are no better than them. I stuck to this advice my whole career, and it never let me down. The only time I broke this rule was when I once lost it with a pair of horrible, gobby, foul-mouthed teenagers who had been terrorising an old man who lived alone in his council flat. They had been posting dog shit through his letterbox and banging on his windows day and night for weeks on end. I had sat with him, holding his hand as he wept, as he told me that he wished that he was dead. When I then found them I had to be restrained by a colleague. I was so angry I could have cheerfully killed them both. When my colleague put me into the police car, I was in tears of rage.

The second type who regularly failed the attitude test were those upper-middle-class types who clearly believed that the law was for everyone else but not for them. Such people would try to bully you into letting them off by name-dropping senior police officers they vaguely knew or magistrates they played golf with, before threatening to get you disciplined by saying that they would 'make sure that you lose your job'. I eventually *really* enjoyed dealing with this type of person because it was amusing to watch someone with a strong sense of entitlement realise, perhaps for the first time in their life, that they weren't going to get their way by being a bully and a pain in the arse.

My advice to you if you ever get stopped by the police for something you know that you've done, which is *definitely* an offence (regardless of whether you think that it should be an offence or not), is the following:

- Rule number one: don't lose your shit.
- If you *do* lose your shit it almost certainly won't end well for you. At best you will get a small fine or a few points on your driving licence. At worst, if you *really* lose your shit you will be handcuffed and helped into the back of a van by several police officers, who will probably enjoy themselves and will have a laugh about you later, whilst you're sat in a cell feeling sorry for yourself. As George Bernard Shaw advised: 'Never wrestle with pigs. You both get dirty and the pig likes it.'

We were all excited and nervous about making our first arrest and for most of us it would be a rather unexciting shoplifter in a high street department store. The staff working in the police control room, which was known as the Computer Aided Dispatch (CAD) room in the Met, would identify calls for service which were suitable for the street duties students to deal with and we would be allocated those jobs – i.e. the jobs no one else wanted to deal with.

Arresting someone for the first few times felt like a pretty big deal. An arrested person was always referred to in Met jargon as 'the prisoner', regardless of whether they had ever been arrested before or been to prison at any time for that matter. Thus, a middle-aged woman who had been arrested for the very first time for drink-driving, after colliding with a bollard on her way home from her book club, was referred to in exactly the same way as a heavily tattooed armed robber who'd spent half his life in prison. It was always amusing to see the look of indignation on the face of middle-class detainees when they heard themselves being referred to as a prisoner.

Back in 1989, pretty much everything was done on paper records. The prisoner would be taken to the custody block and the custody sergeant would book them in, writing the details on a paper custody record, which would contain a record of everything that happened to them whilst they were in custody. The arresting officer would write their notes of arrest in a small notepad, called an incident report book, and anything that had happened out on the street or before arriving at the police station was recorded in the officer's pocket notebook. The prisoner would be kept in a cell and then later taken to an interview room and interviewed by two officers, one of whom would laboriously write down verbatim every question and the answers given by the detainee. Eventually, the custody sergeant would decide whether there was sufficient evidence to charge the arrested person and decide which offence or offences they should be charged with. The arresting officer would then start pulling together a set of case papers, many of which needed to be typewritten on old rickety typewriters. This entire process would take a minimum of three or four hours, and frequently much longer, for even the simplest of offences.

I can remember sitting typing form after form, all of which required much of the same information to be duplicated (arrested person's name, date of birth, address etc.) using carbon paper to create three copies, as this was a time before photocopiers existed. None of us had been taught to type, so it was a horribly laborious process involving two-fingered typing and a lot of bad-tempered swearing.

Shortly after this time, tape-recorded interviews were introduced, which made the process of interviewing a much faster and more natural interaction. Two copies of the interview were made simultaneously – one of which was sealed and could not be opened other than by court order and the other was a working copy. The interview later needed to be transcribed verbatim from the working copy, which was extremely time-consuming, meaning that whilst the interview was more natural and free-flowing, as well as being less open to suggestions that we had made it all up, the end-to-end process took much longer.

As our ten weeks of 'puppy walking' progressed we would be let off the leash a little more and allowed to patrol in pairs without an instructor and eventually alone as our confidence and competence grew.

Occasionally, we would get in hot water, and my first experience of that came from unexpected quarters. I was on foot patrol on the busy high street when I saw a small hatchback which appeared to have been abandoned near a busy junction. It was 'parked' at a 45-degree angle from the footpath and cars were having to drive around it to get down the road. I did a vehicle check on it to make sure it wasn't stolen and it turned out that the registered keeper was local. I started filling out a fixed penalty notice for the offence for 'unnecessary obstruction' (i.e. parking or leaving a car in a way that obstructs the highway), and as I was doing that a very elderly lady pushing a shopping trolley on wheels came scurrying up to me looking agitated.

'Young man... what exactly are you doing?' she asked angrily.

'Is this your car, madam?' I replied.

'Yes, it is, what's the problem?'

'Your car is causing an obstruction; you'll need to move it.'

'It's doing nothing of the sort, and I will not move it. I'm doing my shopping, and I have an exemption as I'm disabled,' she responded.

I could see that she did have a disabled sticker in the windscreen but that didn't give her licence to abandon the bloody car anywhere! I stuck to my guns. She'd failed the attitude test massively and, frankly, I didn't care whether she was eighteen or eighty. She was taking the piss parking like that.

We stood eyeing each other with mutual dislike. It was like a Mexican stand-off. Me, a 23-year-old Metropolitan Police officer in full uniform, a fixed penalty pad and a pen in my hand. Her, a blue-rinsed 85-year-old woman with a bad attitude and a tartan shopping trolley on wheels.

'I'm asking you to move your car because it's causing an obstruction. If you don't move it, I will issue you with a ticket for unnecessary obstruction,' I told her.

She strode up to me and eyed me with genuine venom. 'You will do nothing of the sort, young man!' she exclaimed.

I gave it a moment's thought and said to myself, 'Bollocks to you... you're getting a ticket!'

I carried on issuing the ticket and ignored her increasingly hysterical reaction to me writing it up and sticking it under her windscreen wiper. I walked off with her annoying, whiny voice receding into the distance.

I carried on with my patrol, and in less than ten minutes I heard my call sign on the radio.

'PC Donnelly, can you return to Zulu Tango [Sutton Police Station] and report to your sergeant?'

I walked back to the nick and as I entered the sergeant's office I glanced across into the front office where members of the public came in to tell us their tales of woe and, sure enough, the poison dwarf was there bending the ear of the poor station officer.

My street duties sergeant was a great guy called Mitch Ling and he was stood there grinning at me with Bob, my PC instructor.

'Iain, what's going on? There's an outraged old lady at the front counter who says that you stuck her on for obstructing the highway. She's not a happy bunny, mate! She's a retired headteacher, and she wants to make a complaint about you.'

I told them what had happened and they both started laughing.

'Iain, mate,' said Mitch, 'sometimes, you might be right in the eyes of the law, but it's just not worth it. Have you got the ticket on you?'

I handed him the ticket that I had written out and, to my surprise and genuine annoyance, he ripped it in half.

'Sarge, she was taking the piss! The car was blocking half the high street! She refused to move it, so I was left with no choice!'

'I know, mate… you did 100 per cent the right thing… honestly… but, believe me, it's just not worth the hassle at court.'

This was my first lesson on how to police with 'discretion', but to be honest it really annoyed me. She was an overly entitled, white, middle-class, elderly woman who thought she was exempt from the rules that everyone else had to follow. Having been told that she needed to move her car she had refused and, on that basis, she had been 'stuck on'. Tough shit. We had all taken an oath to uphold the law 'without fear or favour'. It just didn't seem right to back down just because she was old and had an attitude.

However, Mitch had the benefit of knowing how this would play out in court. A poor old disabled woman prosecuted for doing her shopping in the high street. It would be reported negatively in the local newspapers, and the Met would not look good.

As I was leaving the nick to resume my foot patrol I saw her getting into her car, which to my irritation was parked on a double-yellow line outside the police station. She saw me watching her, and she gave me a poisonous glare. I briefly contemplated giving her a parking ticket for the double-yellow line just to really piss her off but I thought better of it and carried on walking.

Before long I was introduced to the local mine of information whose job it was to collate all of the intelligence relating to local crime and criminals. This person was imaginatively referred to as the 'collator' and every police station had one. Generally the collator was a crusty old PC who had an unbelievable ability to remember pretty much anything that had happened in the area in the past 500 years. Frequently, the collator would be assisted by a deputy who was usually a retired collator who could go back a further 300 years. It was almost impossible to ask a question that the collator and deputy collator were unable to answer; they were like a pair of policing Rain Men. You could walk into their office and describe someone you had chased from a burglary over garden fences and lost and they would give you their name, where they lived, their shoe size and what they liked to eat for breakfast. It was impressive to say the least.

The collator's door was always open and the kettle was always on.

The office was lined with steel cabinets and each one was packed with little drawers chock-full of 6x4in. index cards all in alphabetical order as you went round the room. Every single person who had come to the notice of police locally would have a card, and in the case of prolific criminals they would have thick wads of dozens of cards going back many years. The entries on the cards were typed by the collator and indexed by date. Each dated entry would detail the person's offending history and any new intelligence.

It was fascinating to flick through the cards relating to a particular person and look at the passport-sized photos that were taken on arrest to see how they had morphed from being a fresh-faced child of eleven or twelve on their first arrest. You would frequently be able to spot the point when they started using drugs, usually in their late teens, and then they would become more and more gaunt, pale and unhealthy-looking over the years. There would then be a gap of several years when they had been in prison and their next photo would show them looking fitter, healthier and having put on a bit of weight. Then the gradual physical decline would start all over again. Such repeat offenders were often dead by their late twenties.

The pictures of those criminals who stuck to making money and avoided drugs showed a different physical journey. Again there would be a first photo of a young and relatively innocent-looking child, arrested for something like shoplifting or criminal damage, and then gradually they would morph into a hard-faced career criminal looking sullenly at the camera, frequently wearing bloodstained clothing or with a split lip from fighting in the lead-up to their arrest.

The pictures that I found most depressing were those of some of the girls. Again, at first there would be a picture of an innocent-looking teenage girl of thirteen or fourteen smiling at the camera after a silly arrest for possession of cannabis or a trivial theft. They would then be coming into custody regularly over the next five or six years after they had got onto heroin, usually fed by a druggie boyfriend, at which point they would change into a skinny, pasty-faced, spotty drug addict with greasy hair and rotting, black teeth. Often, before they were twenty they would be prostituting themselves on the streets to feed their habit. It was very, very tragic and something that I would sadly witness right up to the end of my police career.

These index cards could be flicked through like some sort of awful flip book that fast-forwarded through a young person's life and you could see them age before your eyes as they descended into an increasingly dark and hopeless place.

Most of these prolific offenders only went in one downward direction, but some managed to sort themselves out. Sometimes they would meet a girl and just grow out of it. Or they would be scouted by a big football club or get into boxing or athletics and decide that running on a track was better than running from the police. I can remember quite a few of the young people from my early years who went on to become household names in the world of TV, music or sport after putting their grim, self-destructive lifestyles behind them.

It's hard to believe now that all this intelligence was stored on little index cards, thousands upon thousands of them, in every police station. It was Dickensian in many ways but it worked really bloody well. The process for submitting intelligence was dead simple. You just scribbled it on a form or in an A4 book in the collator's in-tray and they would do the rest. They would get all the stop-and-search forms and copies of the paperwork and photographs after every arrest and they would monitor the communications on the radio, listening to the stops, name checks and vehicle checks going on out on the street, frequently chipping in with their pearls of wisdom, and collate it all together.

It was far from perfect, of course. The absence of computerisation meant that trying to find out about someone passing through your patch who had offended in a different part of London or in a different part of the country required phone calls to be made to colleagues from other police stations. If someone was committing offences across a wide geographic area it made it tricky to join the dots. We did have the Police National Computer, however, and this was used constantly by patrolling officers to check the names and vehicle details of suspects out on the street.

The street duties course flew by and we ticked off a range of incidents and arrests that would become part and parcel of policing, dealing with the sad, the mad and the bad. Our arrest tally grew and inevitably we all vied with one another for the highest number of arrests.

There was a clear pecking order in terms of arrests. At the top were the quality crime arrests. The arrests that generated the most kudos were (and still are) those catching someone 'in the act' of committing a serious criminal offence as a result of getting there quickly following a call from a member of the public or by using good policing skills. The very best arrests would be for offences of this nature where an officer had arrived on the scene and then chased the suspect on foot, often through back gardens, over fences and walls, before eventually catching them.

The absolute gold-standard arrests were those when there was a fight at the end of such a chase in which the arresting officer came out on top. Maximum respect would be given to the arresting officer in those situations.

Near the bottom of the pecking order were arrests for offences like shoplifting where the suspect had already been detained by store security and it was simply a matter of turning up and going through the tedious process of taking them into custody and bagging up all the stolen gear before escorting them back to the police station. The worst arrests, which generated a great deal of piss-taking from colleagues and filthy looks from the custody sergeant, were for 'drunk and incapable', where someone would be found lying semi-comatose in the street periodically shouting obscenities at passers-by. If it was the chief superintendent or the detective inspector, we'd take them home, but if not the van would be called and they would be detained for their own protection, taken to a cell to sober up and kicked out in the morning. Frequently, they would puke in the van or the custody block and very often they had already shat themselves before we turned up. Strictly speaking, this should have been treated as a medical issue but, in reality, the ambulance crews would refuse to take them for obvious reasons. Occasionally, a new custody sergeant who was a royal pain in the arse would join a team. Someone who would work at a snail's pace, nit-pick every little irrelevant detail and refuse to accept perfectly good arrests. For some inexplicable reason, they would find themselves presented with dozens of filthy, smelly drunks that the PCs had found by scouring every pub car park, railway station and urine-stained underpass for miles around. This would continue until the custody sergeant realised what was going on and 'got with the programme'.

During street duties, we quickly realised how much police officers have to deal with death. In my first ten weeks, I went to lots of non-suspicious sudden deaths. We dealt with fatal heart-attacks in the street, elderly residents found dead at home by family or carers and the occasional fatal road traffic accident. It surprised me how many suicides the police had to deal with and sadly this was an operational reality for me in every uniformed posting at every rank during my time in the force. Some of these suicides live on in my mind many years later. This, together with a lot of other bad stuff that I had to deal with over the years, had a rather detrimental effect on my mental health from time to time.

I will return to the issue of mental health as I recount different stages in my career. It's a massive issue for police officers today in a way that it wasn't when I first joined. This isn't necessarily because we were made of sterner stuff. I think the reason for this is that when I joined we dealt with a lot of awful things but we felt supported by the organisation to get on and do our jobs. We also felt supported by society at large. Today, police officers still deal with all that bad stuff but they feel completely unsupported and unfairly criticised from every side, including from their own organisation. It's very stressful going to work day after day to do a difficult job in that atmosphere. We don't treat the members of the military in this way just before they go off to war. But even though police officers take similar risks every day, a lot of people still feel that it's OK to make them feel like shit.

CHAPTER 7

FIRST RELIEF

After our ten weeks of street duties training we were split up and posted to our first 'relief'. Joining my first proper operational team or relief, as it was called, was even more terrifying than arriving at the police station and going out to meet the public on my first shift. In those days, new probationers tended to be pretty much shunned by the wider team until they had proved themselves in some way.

I can remember well that sense of isolation and loneliness, feeling like everyone hated you just because you were new. Perhaps hate is too strong, but that's how it felt. We were collectively referred to as 'sprogs' or 'probbies', and I was derisively referred to as 'Grad' because I had a university degree, which was quite unusual in those days. Those with degrees were considered interlopers; butterfly-types who would flit from one non-operational job to another on the way up the greasy pole, completely devoid of common sense, generally clueless and not to be trusted. So, I had the double handicap of being both a sprog and a graduate.

It was a generally accepted rule that the probationers made the tea for the relief at pre-deployment briefings and at mealtimes.

This was quite a task as the reliefs could consist of fifteen to twenty officers, and if you gave someone coffee when they wanted tea or sugar when they asked for no sugar you would have to rectify the situation pretty quickly. The only way for someone to escape the tea round was to be so bad at it that they got banned from doing it.

The canteen seating arrangements also had a strict hierarchy. The area car drivers and senior PCs would sit together conspiratorially chuckling about something or other. The rest of the relief would sit in their own little cliques. And finally, the probationers sat together. The sergeants would generally muck in with everyone and sit anywhere, and I recall my relief sergeants being mercifully kind towards the probationers. Most of the sergeants had been very experienced PCs before getting promoted and they had a lot of operational credibility. In those days, few sergeants would get promoted with fewer than five or six years' service, and most of them had somewhere between fifteen and twenty-five years' service. So they'd seen it all.

I spent the majority of my first twelve months as a probationer patrolling on foot. Occasionally, if it was pouring with rain one of the panda drivers would take pity on you and come and pick you up, but I soon learned the well-rehearsed mantra that 'a good police officer never gets wet!' In other words, if you get wet you are an idiot because you have not cultivated enough friendly community contacts or tea stops (or, for some officers, lonely housewives) to drop in on and visit to stay dry. I soon cultivated my own friendly shopkeepers, pub landlords and store detectives who would give me a cup of tea and who would welcome a chat when it was raining or freezing cold.

Eventually, once we had proved ourselves in the rough and tumble of operational policing, and shown ourselves to be reasonably courageous, reliable and hard-working, we would be accepted by the relief and permitted to sit with them in the canteen. You would also know that you had been accepted when the senior PCs took the piss out of you in a friendlier sort of way after you had done something silly out on the street.

For me, this came one Sunday when I came on duty at 7 a.m. after being out on the tiles the night before until about 3 a.m. I left the police station after the morning briefing and started my foot patrol. I was wandering around, still feeling a little worse for wear, when after about half an hour I started to marvel at how quiet (read silent) the radio channel was. This was very unusual, indeed. Eventually, the area car came roaring up beside me and the driver shouted, 'Oi, Grad! The control room has been calling you for ages and you're not answering your radio!' It was at this point that I realised with a sinking feeling that I had left the station without a radio and I had been wandering about aimlessly in full uniform like an idiot with no ability to send or receive messages. Everyone thought it was hilarious. The sergeant gave me a half-hearted bollocking and kindly posted me to the station office for the rest of the shift where, presumably, I could do less damage to myself or to the general public.

The station office was the most unpopular posting for everyone. Back in those days, we had very few civilians working in police stations. Today, it's almost exclusively civilians or 'police staff', as they're referred to, who staff the station office. However, in the 1980s and 1990s, it was usually hapless probationary police officers doing this job. Frequently, they would post an older officer there full-time – someone who'd been ill or injured and who couldn't perform operational policing – however, it was often the poor old probationers who would get lumbered with the station office posting.

Many police stations and front offices have closed now. This is stupid because you end up having to send a fully fit crew of police officers to deal with fairly trivial issues that are reported on the phone rather than encouraging members of the public to go to a police station, which requires a bit of effort on their part, at which point they would usually decide not to follow the issue up. This unwelcome development has increased demand on response officers, clogging up the command-and-control system with trivial nonsense and creates an (accurate) impression in the eyes of the public that the police have lost control of the streets and are overwhelmed. This issue is made much worse by inexperienced civilian call-handlers based in remote call centres who make little effort to resolve issues on the phone and simply create a new problem that some poor PC has to try to sort out.

Trivial nonsense, however, was the staple diet of the station officer, who fielded an almost infinite variety of bizarre queries, questions and complaints from members of the public. Typically, people would come in to produce their driving and insurance documents after a traffic collision or more likely after being required to do so by a 'patrolling' police officer who had been hiding behind a bus stop. The station office was like an amusing social experiment: you would have nervous, law-abiding citizens reporting their stolen lawnmowers and bicycles sat beside sweaty, foul-mouthed young lads who had just been released from custody and who were waiting for their mate to get released so that they could go out and steal some more lawn-mowers and bicycles.

We tolerated very little bad behaviour in police stations in those days and more than once I can remember drunken, abusive youths being physically dragged over the enquiries counter for the offence of 'disorderly behaviour in a police station' (contrary to the Town Clauses Act 1847) and deposited straight into the cells. I don't think this piece of legislation is ever used any more, which is a great shame because arresting people who behaved like this demonstrated that there was a line, and that crossing that line had consequences. It was also very entertaining to watch, particularly if the little scrote had just been released from custody and found himself dragged back over the counter and returned to the nice warm cell that he had been occupying a few minutes before.

We used to get some very odd requests from members of the public who saw us as having supernatural abilities to solve every conceivable problem in life. On one occasion, as a very young and inexperienced station officer, I was visited by an old boy carrying a large cardboard box which he placed gently on the front counter. He told me that he had found an injured pigeon and, opening the box, sure enough, inside was a large, smelly, feral pigeon sitting there with an obviously broken wing. The old boy asked me if I could call the RSPCA and ask them to look after it, so, being unsure about what to do, I suggested that he take a seat whilst I checked with my superiors.

I took the box into the sergeant's office and spoke to the duty station sergeant, who peered into the box, wrinkling his nose with distaste. He picked the box up and said, 'I'll show you what

67

you need to do,' before he carried it out into the rear yard. Then, to my surprise, he took the pigeon out of the box in one of his meaty hands, pulled his truncheon out of the pocket on the side of his uniform trousers and swiftly bludgeoned the bird to death, before throwing it into a skip. 'There you go, mate, sorted!'

Slightly horrified, I asked, 'But what'll I tell the bloke at the front counter, Sarge?'

He rolled his eyes and told me to follow him. He walked back into the front office with me and called over to our pigeon rescuer.

'Hello, mate,' he said to the old boy. 'Listen, thanks a lot for bringing the pigeon in, but there's no need to call the RSPCA now. The wing wasn't broken... just dislocated... so I popped it back in and it's flown away. Good as new!'

The old boy looked delighted, thanked us profusely and off he went, happy as Larry.

I now know that feral pigeons are basically flying rats and that they carry lots of nasty diseases so I don't feel too bad about it.

Station officer night duty was dreadfully dull. There were generally only three categories of people who came into the police station in the middle of the night. Firstly, there were those in genuine distress for some reason or other, and these people were immediately given help. The second category were drunk and thought that we were a glorified taxi service that would take them home, which we refused to do, obviously. Finally, there were those collectively and unflatteringly referred to as 'nutters' (remember that this was 1990 and a long time before political correctness had arrived). They were generally harmless individuals with mental health issues who were fixated with police stations, police officers, police cars, police radios, police procedure – I think you're getting my drift. They were cheerfully tolerated if it was quiet when they would be humoured until they became annoying, at which point you would suddenly pretend to be very busy or you would hide somewhere until they got bored and wandered off. It was often tricky to tell the difference between the nutters and the local MP or some other self-important buffoon of a councillor, who would often pop into the police station to 'raise morale' or show how much they cared about law and order. On one occasion in Birmingham many years later when I was an inspector, I had been humouring a very scruffy, pompous and eccentric visitor to the police station for at least ten minutes before being told that he really *was* a local MP. Personally, I preferred dealing with the genuine nutters.

My favourite nutters were a bloke and his wife in their fifties who used to come into the Sutton station office every night at about 3 a.m. and hand over a thick brown envelope addressed to a specific inspector. I would dutifully put the envelope into that inspector's pigeonhole every time until one night that particular inspector was actually on duty. He came in, threw the envelope on the desk in front of me, and shouted, 'For God's sake stop putting this shite in my pigeonhole! Tell them to address it to the new chief inspector!' I opened the envelope and found about twenty sheets of A4 paper inside. On each sheet there were hundreds and hundreds of car registration numbers written in tiny handwriting on both sides of the paper. That night when the couple came in, I told them that Inspector Taylor was no longer dealing with their information and that in future they should address the envelope to Chief Inspector Roberts, who would be very happy to receive it. And so it would go on until Chief Inspector Roberts had had enough and ordered the envelope to be addressed to the newest inspector on the division.

After a time and once the rest of the team had accepted us, we would eventually be given the kudos of working as the operator in the area car, Zulu 4. This was an incredibly daunting experience for someone fairly new to policing as you were expected to multitask operating both the local radio channel and the main RT set – which communicated with Scotland Yard operators, whose call sign was 'MP'. You also had to navigate for the driver if they weren't sure where they were going and do all the paperwork. A good area car crew was expected to do two things well. Firstly, to respond to 999 calls for assistance and turn up quickly. The second expectation was to patrol their patch proactively day and night to stop criminals on foot and in vehicles.

The skill of the area car drivers was impressive, to say the very least, but it isn't easy to describe unless you've experienced sitting alongside them. The Metropolitan Police Driving School has the reputation of being the best in the world and it routinely turned out drivers who would have likely been able to hold their own against some of the very best racing drivers. Their main skill (and this is what was truly impressive) was that they drove safely in all weathers, in cars that had been designed to take a family of four out on a shopping trip, and had remarkably few accidents on busy public roads. They were powerful cars but they were basically bog-standard models with police livery, blue lights and radio equipment installed. However, the area car drivers squeezed every ounce of horsepower, braking ability and tire adhesion out of those cars to get from point A to point B ridiculously quickly. The best police drivers had an uncanny ability to see and anticipate hazards in the road; pre-empting the actions of the driver of a stolen car or the thinking of pedestrians and other drivers. I loved being the area car operator and never felt more alive than when travelling at high speed on blues and twos on the way to an urgent call, weaving through traffic, feeling the car drifting through corners and wondering what awaited us when we arrived. It was an adrenaline buzz on steroids. Pursuing stolen cars was often frantic. In Sutton, this happened quite regularly and usually involved 'bandit vehicles' being chased at over 120 miles per hour before an inevitable foot chase of the occupants through back gardens, streams and industrial estates. Usually, the suspects would be tracked and found by police dogs or the infrared camera of India 99 before being dragged from their hiding place scratched, muddy and bleeding from running through thorny brambles and crawling under bushes. It always amused me that whilst being handcuffed they would often indignantly protest their innocence, bitterly complaining that they had just been walking home from the pub and that they didn't know anything about a stolen car or a stash of stolen jewellery and watches found ten yards from where they were hiding.

The second task of the area car was to proactively patrol and catch criminals in the act, which was where policing became a real art, and a good police officer eventually developed what to young and inexperienced officers appeared to be an almost supernatural ability to sniff out criminality. Regrettably, these skills have been largely lost in an age where police officers are now either too scared to stop and search people or too busy trying to deal with a multitude of issues that the police service should almost certainly not be dealing with. The withdrawal of funding for a whole range of support agencies in the past ten years now means that the police end up handling all sorts of social issues that they are ill-equipped and untrained to deal with. For example, dementia patients, out-of-control children, those suffering with mental illness and alcoholics and addicts living in squalor. As ex-chief superintendent and author John Sutherland recently stated, 'It makes perfect sense to blame the police for things that go wrong in society. Because it means that we don't have to trouble ourselves with the real causes of the problems we face. Or do anything to address them.'

Most law-abiding citizens just want to know that should they need to dial 999 the police will turn up quickly to help them in their hour of need. Sadly, the police are now generally too busy dealing with petty squabbles over Facebook posts or babysitting people having a mental health crisis to rush to a burglary in progress or proactively spot, search and arrest someone who has just been released from prison and is walking down the street carrying a bag full of drugs and knives.

In September 1989, a couple of months after I arrived in Sutton, the London Ambulance Service went on strike and the police and army were asked to step in and provide a temporary ambulance service until things were resolved with the unions.

A request came out for people to put themselves forward to be trained as paramedics and, like an idiot, I volunteered. This turned out to be a bit of a foolish decision. It was motivated by a desire to do my bit, but it was also motivated by the promise of overtime because we would be on twelve-hour shifts and there would be lots of rest days cancelled so we would definitely make a few quid. I was saving for a deposit for a flat so it was a no-brainer.

The training course was a joke. It lasted two or three days and then we got a big box of bandages and latex gloves and were paired up with an army squaddie driver or a fellow police officer who would drive a station van, which is fine for delivering bread or transporting angry drunks but totally unsuitable for use as an ambulance. The army guys drove green army battlefield ambulances that were based on long-wheelbase Land Rovers. These had the road holding of a large mahogany wardrobe on casters and were absolute deathtraps, particularly when driven at speed. The army guys were completely gung-ho driving these bloody things and they had got it into their heads that because they were with the police they could go straight through red lights at speed without braking or giving way.

I did these shifts exclusively as a temporary paramedic almost every day for about five months and it was really quite traumatic. We had a lot of people die in front of us and we felt totally ill-equipped to help them sometimes. Some calls would involve us having to get very overweight people down many flights of stairs in carry chairs, huffing and puffing and nearly breaking our backs as we went. Sometimes we would only have a stretcher which was made of canvas that had likely been in service since the Second World War. It was frequently like something out of a Laurel and Hardy sketch with the poor old patient desperately clinging onto the sides of the stretcher, sliding up and down it as we negotiated stairs and steep slopes. We probably caused more harm than good most of the time. Other calls would be dealing with someone who had suffered really serious injuries in a road traffic accident or a fall and we had no ability to relieve their pain or treat them properly. I was very glad to get back to police work when the strike finished in the spring of 1990. I have had a massive respect for paramedics ever since those days because it can be a truly horrible job.

I spent about eighteen months at Sutton learning the basics of policing; however, very quickly I became a bit disillusioned. There were plenty of decent, hard-working officers there but there were also a lot who had clearly opted for an easy life in the suburbs. Some of these were officers who had become a bit burnt out from working in a busier part of London and were now bringing up their family in a quieter area. However, many of the Z district officers were just lazy. Some of them seemed to resent doing even the bare minimum amount of work and would dodge confrontation and ignore blatant lawlessness to avoid arresting someone so that they could finish work on time.

I was jealous of many of my old classmates from Hendon who had been posted to grittier inner-city districts. They talked about the busyness of where they worked and some of the crazy situations that they often found themselves in.

To explain this in simple terms, imagine London as an onion. In the very centre you have the well-known, iconic sites which are busy in terms of the 24/7 buzz of shoppers, drunks, night-clubs, businesses and tourism. In pure policing terms, these areas are fairly non-threatening and reasonably peaceful. Then, there are layers stretching outside of the centre where there are greater levels of urban deprivation and poverty which create many of the conditions for higher levels of crime and disorder:

drug dealing, urban street gangs and more serious violence involving guns, weapons and knives. Finally, the outside layers of the onion are a wide band of outer-London areas stretching from the suburbs into the semi-rural districts where you have mixed policing environments similar to Sutton. I'm not a sociologist or a geographer but I suspect that this is a common theme in every major conurbation on earth.

I wanted to experience policing in the middle layers of the onion. So, without hesitation, I submitted a request to transfer to L district on the day I got confirmed as a constable after passing my two-year end-of-probation exams. This came as no surprise to my sergeant, who told me privately that I would probably learn more in a month on L district than I had learned in all my time in Sutton.

A few days later, I discovered that my request to transfer had been successful. I was going to Clapham.

CHAPTER 8

CLAPHAM

From day one, my new posting didn't disappoint. But first a bit of geographical orientation for those who are not familiar with Clapham.

Clapham (or LM as it was referred to by its police call sign) is a region of London about two miles as the crow flies south of central London. When I arrived in 1991, it was surrounded by the three other L district divisions: Kennington (LK) in the north, Brixton (LD) to the east and Streatham (LS) to the south. To the west, Clapham division bordered W district, which included Battersea (WA) and Wandsworth (WW). This is still the case today. Each of these divisions had their own police station with local teams of response officers, community beat officers and CID detectives.

I often smile to myself when I think about arriving at Clapham and the incredibly warm welcome I was given by pretty much everyone I met. It was about as different from Sutton as you could imagine. It was obvious to me immediately that they were a very close-knit bunch. The sergeants were fantastic and the inspectors were incredibly supportive and friendly. However, the single biggest difference was that everyone in the station was so enthusiastic about their job. There was a real buzz in the briefing room and canteen with constant piss-taking and laughter. If you looked up the word 'camaraderie' in the dictionary it should say 'Clapham division in the 1990s'.

Interestingly, I noted that new probationers didn't get shunned by the rest of the team. They were made to feel welcome and nurtured from day one. They still had to make the tea but once they had made it they would sit with the whole team and enjoy the banter.

I had found my policing home.

Very quickly it dawned on me why Clapham division was such a close-knit unit. It was a hectic and frequently dangerous place to work. Demographically it was a weird mix. Clapham was one of the first places in London to become gentrified in the 1990s and there was a strong 'yuppie' population in the well-to-do Victorian and Edwardian villas in the streets surrounding Clapham Common. This era saw the rise of the finance and banking sector whiz kids with their floppy hair, pinstripe suits, mobile phones the size of bricks and bonuses ten times the yearly salary of most ordinary people. Lots of them lived in places like Clapham because they were trendy and offered an easy commute into the City. There were also lots of creative media types who seemed to be attracted to the urban grittiness and loved to hang out with slightly shady characters who made the most of their naïvety and gullibility. These were the sort of people who would throw house parties and open their homes to all and sundry and then find that everything of value had been nicked and human poo had been ground into their Persian rugs before discovering that the culprits had also wiped their backsides on the living room curtains for good measure.

Living cheek by jowl with the upwardly mobile and cash-rich City types, however, were those people living in some of the most deprived inner-city estates in London that had very high levels of unemployment, low levels of educational attainment and generally meagre expectations from life. Kids growing up on these estates were frequently neglected and abused and this taught them that if no one seemed to care about them, they didn't care about anyone else. Sadly, not very much has changed in the past thirty years and inner-city deprivation is just as prevalent now as it was then. Rich people living in expensive homes in certain parts of London are possibly just as oblivious to urban deprivation today as they ever were and still turn a blind eye to the council estate kids waiting for the bus in the freezing rain whilst they take young Cosmo and Tallulah half a mile to prep school in their shiny Range Rover.

Clapham Police Station itself was located right in the middle of one of these council estates in Union Grove and this created a feeling of being surrounded by a lot of people who really didn't want us there. Most of those who lived on these estates were completely law-abiding, decent people who just wanted to get on with their lives and bring up their families. The reality, unfortunately, is that there will always be a hardcore minority who don't want to do that and who will create trouble for everyone, all of the time, everywhere they go. These were our 'customers' – the people we spent most of our time dealing with to protect the decent folk. We targeted them mercilessly until either they went to prison and were off the streets or they decided to behave themselves and stop committing crime. Social justice warriors and champagne-socialist lawyers – who make a very comfortable living out of the criminal justice system – often complain that prison doesn't work. A lot has been written in recent years about the pros and cons of the British prison system. However, what I do know for absolute certain is that criminals don't want to go to prison and whilst they're inside they're definitely not burgling your house or wiping their arse on your living room curtains.

The prediction by my previous sergeant that I would learn more at Clapham in a month than I'd learned in all my time at Sutton proved to be 100 per cent spot on. I had already spent eighteen months as an operational officer learning the basics, but this had just given me the foundations to *really* learn how to be an effective police officer.

It's hard to explain my experience of working at Clapham, even to fellow police officers. I suppose in many walks of life there will always be people, places and times when everything comes together to create something truly exceptional and special. Call it 'excellence' or whatever, but Clapham had those rare and sublime qualities.

If I had to try to put my finger on it and describe it in two words, it would be 'effective leadership'. Every manager from the superintendent down to the sergeants had a crystal-clear understanding of what we were there to do. We were there to protect good people and catch criminals – simple.

However, these leadership qualities were evident across every team at every rank. The senior PCs and the area car drivers were incredibly hard-working, brave and a source of inspiration to the younger officers. The senior PCs had taught those officers who had four or five years' service and they, in turn, acted as role models to the newest probationers. The whole thing was a beautiful, smoothly oiled policing machine that relentlessly pursued criminals and we had the best fun and laughs doing it.

It's fair to say that similarly skilful officers and the same *esprit de corps* existed in lots of other places in those days, particularly in other inner-city divisions like Clapham, because I've heard colleagues wax lyrical about all the amazing 'thief-takers' on their patch.

I immersed myself in this intoxicating spirit, and most days I literally couldn't wait to put on my uniform and go back to work.

I have described how the role of a good area car was to get to 999 calls quickly and also to sniff out criminality and make arrests proactively. There were many Clapham area car drivers who were supremely good at both. My relief ('D relief') were blessed with two of the very best: Derek (Del) Beattie and Phil Weston. They both had what appeared to be supernatural abilities to spot active criminals out and about, morning, noon and night. I learned so much from them and others like them, and I would get very excited if I heard my collar number being paired up with theirs at the start of the shift. I knew it was going to be a great shift.

CHAPTER 9

THE MODEL POLICE OFFICER

I t's important to emphasise that the police service is a large and massively complex organisation that does a lot of things that the public rarely see. The organisation requires a lot of different skills. Not everyone will be a brilliant 'thief-taker' in the same way that not everyone will be suited to interviewing a child who has been sexually abused. However, this chapter is about what a great front-line officer looks like and how these skills form the foundations for all sorts of other specialist policing roles.

Over the years, I've thought a lot about what makes a brilliant front-line police officer and I'm going to try to distil those qualities and skills into a description. I dearly wish that British policing could somehow return to something like this model, because it worked. Do I think that is ever going to happen? Sadly, no. However, in a spirit of optimism, here goes…

A really effective police officer has a number of key attributes. Firstly, at their core, they are a decent human being who genuinely likes other people and who gets on well with almost everyone. They are usually a good conversationalist, enjoy a joke and definitely don't take themselves too seriously.

Secondly, they genuinely care about wanting to do the right thing in the best interests of the public and carry out their duties in a way that fearlessly tackles lawlessness wherever it comes from.

Next, they genuinely don't care whether someone is black, white, straight, gay, male or female. All they care about is whether someone is honest, respectful and law-abiding or whether they are the opposite of these things.

A good police officer also has an excellent memory for names, faces, locations, vehicle registrations and phone numbers. In fact, pretty much any detail that is relevant to policing.

There are a lot of police officers who would score pretty highly in most of these categories; however, it is this next bit that separates the competent police officers from the exceptional police officers, and this is harder to describe.

The truly exceptional police officer is an expert at reading and understanding every nuance of someone's behaviour, body language, eye contact and verbal intonation. Over the years, they have dealt with and spoken to so many people trying to hide their guilt on the street, in police cars and in police interview rooms that they can spot them a mile away in a busy street in amongst the general public. They can almost *smell* the guilt, fear and adrenaline in someone, and they can tell instantly if someone is lying to them. Similarly, they have amazing powers of observation and will spot someone trying to hide an object under their clothing whilst driving past at forty miles per hour. They will spot the foot of someone sticking out from under a parked car where they are hiding 100 yards away. They will spot the metallic flash of someone discarding a knife into a hedge as they drive past them.

They know what 'normal' behaviour looks like and, conversely, they can identify someone whose behaviour just doesn't look right. I used to ask some of the great police officers that I worked with why they had stopped someone who hadn't looked out of place to me at all but then turned out to be wanted for murder in another country, had ten stolen credit cards on them or had a gun in their sock. Often, they simply couldn't put it into words and they'd say something like, 'He just didn't look right.' Others *could* explain it and it was fascinating to listen to their mental processes, what had alerted them initially, why they had asked the specific questions that they had asked and how they knew where to look for the drugs or the weapon or the stolen gear that was stashed nearby.

Such officers will know exactly where to find the bag of discarded stolen property from a burglary by retracing the route taken by the person fleeing from the police. They just know where it's going to be. Why? Because they've learned to think like a criminal without acting like one.

Put all of these attributes together and you have a police officer who is unstoppable. If someone is out in a public space committing a crime when that officer is on duty, they *will* spot them and deal with them in the way that they deserve to be dealt with.

One of the key psychological skills that a good police officer needs to learn and then continually nurture is the ability to sense suspicious behaviour and calculate risk. This is all about tuning into the words, actions and behaviours of other people in order to understand what is really going on and why that person might be behaving in the way that they are. It's all about sharpening your innate human instincts and intuitions that were routinely used many thousands of years ago when human life was nasty, brutal and usually very short.

These skills have been largely lost over time because people generally don't need them. When I was a civilian, I lived my life blissfully ignorant of the fact that there are many things going on in busy places that 90 per cent of people just don't see. After three or four years in the police, I started to see them and it was like having a set of blinkers removed. As I grew in experience, I could see, or rather sense, more and more.

In self-defence training, police officers are taught that people behave in one of three ways: 'green', 'amber' or 'red'. However, this model can also be applied to lots of other areas of policing.

The 'green' state of mind is relaxed and tuned out of the environment. 'Amber' is watchful and waiting but still relaxed. At state 'red' the mind is on full alert and the body is creating massive amounts of adrenaline.

Most members of the public are on green the majority of the time. They don't really notice what's going on around them and when they become a victim of crime, or when something terrible happens in front of them, it comes as a horrible shock and they go from green to red instantly.

A police officer should be on amber most of the time when out in a public space, both on and off duty. Very little should come as a surprise to them because they will have anticipated any problem and mentally prepared a strategy to deal with it. They will only be on green in the comfort of their own home or when lying on a beach on holiday – and even then the very best officers will still spot thieves out looking for purses and mobile phones to steal when lying on a sun lounger!

Another version of this highly observant mindset is taught on police driving courses. Most members of the public only look at a piece of road about ten or twenty yards beyond the front of their car bonnet and they rarely use their mirrors. Good police drivers will be on amber constantly. They are continually raising their vision to look as far down the road as they can, using their peripheral vision to notice what is happening on either side of the vehicle as well as constantly flicking their eyes to their rear-view and wing mirrors. This means that literally nothing should come as a surprise when they are travelling at high speed. They will have seen every single potential hazard and they are continually re-calibrating their speed and position in the road to take account of all of this. Now, imagine doing this at the same time as giving a clear radio commentary, listening to a lot of information coming from others, thinking about where you're going, the best way to get there and what awaits you when you arrive. It's a lot for the human brain to compute, but with experience and practice a good police officer becomes highly expert at doing it.

An experienced police officer can spot criminal behaviour and criminals instantly. Not because they're doing anything dramatic at that moment but because they behave differently to law-abiding people. Like a good police officer, most repeat offenders will also have honed and sharpened their psychological and observational skills but they will use them in a totally different way. They might be looking for opportunities to commit crime, looking at potential victims and mentally weighing them up or looking out for police, CCTV cameras or anything else that might put them at risk of capture.

There were three main things that I was watching for when

assessing and observing potential suspects that I started to hone when working in Clapham.

Firstly, it's all about the eyes. Criminals are watchful and always looking around. If you look at them they will spot it and make eye contact right back at you. Often, they're trying to figure you out just as much as you are trying to figure them out. Sometimes, they'll even smile or laugh and throw you the middle finger because they know that you've spotted them. A key surveillance officer skill is to never, ever make eye contact with someone you are following. All observations have to be done using your peripheral vision and you learn how to look without appearing to look. If you make eye contact with your target, it's game over. This can also work another way – for example, a criminal might try to look too nonchalant when driving past a police car travelling in the other direction. This isn't natural either because most law-abiding members of the public will notice a police car. They will usually flick their eyes towards it with an irrational sense of guilt and worry. However, criminals will sometimes try so hard to look relaxed and innocent that they end up looking even more guilty than if they'd made eye contact.

Secondly, you need to decode unusual body language. If someone is hiding something that they don't want you to know about, either on their person or in a vehicle, they will act in a way that will make you sense that something just isn't right. They might move in a way that is designed to throw you off the scent or distract you. They might flick their eyes to the location of the thing that they're worried about without realising. The most common diversion tactic is to start playing up and creating drama by shouting, waving their arms about, refusing to stay in one place and hoping that by doing this that you'll back off and go away. A good police officer will do the exact opposite but, unfortunately, in a world of mobile phones, social media and a prevailing culture of grievance and entitlement, these tactics often now succeed and many police officers will just leave people alone because it's just not worth the hassle and the complaints. Today, a prolific young criminal can video a confrontational interaction he has had with the police using his phone and instantly upload it to YouTube or TikTok with the title 'More police harassment in Camden' and in no time at all other young people and naïve members of the public will be up in arms about it. The police are on a hiding to nothing because for legal reasons they can't disclose the fact that this particular youth has fifteen previous convictions and that there is current intelligence that he is regularly carrying knives.

The third thing that I learned to look out for was whether someone was about to start running away or start attacking me. In a situation where a suspect is on state red they will be broadcasting many non-verbal cues that need to be read. Their whole body will start to tense up in preparation for the flight or the fight. For example, by looking in their eyes you can tell if they are either closing down their field of vision and looking at you very intensely as the target for violence or looking around at their escape-route options. As soon as I noticed this, I would get in very close if I thought they were just about to leg it or I would put some space between us if I thought they were about to swing a punch.

As a rule, I never let people talk to me with their hands in their pockets. If I had told someone to keep their hands out of their pockets, or where I could see them in a car, and they refused, I would immediately consider that they had either a concealed weapon or something else that they were trying to hide or dispose of. I didn't care if they were unhappy about it, I didn't want to get stabbed or shot.

Working in Clapham taught me all of this but, later in my career, when working as a member of a surveillance team, it was interesting to dispassionately watch this behaviour unfolding in front of me. As a photographer hidden away, I had the luxury of zooming in on facial expressions and trying to lip-read what people were saying. In the same way that good police officers are always on amber, so are serious criminals and terrorists. You could see their body language changing as they moved up a gear into the preparatory stage of doing something that they knew could land them in prison for a very long time. This change in behaviour would get picked up instantly by a surveillance team and they would be able to tell that something significant was just about to happen. As soon as you heard a team member saying something like, 'OK, all units… he's eyes all around. Now walking with purpose. Standby, standby…' we would all perk up and be on full alert. Armed robbers would typically conduct a recce of a location where they planned to commit an offence, often in the vicinity of a bank or cash machine. Their body language would be fairly relaxed, but they would be looking everywhere and taking everything in. However, when coming back to do the real job they would look completely different. They would be moving more purposefully, usually with a serious facial expression and they would constantly be scanning for police. Terrorists would do the same. They would conduct hostile reconnaissance of a location, sometimes several times before an attack. For example, we would be watching a team of serious criminals preparing for a robbery and providing a second-by-second commentary of what was happening for the benefit of the supporting firearms team. Everything would be looking good, the Securicor van would pull up outside the bank and then suddenly the baddies would just walk away and split up because one of them had seen something that had spooked him and the job had been aborted. This could be really frustrating, and we would never know why the robbers had changed their mind. Often, it was a case that they'd seen what they thought was a police officer, or maybe they'd seen a car with three or four occupants on the other side of the street and they thought they could be firearms officers. Such criminals were tuned into their instincts in exactly the same way that we were tuned into ours. It takes many years of working in tough policing areas as uniformed officers to develop this knowledge and situational awareness.

The things that people say are obviously important too. A good police officer will often know when someone is lying to them because they will delay answering a very simple question to give themselves some thinking time. An ex-colleague from Clapham had a rule that he called the 'Who, me?' rule. If he asked someone their name and they came back with, 'Who, me?' it was usually a sure sign that that person was just about to offer up a false name. It might not just be 'Who, me?' but could also be some other utterance that served the same purpose of buying them a bit more thinking time. Generally speaking, there are only three types of people who don't tell the police their real name immediately upon being asked: criminals, left-leaning types and conspiracy theorists. The police aren't remotely interested in left-leaning types or conspiracy theorists, but they need to be interested in criminals. If they're not, they're in the wrong job.

Typically, when I stopped a car with multiple occupants or spoke to a couple of likely lads in the street with a colleague, I would split them up and we would individually weave the following questions into the conversation:

- What's your name and date of birth?
- Where do you live?
- What's your mate's name?
- Where have you just come from?
- Where are you off to now?

We would then swap over and ask the same questions of his mate and see if the answers bore any relation to each other. If they'd been through the system plenty of times, they would often start playing up and creating drama if they had something to hide rather than just answering the questions, or they'd start giving you lots of 'Who, me?' type answers. I would also ask their date of birth at the start of the interaction and then ask it again a few minutes later. If it was made up they rarely got it right the second time or they would have to think about it, which told me everything I needed to know.

Politely and professionally asking lots of questions and then remembering or noting down the answers given is really important. Frequently, out on the street, suspects would tie themselves up in all sorts of knots and forget what they said earlier. I used these skills in a more advanced way later in my career when interviewing serious criminals and sex offenders. Often, people will say something that indicates guilt or knowledge of some aspect of an offence that they have committed and somehow it just 'leaks' out of them, almost as if their brain just cannot keep it in. A good investigator will spot these comments and mentally bank them for later. Sometimes, in between interviews we would discuss these psychological leaks and ensure that they were explored deeper in the next interview. Often, the interviewee hadn't even realised that they had said that thing, but it would provide a real insight into what was going on in their head. We would bring it back up later by saying something like: 'When you were being booked into custody you said X, which struck me as a slightly odd thing to say. Can you maybe just tell me what you meant by that?'

We also conducted intelligence interviews after someone had been charged or by going to interview them in prison after conviction. Frequently, these conversations would yield lots of valuable information that could be used to help us understand offenders better. These mental leaks happened in this setting too. For example, we might ask a sex offender, 'You've already told us that your primary sexual attraction is to girls under ten years old. Are you also attracted to boys of that age?' If they answered, 'No, not really,' that probably meant, 'Yes, I'm very attracted to boys of that age, but you haven't caught me for any offences against boys, so I'm not going to talk about that.'

A lot of what I have described above about what I started to learn on the beat in Clapham is really quite basic stuff. However, towards the end of my service, I found it surprising and worrying how few police officers did any of this. I got the sense that they were afraid to talk to people and afraid to put anybody under even just a little bit of mental pressure. When I was a uniformed sergeant and later an inspector, young officers used to say things like, 'What reason would I have to speak to that person?' I would tell them in no uncertain terms that as a Crown servant of Her Majesty the Queen they had every right to speak to a member of the British public and, provided that they behaved professionally, they had nothing whatsoever to fear.

Unfortunately, quite a lot of police officers never really learn these skills because they're probably in the wrong job or they're working somewhere too quiet. No matter how good you *could* be at these techniques, you would never learn them in a sleepy part of the country. You need to be somewhere with a bit of life and grit. Some police officers are exceptionally good at it and they are the ones who will routinely generate their own arrests of quality criminals just by seeing something that didn't look right and by trusting their instincts.

Many years ago, most traffic officers only dealt with traffic offences, vehicle defects, accidents and speeding. Occasionally, us local officers would find ourselves posted to assist them with an initiative to tackle dangerous vehicles or some other traffic-related issue. The local officers from places like Clapham would get really frustrated because the traffic officers just didn't seem to see that many of the people they were stopping for trivial issues, such as displaying an out-of-date tax disc, were clearly criminals who probably had drugs, guns or God knows what else in their car. They would issue them with a ticket, having been given almost certainly a false name by the driver, and then send them on their way, never to be seen again. It used to drive us nuts!

Today, this is no longer the case and traffic officers are one of the very few small groups of police officers who have the time, inclination and ability to proactively get out there and disrupt criminals. Everyone else is too busy handling routine calls for service, sorting out trivial issues or dealing with time-wasters.

Some of the most ineffectual operational police officers that I worked with over the years were a bit hopeless at proactive policing. They weren't aware of what was going on around them and they were too trusting and fell for obvious lies. They tended to over-intellectualise problems, failed to understand things that were basic common sense to most cops, and they couldn't spot the signs of impending violence. They were a liability to themselves and, more importantly, they were a liability to their colleagues. Frustratingly, quite a lot of them ended up in very senior ranks and became a barrier to our ability to fight crime.

I always found the dynamic between good police officers and criminals in the street fascinating, and this also applied off duty. I would regularly spot someone who was up to no good when I was off duty. We would make eye contact and they would know that I was a police officer. I knew what they were up to and they knew that I knew.

It's very hard to describe this sense that someone is up to no good, particularly when giving evidence in court. A court focuses solely on evidence, facts and verifiable events. More than once, I had barristers berate me in court when I stated that I had initially stopped and spoken to their client because their behaviour had raised my suspicions. In reality, most barristers know exactly what you mean when you say this because they deal with criminals all the time and they know perfectly well what most of their clients are like. However, it's all part of the game to feign shock and surprise at the actions of the nasty police officer who has picked on their client for no good reason. It's all about persuading the more gullible members of a jury to acquit their client.

There are still police officers in every force who are great at proactively catching criminals, and it's encouraging to see evidence of that in some of the fly-on-the-wall TV shows, but back in the 1980s and 1990s, there were lots and lots of them. But then the bureaucracy screwed everything up and now everyone's too busy dealing with time-wasters to catch real criminals.

If policing does somehow rediscover some of its true spirit, it's incredibly important to emphasise that good policing skills don't appear overnight. It takes many years of experience and passing on that experience to younger officers to create a place like Clapham in the 1990s. Even if we decided tomorrow to try to recreate this dynamic, empowered, 'can do' mindset, it would probably take almost as long to recreate it as pointless bureaucracy and clueless politicians took to destroy it.

In those days, the organisation generally discouraged reporting a crime unless the issue that you were sent to was serious enough. Generally speaking, 'proper' crimes would get reported and investigated: if you got badly assaulted or had your car stolen or broken into or had your house burgled it would be treated seriously and you would get a fairly consistent standard of investigation. However, if your complaint was deemed to be frivolous or trivial you would be given 'words of advice' and the matter would go no further. For example, if we attended a complaint of two neighbours arguing the toss over a damaged garden fence and this resulted in a bit of pushing and shoving, we would have advised both individuals to wind their necks in and stop behaving like children. Today, we would end up with two crime reports for common assault, another crime report for criminal damage and a full investigation. This would probably take several days and would almost certainly result in no further action – i.e. a complete waste of everyone's time and effort. Arguably, this over-zealous approach (which is mandated by the Home Office) worsens and prolongs the conflict between the neighbours rather than nipping it in the bud.

In the 1990s, if an inexperienced officer returned to the police station and tried to submit a crime report for a trivial matter – commonly referred to at that time as a 'load of bollocks' (or, usually, LOB) – they would be told in no uncertain terms by a sergeant not to do such a thing again and the report would be ripped up and thrown in the bin.

The basic attitude was that we should always be focused on crime and that we should be out and about, patrolling the streets and sniffing out criminality day and night. We obviously couldn't do that if everyone was tied up back at the station filling out paperwork. This culture created a real zest for policing and we all couldn't wait to get to work to get stuck in. It also generated healthy competition between the teams within the division. If you were out in the community committing crime there was a very strong chance that you'd be caught. Sadly, that is very much not the case today.

The major downside of this culture, however, was that it gave a licence to lazy or unprofessional officers to ignore lots of quite serious incidents because they couldn't be bothered dealing with them properly or because a victim had been rude to them. It also created the risk that a member of the public could come to very serious harm at a later date because the police hadn't done their job properly or failed to help them when it should have been obvious that they were at risk. Therefore, a very inconsistent level of service was created. However, this did not become a problem for the force because at that time no one was interested in modern notions of 'customer service' or performance metrics and data quality. In the early 1990s, if someone had asked a police constable or sergeant how the 'police performance' was in Clapham or elsewhere, they probably would have assumed that they were asking about the top speed of the cars.

During this time, the dispatch of officers to incidents was carried out by staff who worked from a control room in Clapham Police Station and these people were members of our team. Therefore, it was common practice for these staff to screen and paraphrase what was said by an officer out on the ground and turn it into something on the electronic log that would be acceptable in an audit. This meant that what got recorded on the log often bore very little relation to the reality of what had actually happened. I'm not talking about blatantly covering up bad behaviour on the part of officers because I never saw that happen. No one in that position was willing to risk losing their job or potentially going to prison to cover up something carried out by someone else. It was more about ensuring that dealing with time-wasters did not turn into us spending our whole time doing pointless paperwork.

I'll give you another example. You are sent to a disturbance outside a local convenience store and on arrival you find two blokes who are both worse for wear having clearly had a bit of a drunken scuffle. Both are effing and jeffing at each other and one has a bloody nose. So, you and your colleague separate them and pretend to be interested in what they are telling you about why they were having a scrap. Both make allegations against the other and it is clear that if you do nothing it would all kick off again. So, you tell the less pissed one to clear off and put the more pissed one in the back of the car. You then drive him home and let him out of the car, telling him that if you got called back again he'd be getting nicked.

In this scenario, you have at least three criminal offences that have been committed: drunk and disorderly, assault causing actual bodily harm, and affray. If you arrested both men, two officers would be taken off the street for at least four or five hours. Nowadays, those same officers would be off the street for a further day to attend court and, if adjourned at court, more than one day. The final outcome would be of little interest to anyone and would probably result in a 'bind over to keep the peace', which is basically an undertaking to the court not to do it again, or a trivial fine that neither protagonist would ever pay. It would be cheaper for the British taxpayer to take them both out for dinner at the Savoy rather than the ridiculous rigmarole now expected by the Home Office.

The most sensible and cost-effective approach would be to

separate both parties and get back on to the street to deal with real criminals. In Clapham, we would have dealt with that incident from start to finish in about twenty minutes rather than three days. The assessment given to the staff in the control room would have been along the lines of: 'Two piss-heads having a punch up, we told one of them to foxtrot-oscar, and we took the other one home.' The electronic log would probably have read: 'Police attended, no offences disclosed, both parties suitably advised and no further cause for police action.' Sorted.

In the 1990s, there were no camera phones to shove in cops' faces every time they spoke to someone and barely any CCTV cameras. Therefore, if someone wanted to make a complaint about poor service, these were usually 'squared up' quickly by the sergeant or inspector, unless the complaint was really serious.

CHAPTER 10

INSTITUTIONALLY RACIST?

It was around this time that the murder of Stephen Lawrence changed policing in the UK for ever. In the unlikely event that you don't know who Stephen Lawrence is, he was a young black man who was brutally murdered by a gang of white racists in Eltham in London in April 1993.

I'm not going to say very much about the actual investigation itself for the following reasons:

- I was never involved in it in any way and I'm therefore not qualified to talk about it.
- So much has already been said and written about it over the past twenty years that there is probably nothing more to add.
- It seems to me that everyone is allowed to have an opinion about these incidents apart from the police officers who are the ones who routinely have to actually deal with the fallout from chaotic and violent events, unlike the vast majority of commentators who have never had to deal with such things and also have the luxury of many years of hindsight.

The murder was horrific and the people who carried it out were abysmal criminal low-life. Stephen Lawrence was a good lad from a good family with a very promising future, and he was brutally murdered for no other reason than the colour of his skin and for being in the wrong place at the wrong time. There were all sorts of mistakes made in the investigation into his murder. Everything from the initial response, the management of the crime scene and the follow-up enquiries that were conducted over many months and years. Undoubtedly, there was a clear need for an inquiry into the failings in the investigation so that lessons could be learned. However, in policing, there was (and still is) a profound, raw sense of unfairness that the entire organisation from top to bottom had been damned because of a single badly managed investigation that then became highly politicised. As a result, my colleagues and I collectively found ourselves in the position of having our entire organisation labelled as 'institutionally racist' in the 1999 Macpherson Report that was released after the inquiry into the murder. This clumsy accusation has been used again and again by the critics of policing to suggest that every police officer in the UK is a racist; something that could not be further from the truth.

There were a great many positive things that needed to be changed and did change in policing in the years after the Stephen Lawrence Inquiry. The professionalism with which serious investigations were dealt with, particularly murder investigations, improved beyond recognition. The actions that police took in the initial response to critical incidents, termed the 'golden hour', dramatically improved. The way that police dealt with bereaved families and how they communicated with witnesses and local communities radically changed for the better. However, I believe that from that time onwards British policing lost its confidence and became a deeply fearful, risk-averse institution in which officers started to anticipate calamity around every corner, even when dealing with quite trivial incidents. Police managers had seen the way that anyone even loosely involved with the Stephen Lawrence case had been treated by the courts and by the media and they became terrified of finding themselves in the same position.

It was really shocking to all of us in policing at that time to have the organisation treated in this way. For many years afterwards, police officers were very nervous about dealing robustly with minority ethnic men who they knew, or who they believed, were involved in crime. I believe that this risk-averse culture in policing and the constant fear of accusations of racism helped to lay the foundations for the knife-crime epidemic some years later that has tragically taken the lives of scores of young people. After the Macpherson Report, police officers found themselves (and still find themselves) in an impossible position in respect of issues of race in Britain. They are vilified if they stop and search or arrest too many minority ethnic offenders, but if they fail to deal robustly with those same offenders they are vilified for 'tolerating' crime committed against minority ethnic victims. So, what does the average 23-year-old police officer do when he is confronted with this situation when policing our streets? Sometimes, it's just easier to ignore things because, in the current climate, getting involved can end very badly for police officers.

The subject of police racism was a constant issue throughout my time in the service, and I find it frustrating that even now, following the Black Lives Matter movement and the death of George Floyd, there is still a routine perception that the UK police is institutionally racist. The Black Lives Matter movement tried to equate the UK police with the US police, which is just wrong and foolish in all sorts of ways. The way that policing is done in the UK could not be more different, and anyone who thinks that it's the same is totally deluded. Our US colleagues operate in an entirely different context. As a society, the United States is awash with legal and illegal firearms and this has inevitably shaped the policing style. This situation has made US police officers deeply fearful about getting shot and they therefore adopt a much more aggressive approach to members of the public. Whereas, in the UK, police officers patrol unarmed in over 90 per cent of cases.

To illustrate my point, the UK has one of the lowest rates of fatal shootings by police in the world, with a consistent level of 0.5 people killed by police per 10 million of the population. In the US, the rate is twenty-eight people per 10 million – nearly sixty-times more than the UK. To put this figure in a European context, the Dutch police kill five times more than their UK counterparts, the French police eight times more and the Swedish police kill twelve times more of their citizens than the UK police.

Without a doubt, perceptions of policing and levels of trust in policing differ between communities, and the service has been working incredibly hard for many years to try to ensure that the police workforce better reflects the communities that they serve. Ethnic minority communities have much lower levels of trust in the police than white communities; however, the question I would ask is this: to what extent do lower levels of trust result from the actual words and actions of police officers and to what extent is that a product of many years of negative media stereotyping of police officers as racists? The toxic and corrosive impact of this reporting should not be ignored. It's a lazy and generally false narrative and it does no one any good to keep repeating that message.

This is exacerbated by the self-appointed 'community activists' who whip everyone up after incidents involving police. MPs such as Diane Abbott or, for those with longer memories, Bernie Grant, who was dubbed 'the high priest of conflict' by Douglas Hurd when he was Home Secretary, repeatedly attack the police, undermine trust in ethnic minority communities and encourage a mindset of perpetual grievance and victimhood. It's hardly surprising that the police struggle to create a more diverse workforce when there are so many unhelpful voices undermining recruitment efforts.

I have seen the organisation go to extraordinary lengths to demonstrate transparency and try to gain the trust of ethnic minority communities; however, time and time again all this hard work is undermined by a small number of vociferous individuals.

The only conclusion that I can come to is that in the UK there's something of a cottage industry that encourages a sense of grievance. This community of activists, quangos, advisors and 'experts' now provides a livelihood to people who have a vested interest in maintaining the status quo. Frankly, they will never be supportive of policing. It's not in their interest.

Do the police sometimes get things terribly wrong? Yes, of

course they do. Why? Because it's an organisation made up of human beings who make mistakes for all sorts of reasons – usually these are honest mistakes but some are inevitably made out of stupidity or malice. Are there still a small number of individuals in the police who have unacceptable attitudes towards ethnic minorities? Yes, there are. Why? Because you will find that in every organisation and its impossible to know what someone is thinking 24/7. There will always be a small number of covert racists in the police, in the same way that there will always be racist individuals in medicine, teaching, the church, politics and journalism.

In 2009, Trevor Phillips, the Equalities and Human Rights Commission chief, stated in a speech marking ten years since the Stephen Lawrence Inquiry that the police had changed massively and that Britain was 'by far the best place in Europe to live if you are not white'. Phillips went on to say:

> On balance, the positive changes provoked by Macpherson have outweighed the cost of the political turmoil. But does this mean that I believe that the Met, or any force for that matter, should be pilloried with the single blanket accusation of being institutionally racist? I don't think so. That would imply that nothing has changed.

And yet, the relentlessly negative media narrative persists. Certain journalists listen only to ex-police officers with a specific agenda and an axe to grind. There's no balance. It's such a shame that they don't speak to black ex-police officers like ex-Met Inspector Chris Donaldson, who has talked about how he did not experience racism during his time in the Met – for example, in an interview for the Triggernometry YouTube channel.

They should also speak to Keith Fraser. When I interviewed my ex-colleague Keith, who is now the chair of the Youth Justice Board for England and Wales, on my *Tango Juliet Foxtrot* podcast, he described how he experienced no racism whatsoever in the Met despite being posted to a predominantly white community in Barking and Dagenham in 1988. Keith was a young black man from Birmingham landing in a part of London unused to seeing black people, never mind black police officers, and he received nothing but love and support from his colleagues. So, why don't the media and journalists speak to people like Keith? I can only conclude that it's because many of them have an agenda and they don't want to hear anything that challenges their thinking.

I have been in the thick of it operationally for many years, in a number of ranks in some of the busiest places in two different urban forces, and I have never, ever seen a police officer obviously pick on someone or treat them badly simply because of the colour of their skin. I've just never seen it.

However, I've seen *thousands* of incidents involving confrontations with members of the public of all ethnic backgrounds, many of them very violent indeed, and there was always a good reason that this had happened and it was never because an officer just decided to target them because of their ethnicity. To an onlooker or someone watching phone footage after the event, the sight of three or four white police officers trying to physically restrain a young black man in the street will often create the impression that they're acting oppressively. There are so many possible reasons why something like this might be happening.

The man may have been pointed out by a recent victim of crime as a suspect. He may have been seen buying or dealing drugs and the officers had reasonable cause to conduct a search. He might be wanted on warrant or wanted for an offence and the police had been trying to track him down to arrest him. He might even be suffering from a serious mental illness and was therefore being detained for his own safety. But, of course, all that passers-by see, and what is frequently then replayed on TV or on social media, is three or four white officers appearing to assault a young black man for no reason.

There have also been a number of deaths in police custody involving black and minority ethnic members of the public that have been alleged to have resulted from police brutality. Every death is a terrible tragedy for a grieving family and I certainly don't underestimate the damaging effect of these incidents. However, if you genuinely believe that the only possible explanation for those deaths is that the police murdered them or, at the very least, set out to deliberately cause serious harm to that person, this is not the case. Many of these deaths resulted from a tragic combination of drug ingestion, alcohol intoxication, severe mental health issues and sometimes underlying health vulnerabilities. When you add a violent physical struggle into this mix it can sometimes end very tragically with a condition that is known as 'excited delirium' or 'sudden death in restraint syndrome', which can lead to cardiac arrest.

There is a clear issue of disproportionality across the entire criminal justice system. Young black men in particular are significantly more likely to be stopped and searched, more likely to be arrested and charged and more likely to be sent to prison. There is therefore a correspondingly disproportionate number of young black men who are likely to die in police custody for all sorts of reasons that do not necessarily have anything to do with police misconduct. However, the question that everyone needs to ask here is, 'Why is this the case?' I'm not even going to try to answer that question comprehensively because that is one for sociologists, psychologists, educationalists and economists. All that I will suggest is that there is an unbelievably complex situation that needs to be seen as a whole to be appreciated. We need to look at how social deprivation, low levels of educational attainment, poor housing and other factors such as drugs, addiction, broken families and poor mental health have all contributed to this situation.

So, what are the options for police in the following hypothetical, yet typical, situation?

Police are called to a public place to deal with a disturbance. A man is pacing around in an agitated state, shouting incoherently at passers-by. On their arrival, the officers try to engage him in conversation to calm him down but he continues to shout at and threaten people in the street. By his general demeanour the officers assess that he is either under the influence of drugs or suffering from mental health issues and that he needs to be detained under Section 136 of the Mental Health Act for his own protection and for the protection of the public. He is a big and strong man and the officers know from experience that they will need help, so they call for another unit to attend. On the arrival of the second car, the officers attempt to take the man by the arm and lead him to the car but he violently resists. This man has a long history of severe mental health problems, several convictions for violent offences and he has not been taking his medication. He has also recently smoked several rocks of crack cocaine. What should the officers do? Ignore the man and walk away? That is not an option. They must deal with the situation as carefully as they can. But the officers know that things can go horribly wrong in such a situation.

I've experienced this many times and, believe me, it's not enjoyable.

Professor Larry Sherman leads the Cambridge Centre for Evidence-based Policing. Research he conducted in 2020 into UK homicides found that murder rates across the UK are between 200 per cent and 800 per cent higher in black communities than they are in white communities. Even more shockingly, in the 16–24 age group young black men are twenty-four times more likely to be victims of homicide than white men of the same age. Sadly, the majority of these victims will be killed by other young black men. It is therefore clear to me why young black men are disproportionately impacted by police use of stop and search and I have no doubt that many young lives have needlessly been lost as a result of politicians undermining the use of this tactic by police.

Indeed, rather unbelievably, Sadiq Khan pledged to 'do everything in my power to cut stop and search' when he was campaigning to be London Mayor in 2015. By 2018, in the face of spiralling numbers of fatal stabbings in London, he pledged 'a significant increase in stop and search' as a 'vital tool for police to keep our communities safe'. However, by November 2020, he again pledged to overhaul the disproportionate use of stop and search and the way that it was affecting black Londoners. A typical example of shameless political opportunism and hypocrisy that has ended up costing lives.

Will anyone ever hold politicians responsible for their recklessness? Will they ever get dragged through the courts the way that police officers regularly do when something goes wrong? I definitely won't hold my breath on that ever happening.

Many police officers are now talking openly about *never* stopping and searching people, particularly minority ethnic suspects, because it simply isn't worth the hassle. The police obviously can't ignore criminality because that would be a disaster and many lives would be lost. Nonetheless, I believe that if this nonsense persists there is a real possibility of just that happening. There needs to be more of an open and honest discourse about this issue and an acknowledgement that, for all sorts of complex reasons, young minority ethnic men in some of our major cities are disproportionately both victims and perpetrators of violent crime. The police can either deal with the situations they find themselves in or they can ignore them. What should they do?

The assertion that the British police are a bunch of racists shows no signs of going away. I have always found it deeply offensive to have the institution that I worked for labelled in this way. I believe that many of the people who continue to make this claim have an ideological agenda that is at odds with the harsh realities that police officers and many other public servants have to deal with. They're not interested in hearing the side of the police or considering other explanations because they do not fit their one-sided narrative. Most senior police officers are too timid to challenge this properly; preferring to throw their own people under the bus rather than say it how it is. However, one thing that is clear to me is that by continuing this narrative, police critics are condemning many, many more young black men to violent deaths before their lives have even started.

CHAPTER 11

INNER-CITY VIOLENCE AND DEPRIVATION

Clapham was an eye-opener for me even though I had already done eighteen months of operational policing at Sutton.

Inner-city policing involves dealing with the human consequences of trauma, poverty, deprivation, addiction, low life expectations, violent and abusive relationships, inadequate housing, poor mental health and highly dysfunctional families 24/7. As police officers, we tend to intervene in people's lives when things have reached or gone beyond crisis point. Crisis point for many people only comes along with events like the loss of a well-paid job, finding out that a long-term partner has been having an affair or learning that a loved one has an incurable illness. All these things are individually horrible, but the people we were dealing with had much of this going on as well as other chronic issues that made their lives pretty hellish.

There is often a sense of inner conflict for police officers working in these kinds of areas. On the one hand, you desperately want to work in these places because you know it's going to be interesting and exciting. On the other hand, you will frequently go home despairing at the injustices served up by life and the hostility with which you are treated by many fellow human beings.

The police get sworn at, spat at, lied to and frequently physically assaulted because they are the only people in society who will stand in front of someone and say: 'No, you are not going to do that as it's against the law and if I have to I will physically stop you from doing it.' When there is a crisis we are the ones who get called and we have to sort it out.

Many people simply do not want to abide by the standards and systems that make Britain a functional and tolerably peaceful place to live. For such figures, it was often the case that their parents or carers had little control over them; their teachers were so exasperated with their disruptive behaviour that they had to exclude them from school; and they challenged every authority figure they came across. For these people, it is down to the police to enforce the law and tell them 'No'. And if the police can't do that, then we are all in trouble.

And it is not just people from low socio-economic backgrounds who behave in this way. I regularly dealt with entitled, obnoxious people (usually men) who had good jobs, drove expensive cars and lived in nice houses. Their offending tended to be less obvious, however, and either took place behind closed doors at home or in the workplace or in the form of aggressive or drunken behaviour on the road.

Academics and journalists often criticise the police and provide explanations about how bad behaviour can be the result of environmental factors, such as deprivation, neglect, foetal alcohol syndrome and social exclusion. I understand that these can all influence an individual's behaviour. However, such assessments do not provide practical advice for how the police should actually act. For example, how should they deal with a very angry, alienated, intoxicated seventeen-year-old who has tried to assault a doctor trying to deliver his sixteen-year-old girlfriend's baby simply because he takes exception to the doctor touching her vagina? I use this example because I actually dealt with this exact situation, but there are thousands more situations just like this.

It's frustrating when you read agenda-driven headlines in newspapers by journalists, who do not provide or have access to all of the facts, pontificating on situations that they have never had to deal with and offering judgements on the actions of police officers who have made split-second decisions in a chaotic situation playing out in front of them at 2 a.m. I would love to take a journalist on a normal, bread-and-butter policing call and see how they deal with such a situation:

'There you go, see that really angry-looking, coked-up bloke over there in the corner of the pub with the broken bottle in his hand threatening customers? I want you to approach him, talk to him and if necessary bring him into custody in a way that is lawful and where neither you nor he sustains unnecessary injuries.'

Or:

'See that seventeen-year-old with eight previous convictions for violence running away from that stolen car with his pockets full of cash and a Rolex from a robbery victim? I want you to chase him through the streets and then arrest him without being heavy-handed.'

When I was in Clapham in the early 1990s, police officer safety (or rather the lack of it) became a massive issue, particularly in the major cities. It's hard to believe it now, but at this time we patrolled day and night unarmed with no body armour, no CS gas, no baton worth talking about and no GPS-enabled communications device that showed exactly where we were when we got into trouble. I can remember hearing police officers screaming on the radio trying to summon help. All that we could do was quickly get to the general location that they had been sent to and try to find them or wait for a member of the public to dial 999 to tell us what was going on and the exact location of where it was happening. In hindsight, it was disgraceful that this situation was never challenged properly or remedied by those in positions of power.

During this period, many Met officers were killed or seriously injured on duty. In November 1991, Sergeant Alan King was stabbed to death by Nicholas Vernage, who had just been released from prison. Vernage had murdered his girlfriend days earlier and then murdered a man whose home he was burgling. Alan, who was patrolling alone, had become suspicious of Vernage and challenged him. Vernage turned on him and stabbed him multiple times. The following day, on the other side of London, patrolling officers John Jenkinson and Simon Castrey spotted Vernage in a car and challenged him. Vernage stabbed them multiple times, causing horrendous injuries to both officers. They survived only as a result of receiving rapid medical attention. Shortly after, Vernage was apprehended and later sentenced to twenty-five years.

Shortly after this in December 1991, Detective Constable Jim Morrison was stabbed to death whilst trying to detain a handbag thief in Covent Garden, central London. Jim's killer has never been brought to justice.

Then, tragedy came to Clapham in October 1993 when my good friend and close colleague PC Pat Dunne was shot dead in cold blood by notorious gangster Gary Nelson, who moments earlier had murdered William Danso in his home. Danso had been a bouncer and was murdered for the crime of 'disrespecting' Nelson by refusing him entry to a nightclub. Pat had been attending a routine incident in the house opposite and on hearing gunfire walked outside just as Nelson and his two accomplices were leaving Danso's house. They shot Pat dead and ran away laughing.

Four months later in February 1994, Sergeant Derek Robertson was stabbed to death when he tackled three men who were escaping from an attempted post office robbery in Croydon, south London. And in April 1995, PC Phillip Walters was called to assist in a domestic disturbance in Empress Avenue, Ilford. As he was attempting to handcuff the suspect, a gun was drawn and PC Walters was shot dead.

In October 1997, 25-year-old PC Nina Mackay was stabbed to death by a paranoid schizophrenic in Stratford, east London, during a routine arrest.

The murder of a police officer on duty anywhere in the UK has a huge impact on all serving officers, who collectively grieve for their fallen colleague. However, the impact of Pat's death on everyone at Clapham was profound. We were a very tight-knit policing 'family' and we went out day after day to deal with difficult and dangerous incidents across south London literally in our shirt-sleeves.

This murder was particularly despicable. Pat was not trying to apprehend Nelson but had heard the gunshots and arrived on the scene. He was outnumbered three-to-one, and the trio were armed with two guns. They shot Pat in the chest, who was unarmed with no protective equipment. He literally didn't have a chance.

Pat was one of the kindest people I have ever met. He was a very gentle man, in many ways totally unsuited to policing, but this 'weakness' was also his strength because he inspired great trust in those he dealt with. He had joined the police rather late in life after a career in teaching. He was very softly spoken, had an easy-going manner and great wisdom as a result of spending over twenty years in the classroom. He was particularly great with kids and older people and this made him a natural fit for the role of the permanent beat officer, sorting out the daily issues that arise in local communities with patience and good humour.

It was an appalling injustice that Pat was murdered in such a callous way. Nelson managed to evade justice until twelve years later in 2006 when he was finally convicted and sentenced to thirty-five years in prison. I hope that every day of those thirty-five years is a thoroughly miserable experience. He'll certainly have plenty of time to think about what a complete coward he was; unfit to even stand in the same room as a good man like Pat Dunne.

Pat's death and avoidable deaths of serving police officers before and since made many in the police believe that legislators and opinion-formers were ultimately not interested in supporting and protecting them. This would be proven to be much more than just a suspicion twenty years later (during Theresa May's time as Home Secretary and Prime Minister) when everyone finally realised that the protective 'covenant' between the British police service and the government had irretrievably broken down.

The debate over whether the British police should be armed rumbled on for the length of my time in the police. I'm convinced that the police should not be routinely armed and there are several reasons that I believe this. Firstly, I believe that the routine carrying of firearms would create a barrier between the police and the public because most of the police's interactions are non-confrontational – whether with victims, witnesses or people just going about their business. It is not just the mere appearance of firearms that has this effect. It is the fact that police officers would inevitably have to change their behaviour and approach when responding to crime to take account for the fact that they're carrying a deadly weapon. Secondly, if the police are armed there is substantially more risk of innocent members of the public being mistakenly shot or, for that matter, police officers being disarmed and shot with their own weapons. And finally, there are some police officers that I have worked with over the years who I wouldn't trust with a sharpened stick never mind a gun.

In Clapham, we had run-ins with very dangerous people almost every day and, because the policing culture was about proactivity at that time, we actively sought these people out. We didn't get tied up in ridiculous risk assessments in the way that police officers do today. We just got on with it.

Clapham and Brixton were home to many major drug dealers who supplied a small army of street dealers. Many of them carried guns and they were not afraid to use them on rivals or on the police if we got in their way. We hunted these people down day and night, as well as the scores of active burglars, street robbers and car thieves who were offending on our patch. But it was the drug dealers who posed the biggest risk to everyone. They were collectively referred to as 'Yardies', which was derived from the Jamaican patois term for 'back yard'. Many Yardies were British born and bred, but just as many shuttled backwards and forwards across the Atlantic and had connections in the United States as well as other parts of Europe.

Some of the most experienced officers in Clapham had an encyclopaedic knowledge of these drug gangs and had dealt with some of them many times between periods of imprisonment and periodic deportations, but they would then pop back up in London using a new name, with a new set of identity documents. The Met introduced a number of major initiatives to try to stem the increasing violence and murders arising from Yardie activity. Operations Lucy and Dalehouse were set up, and later came the long-standing Operation Trident, which focused on wider issues of drug-related gang violence. These initiatives were frequently criticised as being discriminatory to black members of the community; however, such criticisms never offered a more effective solution to the problem – in the same way that today's police critics do not offer a solution to the knife-crime epidemic.

I often think about how many close shaves I had over the years, but in Clapham these were a fairly regular occurrence. But there is one event that particularly sticks in my mind.

I was working as the operator in 'Lima 2', the Clapham area car, on a night shift in the summer of 1993. It had been a hot day and it was still fairly warm as we cruised around the south of our patch. I was crewed with the driver, Phil Weston, who was a Clapham legend and without a doubt the best proactive thief-taker that I ever worked with. He was a fairly small, but incredibly tough, Welshman with an unbelievable ability to sniff out criminality and an amazing memory for names, faces and vehicle registrations. He had been at Clapham for over twenty years at this time and he later went on to work as a detective on the Met's serious and organised crime team. It's worth emphasising as an aside here that these professional policing skills are not acquired overnight. They take many, many years to learn, which is why flooding the current police service with inexperienced rookies is incredibly risky.

It was about 2 a.m., and I can remember sitting in the car with the window wound down, listening to the intermittent transmissions coming from the 'mainset' radio, as well as the local Clapham channel on my personal radio. Phil was always on the lookout and missed absolutely nothing. He could do this whilst also making me laugh with a constant stream of amusing anecdotes that would generally be triggered by passing a point in the road where something funny had happened to him many years before. As we were driving along, suddenly he gunned the engine and went off at some speed, turning the lights of the car off. He'd obviously seen something that he wasn't happy about and he often did this to buy us a few moments of time so as not to alert the suspect.

I asked him what he'd seen and he told me that a car had just turned rather too quickly into one of the council estates – often a sign that someone wanted to avoid the attentions of the police. We turned into the estate and found the car parked in a dead-end. We pulled up about twenty yards away from it and just sat there watching, with the engine ticking over. After a couple of minutes, the doors opened and three very large, scary-looking men got out of the car. Phil immediately recognised the front-seat passenger as a prominent Yardie gangster. They went into a huddle for a moment, and then all three started walking away from their car towards our car. They were walking very purposefully, very determined and all were grim-faced. The driver had a long black leather coat on which came down to his knees. As they drew closer, the man in the leather coat began to reach inside his coat, but before I could see what he was reaching for, Phil slammed the area car into reverse and drove at top speed away from the trio, spinning the car around to face the other direction before driving away. We both knew that if we'd stayed there we would have been shot. I have no doubt whatsoever that they were carrying guns and, by the way that they were walking, they had made the decision to shoot us. Why? Probably because there was a large quantity of drugs or guns in the car, or perhaps because one or more of them was wanted for serious offences that would guarantee a long prison sentence.

I can't prove that we would have been shot, but every instinct in my body told me that we were in very great danger. As every good police officer knows, sometimes you've got to tactically withdraw until the odds are stacked more in your favour, and as we used to say, 'They'll come again'; in other words, 'They're criminals, we'll get them eventually.'

The need to protect police officers became increasingly clear and in the mid-1990s hundreds of officers in the UK were asking law enforcement colleagues in the United States to send them their second-hand body armour. This was obviously incredibly embarrassing for senior officers and the Police Federation. However, it was not until the early 2000s that the wearing of stab vests was mandated for all operational officers.

During my time in the Met, the only time that I felt a little better protected was when we went to Hounslow to do our twice-yearly public order refresher training, otherwise known as riot training. We would spend two days there in our flame-proof suits and NATO helmets, running through various tactics, working as a team to deal with all sorts of scenarios in a massive fake town that had been constructed with its own houses, shops, streets and vehicles of all types. I loved the training; it was great fun. At the end of the two days we would have a full-on riot with hundreds of petrol bombs being thrown at us by the instructors alongside wooden 'bricks' that bloody hurt if they hit an unprotected part of your body. The students would be split into two groups: rioters and cops. I particularly enjoyed being one of the rioters. We always used to focus our aim at the inspectors and chief inspectors in command, who wore orange epaulettes on their shoulders, which was hilarious because scores of bricks would all end up being thrown at some poor inspector. I found this less funny when I was an inspector myself many years later and was in that exact situation.

At that time, one of the instructors was a slightly terrifying warrior of an officer called Tracy Axton. She was stunning, with long auburn hair, about 6ft tall, built of solid muscle and she kicked the living crap out of everyone, me included. We called her the Ginger Ninja. One of the exercises we trained for was to go into a room in threes with shields and deal with an armed assailant. I remember going into the room with other officers to try to deal with her. She was armed with a baseball bat and an iron bar and she literally pummelled all three of us into the ground.

When working in Clapham (and this applied in any deprived inner-city location in London), there was almost constant aggravation and conflict. Very few people cooperated with the police voluntarily. Anyone who had been through the system would generally refuse to tell you their name when stopped and frequently gave false names. This situation generated a lot of friction and distrust on the street between the police and young people, particularly those who lived in tough neighbourhoods. This sense of distrust was made worse by annoying left-wing radical types who would often interrupt conversations on the street between police officers and young people. Frequently, they would tell the young people we were talking to not to speak to the police as, in their eyes, we were the worst kind of fascist oppressors. I can remember one comical incident in Brixton when we were trying to help a couple of young black lads who had been attacked by a group of youths. We were taking their details and writing down the descriptions of their assailants when a car stopped beside us. Out jumped a pair of humourless activists in their usual uniforms, which consisted of John Lennon glasses, dodgy tie-dyed T-shirts, jeans and Doc Marten shoes. The only thing they didn't have were copies of *Socialist Worker* in their back pockets. They immediately interrupted us (or 'put their oar in', as we would have said) and tried to pull the two boys away. I told them to clear off and tried to explain that these lads were victims of crime and we were trying to investigate what had happened. They refused to listen to us and kept telling the boys not to talk to us, before trying to shove 'know your rights' leaflets into their hands. Eventually, one of the lads turned around and told them to piss off and mind their own business. So, looking confused and downhearted, the pair got back into their car and pissed off to wage war against the fascist state somewhere else. This used to happen quite a lot in south London and it was especially irritating when such people also had video cameras that they shoved in your face. Many would try to goad us into arresting them for obstruction. This would have been legally justified but it just wasn't worth the hassle, complaints and inevitable civil action. I can't even imagine how horrible it must be now with camera phones everywhere.

By the start of 1994, and after four years on the beat, I felt that I was ready for a new challenge. Life at Clapham was great, but the police service has so many opportunities to try different things and I had started to think about my options.

Metropolitan Police Special Branch, or 'SB' as it was referred to, held a strong attraction for me. It was the only department in the Met that required applicants to pass a demanding set of tests, an interview and an exam to permit entry. The selection procedure was rigorous and potential applicants were advised to spend a minimum of six months preparing to apply as there was an expectation that candidates had a comprehensive knowledge of UK current affairs, politics and world events.

In due course, I sat and passed all of the tests and after a tough interview I was offered a posting as a detective constable in Special Branch. After the mandatory leaving drinks with my Clapham comrades, who took the piss mercilessly about me leaving to become a 'spy', in June 1994, I turned up for work at New Scotland Yard in my smart new suit and tie.

CHAPTER 12

SPECIAL BRANCH

Special Branch was formed in 1883 and was originally called the 'Special Irish Branch' because it had been set up to combat the activities of the Irish Republican Brotherhood, who conducted a bombing campaign in England between 1881 and 1885, targeting iconic sites, including the Tower of London and the Houses of Parliament, in an attempt to force the British out of the island of Ireland.

The role, remit and size of SB grew over time. Eventually, it became a large intelligence-gathering organisation charged with tackling all types of national security threats, including from domestic and foreign terrorism, extreme left- and right-wing threats, hostile foreign powers and later the threat to public order from environmental groups and animal rights activists.

Special Branch was a unique entity as it had one foot squarely in the policing world and the other in the world of national security, working very closely with MI5 (the UK domestic security service), MI6 (the UK foreign security service) and GCHQ (the government communications intelligence agency). However, at Special Branch first and foremost we were police officers primarily accountable to the Metropolitan Police commissioner, police regulations and the courts. Our formal name was SO12, where 'SO' stood for 'specialist operations'. There were lots of other renowned specialist operations departments in the Met, such as SO8, otherwise known as the 'Flying Squad', who dealt with armed robberies, and our sister department SO13, the Anti-Terrorism Branch, who arrested and built the criminal case against terrorists once we told them who they were, what they'd been doing and where to find them. SO13 also investigated terrorist incidents that had already happened, which arguably meant that SO12 and MI5 had failed to stop those attacks from happening. Whilst such obvious 'intelligence failures' had tragic consequences, due to the nature of the work, 90 per cent of our successes never became public knowledge simply because to do so would have exposed secret sources and sensitive intelligence-gathering techniques.

On my first day at Scotland Yard, I was shown around by a charming but slightly ageing sergeant who had obviously been in the Branch for about a thousand years. I remember him telling me that when he was asked by his kids and grandkids what he did at work, he told them, 'I keep an eye on the people who would be on the side of the enemy if we went to war.' He said this with a twinkle in his eye but, over the years, I found this overly simplistic explanation actually quite accurate. Ultimately, apart from the extreme right-wing Nazis that we investigated, none of these people would have been happy to stand up and sing the national anthem. Most of them worked to an agenda that was in some way about undermining democracy and the rule of law.

At this time, SB was divided into several squads that were

responsible for different thematic issues. B squad was charged with countering the activities of the Provisional IRA (PIRA) on the UK mainland and C squad was focused on domestic extremism, including extreme left- and right-wing activists, animal rights extremists and environmental groups. Most of the groups and individuals that C squad investigated and monitored didn't pose the same level of risk as terrorists. However, they were still dealing with individuals who were perfectly happy to commit quite serious criminal offences to further their aims. Such individuals posed a threat to public order as well as disruption to legitimate businesses.

There was also E squad, who investigated hostile foreign intelligence agencies that wanted to spy on the UK or mount attacks on political dissidents in exile in London. Historically, E squad was focused on frustrating the efforts of Cold War adversaries, including the Soviet, East German and Czech security services. After the Cold War and the fall of the Berlin Wall in 1989, E squad started to take a greater interest in emerging threats from other parts of the world. The focus turned to Palestinian terrorist groups as well as the growing threat from battle-hardened Islamists returning from conflicts in Afghanistan, Chechnya, Algeria and Bosnia.

A squad was the department that provided 24/7 armed protection for the Prime Minister and other key government personnel as well as any foreign dignitary deemed to be at risk of terrorist attacks, such as the US ambassador or the Israeli ambassador to the UK.

P squad monitored individuals leaving from or arriving at an international port, such as Heathrow airport or the Eurostar terminal. These officers would stop people of interest to the security services and detain them under anti-terrorism legislation. They also had an important role to play with checking or arresting wanted criminals entering or leaving the UK and safeguarding children being unlawfully taken out of the UK.

Finally, S squad conducted all of the surveillance activity associated with ongoing operations. Typically, this surveillance was directed at suspected terrorists or their support networks. Any part of Special Branch could task S squad and their work was therefore extremely varied.

I am not going to discuss sensitive aspects of Special Branch work, primarily because I am still bound by the Official Secrets Act, but also because this book is more about how the police service changed during my time as an officer. There are plenty of books out there about national security policing. Some are quite good but many are written by Walter Mitty-types who briefly passed through the intelligence world before moving on or getting kicked out.

I was introduced to my new team and I was ecstatic to find that I had been posted to B squad, the biggest and busiest department in Special Branch. B squad had a fantastic reputation, having more or less been on a war footing since the early 1970s, and had investigated every significant Irish terrorist conspiracy over that period of time.

Over thirty years until the late 1990s, the Troubles in Northern Ireland resulted in the deaths of nearly 4,000 people and caused innumerable serious injuries and enormous destruction. The majority of deaths were caused by Republican paramilitaries, including PIRA, who targeted police officers, military personnel, high-profile individuals and locations of perceived economic value to the British state. They were a competent, ruthless and well-organised terrorist organisation that was configured into local geographic units led by an officer commanding (OC). Each geographic unit had a team of senior members responsible for defined tasks, including recruitment, training, logistics, intelligence, operations and discipline. PIRA operated on a cell structure which maximised operational security by ensuring that only a small number of individuals would ever be privy to operational intelligence or, for that matter, the membership details for each cell.

PIRA was well-funded from overseas donations, extortion, fraud, organised crime and the smuggling of alcohol, cigarettes and diesel fuel across the Irish border. It was also well-equipped and had acquired an extensive arsenal of modern weapons and explosives from sympathetic foreign powers and criminals across the Middle East, eastern Europe, north Africa and the United States.

The focus of B squad was to gather intelligence and evidence to facilitate the arrest of PIRA members covertly sent to the UK mainland to carry out assassinations and bombing campaigns. These PIRA teams were referred to as active service units (ASUs) and the individuals sent to the mainland were generally some of the best people the group had. In the early days of the PIRA mainland bombing campaign back in the 1970s, the calibre of terrorists sent to the UK wasn't the best; however, by the time I joined Special Branch in 1994, PIRA had become extremely experienced at operating on the mainland and they had learned the lessons from many years of successful and unsuccessful operations.

Many of the detectives I joined had been around for a very long time and knew this murky world intimately. They talked with great authority and passion about operations from years before and about what individuals had been in the different PIRA ASUs and how they had tackled them.

The risks taken by ASU members were significant and they had it drilled into them that they faced two likely outcomes by volunteering for mainland or overseas duties. They faced either death or imprisonment and that was the fate that awaited most of them. It was possible for ASU members to conduct mainland attacks successfully and then slip back to Ireland. However, the odds of compromise and arrest grew over time and sooner or later most of them would make a mistake and leave a forensic trail, come to the attention of the intelligence services one way or another or just run out of luck. We may not have agreed with what PIRA was trying to achieve, or the violent methods they used, but in SB we had a lot of respect for our adversaries, as I suspect they had for us. Many years later, long-standing counter-terrorism officers all agreed that if Islamist extremists in the UK had displayed even a quarter of the logistical skills and operational tradecraft that PIRA had displayed, we would have been in a lot more trouble as a nation.

Shortly after I was posted to B squad, a long period of negotiations between the British government and the leadership of PIRA finally led to them announcing a cessation of military operations in August 1994.

This was a bittersweet moment for many of us involved in counter-terrorism. On the one hand, we were pleased that PIRA would (at least, for the moment) no longer be killing and maiming innocent people, but on the other hand, our *raison d'être* as Special Branch officers was to pit our wits against terrorists to stop attacks. It was a bit like soldiers training for combat and then being told they would not be going to war after all and would be staying at home in their barracks.

Once it became clear that PIRA was semi-serious about a ceasefire, B squad was slimmed down and many officers were redeployed to other SB teams.

Thanks to the IRA ceasefire, and to my slight bemusement, I found myself transferred to the Islamic fundamentalist desk of E squad. To say that this was a steep learning curve for me was an understatement, because I knew next to nothing about Islam or for that matter about Islamic fundamentalism at this time. Fortunately, I would be working with some people who knew a lot and I, therefore, immersed myself in the subject matter, asked some really dumb questions and absorbed lots of books very quickly.

It's hard to believe it now, nearly twenty years after 9/11, but back in the mid-1990s, hardly anyone was interested in Islamic extremism. Our desk was one of the poor relations of the much sexier Irish Republican terrorism desks that swanned around with their new-fangled mobile phones, pagers and unlimited overtime budgets. However, very quickly we saw the increasing threat from fundamentalist fighters returning from foreign warzones and how 'Londonistan' (as the French government referred to the English capital at the time) was emerging as a safe gathering place for Islamist radicals from around the world. It was clear that these people were exploiting the British respect for civil liberties and the tradition of providing protection for political activists, whilst at the same time espousing contempt for democracy and 'decadent' Western values. However, hindsight is a wonderful thing, and it would have taken something of an intergalactic leap to successfully predict the cataclysmic events that would play out in the years that were to come.

Daily life in SB was great fun. The work was fascinating, the people were knowledgeable, and frequently hilarious, and the camaraderie was amazing. We got invited to some fantastic places around London, and we enjoyed being part of a much wider national security community that I never really knew about. We also worked closely with our counterparts from friendly nations across the world, and barely a week would go by without an invitation to meet someone interesting or host an overseas colleague.

Fellow SB officers could not have been more welcoming towards newcomers like me, and there was definitely the sense that I had joined quite an exclusive club in which we were all bound together by a strong sense of history and a need for great discretion because of the nature of what we did. It's always the people who make or break any job, and the people in SB were often true characters; many were larger-than-life personalities with great charisma who could hold their own in any company. They were quite capable of chatting comfortably to homeless alcoholics one moment and government ministers the next, and this was their particular skill, which had been honed during the critical years of front-line uniformed policing that everyone in

SB had in common. There was a definite mystique surrounding Special Branch and this created animosity amongst some police colleagues outside the department. The people who had the biggest chips on their shoulders towards SB tended to be senior officers in other departments who at some point had tried and failed to get in. They were frequently bitter about this many years later, and they really hated the fact that there was sensitive information that could not be shared with them, no matter how much they tried to pull rank or bully junior officers.

They frequently didn't understand that a typical SB report written by a junior officer was often an amalgamation of information and intelligence drawn from lots of very sensitive sources. Some of it could be from human informants, some from technical sources, some from covert surveillance deployments and some from information supplied in confidence from other government departments. Mostly, it was a case of filling gaps in your understanding of a particular issue by going out, discreetly speaking to contacts in the community or using your common sense and policing skills. My first two years in Special Branch were spent learning to write these reports. It was a real skill, and most of my early efforts were returned by my sergeants with schoolteacher-like red pen through entire sections that had to be re-written. The trick was to write a report that told the reader everything they needed to know about a person or an issue in about three sides of A4. SB had rigorous standards in terms of style, format and content. The reader needed to be unable to guess where information had come from to protect sensitive sources.

Everything was produced on paper; each report would be

printed out and checked thoroughly by a sergeant before being submitted to the detective inspector. If they were happy with it, it was attached to a paper file relating to that person or organisation and stored in SB Registry, which was a huge room filled from floor to ceiling with row upon row of files, many of which went back as far as the First World War.

We gleaned our intelligence from all sorts of places; from the most mundane to the most secret and sensitive. Unlike today, we did not rely on technology and most of the devices that would have been considered super-secret in those days you could probably have bought in Currys or Argos ten years ago. I can remember us all gathered around a single, brand-new Special Branch desktop computer with its 33K dial-up modem back in 1994. We looked on, gobsmacked at the wonders of this new bit of kit that could produce information out of the ether like magic. There was only one person who was authorised to use it and he guarded this privilege jealously.

Ultimately our 'customers' were the security services who would set the intelligence requirement and we would go out and fulfil it. At this time, the relationship between SB and MI5 was quite a tense one. MI5 had been left with relatively little to do at the end of the Cold War in 1989, and they needed to find a role that ensured that the Treasury didn't start looking too closely at their budget. At this time, SB was responsible for all intelligence gathering that related to Irish Republican terrorism on the UK mainland; however, around this time, MI5 successfully lobbied the government to take on that task.

The relationship between the two agencies had always been complicated, but this decision went down particularly badly in

Scotland Yard. Relationships are thankfully a lot healthier today than they were in the 1990s. At the time, many in SB felt that MI5 had a condescending and paternalistic approach to us; they would disparagingly refer to us as 'Plod' and treated us as if we were all a bunch of knuckle-dragging morons when, in reality, many of us were more educated than they were. There was long-standing irritation in SB that MI5 continually reaped the benefits of all our hard work by merely changing the letter-heading on the reports we had compiled and then, to add insult to injury, frequently tried to shift the blame onto us when any-thing went wrong. We referred to them as the 'Toads' and their HQ at Thames House as 'Toad Hall' because of the way that we saw them toadying sycophantically to civil servants and govern-ment ministers.

Many MI5 desk officers were barely out of university and were quite naïve about how the world worked. We saw it as our job to try to educate the slow learners. This involved taking them out to the pub, telling them a few home truths and then getting them drunk. Working relationships were usually better after that.

I remember one amusing incident when an enthusiastic young desk officer had asked to do a two-week attachment to SB. This wasn't a common occurrence; mainly because senior officers were worried they would run back to Thames House telling tales about those 'nasty, thick coppers', although it probably had as much to do with mutual antipathy. However, during my time there was a growing realisation on both sides that we all needed to build more bridges and play nicely.

A few of us had been asked to look after this lad, take him out and about and show him what we did and how we did it. And so it was that after about ten days, a couple of us got called into the DCI's office and he asked us how it was going. This particular DCI was much loved, extremely competent and hugely respected by everyone. He was a great guy, but he didn't suffer fools gladly. We told him what we'd been doing with this lad, telling him that it had gone pretty well and we hadn't given him any reasons to tell any tales to his superiors that would paint us particularly badly. The DCI sat listening and nodding on the other side of the desk. At the end of our account, he leaned back in his chair and said, 'Yes, I've had a couple of chats with him and to be fair, apart from being a complete tosser, he's not a bad lad, is he?'

We both fell about laughing because we knew exactly what he meant. The lad's heart was in the right place, he seemed keen to learn and didn't appear to have any hidden agenda, but he just wasn't the sort of bloke you'd want to go to the pub with or, God forbid, back you up if you got in a tricky situation. The DCI had made the same assessment straight away. In many ways, that single remark summed up the difference between MI5 and Special Branch during the period that I was an officer.

I was lucky to work alongside some true non-conformists in Special Branch. This sounds counter-intuitive, but I can honestly say that some of the people I worked with were genuine one-offs, and I had absolutely no idea how on earth they had ended up joining the Met in the first place. I won't name them, but I don't doubt that my ex-colleagues will know exactly who I'm talking about.

We had a guy who had been in the Australian Army during the Vietnam War and had been a 'tunnel rat', crawling through miles of pitch-black Vietcong tunnels armed with a Colt 45 handgun. He actually had a medical certificate to prove that he had been clinically assessed as being sane that he would proudly show people.

One of the older chaps I sat close to in the office for several years was convinced that his brain was being fried by the computers in the office and he also complained bitterly about others talking on the phones because his hearing aids would play up. He therefore surrounded himself with a wall of cardboard boxes covered in tinfoil, turning his workspace into something that looked like a miniature shanty town.

We had an ex-scriptwriter for many of the earliest episodes of *Doctor Who* on the team. He still gets mobbed when he goes to *Doctor Who* conferences and events around the world.

Another very eccentric SB DC had auditioned to be the gong-striking muscle-man at the start of the Rank films and had ultimately been pipped at the post by Ken Richmond, the Olympic wrestler.

We also had quite a few very posh characters, who spoke with plums in their mouth and could easily have passed for minor royals or members of the aristocracy. One of them used to get called away to do undercover jobs for the art and antiques squad, flying across the world and staying in very upmarket hotels, posing as a wealthy buyer for stolen masterpieces. Another of them was a rather lovely classically trained pianist, who I would address formally as 'Lady Katherine'. I could never figure out why on earth she had joined the police, but she was fantastic at her job and great fun to be around. She would tell amusing stories of dealing with violent, gobby detainees as a sergeant who she would quickly have eating out of her hand as she treated them like naughty schoolboys caught having a midnight feast after lights out.

However, my absolute favourite character was someone called Andy. Andy had served in the Royal Marines and in the Special Boat Squadron in the Falklands War. Andy was a practical joker with a wicked sense of humour and, on one occasion in 1998, I was one of his many victims. He was based in Thames House, the MI5 HQ for a period of time, and I needed to go there for a meeting about something or other. At that time, he was very slowly building his own house from building materials that he collected by rifling through skips on people's drives. We joked with him that he was like the Old Woman Who Lived in a Shoe.

He met me in the foyer and, after getting through the inevitable security processes, we walked through the building chatting. I had been there quite a few times, but I was grateful for his company because the building is huge and it's probably one of the most confusing places that I've ever been in. Everywhere looked exactly the same. All of the corridors were painted the same drab light grey, and all of the offices that we walked past looked exactly the same, making it a rather disorientating place to be.

Eventually, we walked into an office where there was a single occupant; an attractive girl in her late twenties, sitting at a desk, typing away on a computer. I had never seen her before. She looked up and smiled politely. There was then a rather long and awkward pause, with Andy standing there saying nothing, and me stood there wondering why we were in this particular office. The girl looked quizzically at us both.

Andy then rather formally cleared his throat and said, 'Iain, this is Suzanna. Suzanna, this is Iain.'

I smiled and nodded at her and said, 'Hello, Suzanna,' and she returned the greeting.

Andy carried on standing there, saying nothing, and I began to feel very uncomfortable and a little confused. After another ten seconds of silence that felt about ten minutes, he said to me, 'Go on then...'

I said, 'Sorry, Andy, what do you mean, "Go on"?'

Andy said, 'I think you have something to say, Iain, don't you?'

I looked blankly at him and said, 'Sorry, Andy, I have no idea what you're talking about.'

He rolled his eyes and smiled apologetically at Suzanna and said, 'Suzanna, Iain has something that he would like to say to you, haven't you, Iain?'

By this time I was starting to feel a rising sense of panic, combined with confusion. I could feel my face turning red at this ridiculous and baffling situation. I could barely even look at Suzanna, but eventually she started giggling and I realised that this was obviously a prank that Andy had cooked up.

Andy spun on his heel chuckling and, still feeling embarrassed and calling him all sorts of names, I followed him along many more non-descript corridors, up and down stairwells and finally we ended up in an empty office. He suggested I take a seat and told me that he'd go and collect the person that we were there to meet.

I sat waiting, and waiting, and waiting. After about fifteen or twenty minutes, I realised, with a horrible sickening feeling, that he'd abandoned me there. The horrible bastard had led me into the bowels of this awful, huge, grey, anonymous building where everywhere looked the same. I had no mobile phone because mobiles had to be handed in at reception. I had no idea where I was and no idea how to find my way back. We had passed through numerous electronically locked doors that he had opened with his security swipe card, so it wasn't as simple as just wandering around until you found your way out. James Bond would have been flummoxed.

I humiliatingly wandered into at least half a dozen offices, trying to explain to suspicious members of staff who I was and that I needed to get back to the foyer. No one knew who Andy was and they couldn't find him in internal phone directories. I began to fear that I would spend weeks marooned in this ghastly building.

Eventually, someone took pity on me and helped me find Andy's office. I walked in and found him sitting with his feet up on the desk, shoulders shaking with laughter. I wasn't amused. I noted that his was the only office in that dreary building that had any spark of individuality. Above the door in large Gothic lettering was written: 'Abandon hope all ye who enter here.'

I loved working with these quirky characters. They could run intellectual rings around many of our MI5 cousins, who treated police officers as if they were all a bit thick.

The demise of Special Branch in the years leading up to its disbandment in 2006 was, by all accounts, a very sad, frustrating and difficult time for the many hundreds of intelligence officers who had served there for such a long time. There was a definite suspicion that scores were finally being settled by the CID, specifically some senior people in SO13 who didn't really understand or value what SB officers did. They didn't appreciate the variety and seriousness of the national security threats that the department was responsible for investigating. Nor did they understand the political context of working alongside the wider security service community. CID officers dominated the newly created Counter-Terrorism Command (SO15), and many of their senior officers appeared to nurse long-standing, irrational resentment towards ex-Special Branch officers. I don't really know why this was the case, but many people believed that it was because of three things. Firstly, the CID had always resented the fact that Special Branch officers were given the title 'detective' as, in the eyes of most of the CID, *they* were the only ones who should be allowed to use that title. Secondly, over the years, many of them had tried to get into Special Branch but had been unable to pass the exam. Consequently, they nursed a grievance towards the department. Finally, CID officers hated the fact that much of the work of Special Branch was by definition 'secret' and they bitterly resented being kept out of the national security 'circle of trust'. This is obviously very childish, but these inter-departmental rivalries exist all over the world in law enforcement.

CHAPTER 13

TERRORISM

On 9 February 1996 at 5.30 p.m., PIRA announced that they were ending their seventeen-month ceasefire. Shortly after this announcement, a number of calls were made to media organisations warning that a large bomb had been left near South Quay station in Docklands and, sure enough, a large, unattended truck was found close to Marsh Wall. This bore all the hallmarks of an imminent PIRA attack, and the police therefore urgently began evacuating the area.

At about 7 p.m., the lorry-bomb exploded, killing two people and destroying the surrounding area. If you want to see the devastating results of the explosion, search online for the 'Marsh Wall bomb'. Whilst you're at it, have a look at the damage caused by the Baltic Exchange bomb in 1992 and the Bishopsgate bomb in 1993, which preceded the PIRA ceasefire in 1994. The IRA didn't mess around.

These massive bombs were manufactured using homemade explosives (HME), which are made from mixing nitrate-rich fertiliser with sugar, which is then initiated using detonators attached to a time and power unit (TPU). The TPU is basically a box with some sort of timing mechanism attached to batteries with sufficient electrical power to set off the detonators. A driver would simply park a lorry with the bomb in the back near their target and flick a switch to arm the device on a timer, before walking away and getting picked up by an accomplice waiting nearby. Typically, these bombs were made of several thousand pounds of HME and by containing the explosion within the confines of a steel-sided lorry their explosive power was massively increased. They are referred to as large vehicle-borne improvised explosive devices and were used by PIRA throughout the 1980s and 1990s to devastating effect in Northern Ireland. Once the device had been armed, warning calls would then be made to the authorities in which a codeword was given with an approximate location of the bomb. Theoretically, this warning would give the authorities time to start clearing the target location, but often the warnings were unclear or the location was deliberately ambiguous, making it a race against time to find the bomb and get people away from it.

With the South Quay bombing, PIRA was back at war with the British state, and as the policing organisation responsible for defeating them, SB was therefore back on a war footing with them.

I can remember feeling incredibly excited at the prospect of getting stuck in, but I was also conscious of the fact that I was still working on Islamic extremism. Therefore, on the basis that shy children get nothing, I spoke to my boss on E squad and asked him if I could get redeployed back onto B squad. I remember him rolling his eyes and laughing but agreeing to let me go at the next movement of staff between squads. This came within days after the management of Special Branch directed a significant increase in B squad capacity in response to the resumption of hostilities. Therefore, the week after the bombing, I was back where I wanted to be.

The entire atmosphere within the department changed overnight, and there was a real buzz of activity and excitement. I was posted to one of the 'operations' or 'ops' teams on B squad. We were responsible for developing incoming intelligence on potential threats to try to firm up what we were dealing with. The intelligence might have been from a highly sensitive source or it might have been something as simple as a member of the public ringing up to report unusual activity at an address. It all had to be bottomed out in order to be either confirmed or eliminated. Much of the information that we were given in good faith by police officers or members of the public would turn out to be of no security interest whatsoever, but this could not be assumed. In the past, PIRA ASUs had been identified as a result of a seemingly trivial snippet of information being passed to a local bobby on the beat, who then fed this into the intelligence system, before it found its way to someone on a B squad ops team. So, everything had to be meticulously investigated.

B squad detectives who had been around for a long time had lots of examples of PIRA compromising themselves as a result of what we called the 'Paddy factor'. These were moments when a highly trained and experienced terrorist would give himself away in a silly lapse in operational security or tradecraft. For example, they might get sloppy and leave valuable forensic evidence behind or do something in a moment of foolishness that caused alarm bells to ring with Special Branch and someone who had seen something similar before in a different investigation would put two and two together.

The next few months flew by and I spent long days and weekends at work, chasing down intelligence leads with my team and improving my craft as an SB officer. However, we had a lot of fun, and there was very much a 'work hard, play hard' mentality with lots of clever, funny people bonding over police war stories, carrying out cruel practical jokes on each other and drinking a lot. In between operations, we would have enormous, raucous after-hour squad piss-ups where an entire floor of Scotland Yard would be filled with scores of detectives of every rank drinking, laughing and bickering amidst a thick fog of cigarette smoke. Interestingly, during such drinking sessions a lot of good work was done because this very democratic, 'rank-free' environment created a flow of ideas, theories and tactical discussions where everyone's views were listened to. Frequently, the ideas put forward the night before would be put into action over the following days.

Occasionally, the job could be pure tragicomedy, and on one occasion in 1996 I was on the receiving end.

Today, the police's ability to gather video evidence of terrorist activity has become very sophisticated; however, back then, it was fairly rudimentary. We would find a friendly occupant of a premises that had a view of the target address and staff it with eagle-eyed B squad officers who would maintain a running log of what was happening and then direct the subjects to the surveillance team when they left the address. There would also generally be a video camera to record comings and goings 24/7. This would support the account of the officers in the observation post (OP) and ensure that if we had to go to the loo or had a severe sneezing fit nothing would be missed.

The video recordings would be made on old-style VHS tapes that would periodically be collected and returned to Scotland Yard to be stored as evidential exhibits. There's nothing sensitive in telling you this because the defence teams in every trial get shown footage from these tapes so that they can check that the police have not made the evidence up. They obviously don't get told where the actual OP was or who lived in the address and we were always careful to ensure that the intelligence could have been gathered from any one of a dozen addresses.

On this occasion, I was dispatched from the Yard to go to an OP and pick up some VHS tapes that were required quite urgently. Two of my B squad mates were physically in the OP so I left a message for them on our pagers and told them that I'd be there in about twenty minutes. I'd never been to this particular OP before so, just before I left, I popped my head round the door of the operations room and scribbled down the address that was written on a whiteboard.

I jumped on the Tube at St James's Park and made my way towards that part of town. On arrival at my last Tube destination, I paged them again to say I'd be about two minutes so they could be at the front door ready to let me in quickly so that I wouldn't be hanging around in the street in plain view of our terrorists. Simple things like that could make the difference between compromising a job and maintaining cover.

I walked up to the door and knocked a couple of times. I waited for what seemed like an eternity, getting annoyed that the guys hadn't opened the door immediately because they knew that I was coming. Then, I heard footsteps approaching inside and the door swung open. To my indescribable horror, I stood looking into the face of one of our terrorists and instantly realised that I had mistakenly knocked on the door of the target premises rather than the OP. My mind was whirling and I could feel the blood draining from my face. Very quickly I stammered, 'Hello, sorry to bother you, but is Steve in?' He looked at me blankly and in a broad Irish accent replied, 'There's no Steve here.' I apologised and said something about Steve the plumber and how I thought he lived there, or some such nonsense, and then turned on my heel and walked off up the street trying to look as casual as possible.

As I was walking away, I was swearing under my breath as my pager started vibrating. The message said, 'You idiot! What the hell are you doing?' The guys in the OP had been watching me knocking on the door and were doing their nut. I walked around the corner out of sight of the address and smacked my head hard with my hand, cursing my stupidity. I rang the OP and my mate John answered. 'What the hell were you doing?' he asked in disbelief. 'Oh, God, John, I feel like such an idiot! I wrote down the address of the target when I thought I was writing down the address of the OP!' I explained.

In the end it was fine. The subjects carried on quite normally and clearly hadn't been spooked. The operation ended successfully so I'd got away with it, but I received so much grief for my stupidity for months after. It was a story that got told and retold in the pub.

From that time on, there was a policy that the address of the target address was always written in red on the whiteboard and the OP address was double underlined in black.

On another occasion, I was leaving a different OP in the middle of the night carrying a holdall full of camera gear and videotapes when suddenly a police response car came roaring up beside me, screeched to a halt and two uniformed PCs leapt out and almost rugby tackled me.

This was all in full view of the target address so my attempts to leave the address silently and unobtrusively hadn't quite worked out as I had planned.

I hissed at them, 'Guys, I'm police... Special Branch. Let me go and I'll meet you 100 yards around the corner because we're all going to blow this bloody operation.'

But they refused to believe me, thinking it was a clever ploy to get away with a bag of stolen gear, so I decided to go along with them. 'OK, then, I'll get in the car and you can pretend to arrest me so at least if anyone's watching it just looks like you're doing your job,' I said.

I got into the back of the car and the driver spun it around and they took off at speed with their 'prisoner'. We pulled over at the side of the road a few hundred yards away and I fished out my warrant card from my wallet, at which point they both looked a bit embarrassed. In the end, we all had a laugh about it and they went off looking for some real criminals.

Officers tended to spend a large part of their careers in SB, which meant that it wasn't unusual for a senior officer of super-intendent or chief superintendent rank to have worked with many of the lower-ranking officers since the time when they were all DCs. This created a more effective team and made it much easier for all ranks to have an honest conversation about either a personal or an operational issue. This culture was destroyed some years later by a policy known as 'tenure', which required everyone to move out of specialist departments after a set period of time. This policy diluted the deep subject-matter knowledge in specialist departments, and it resulted in the recruitment of some senior officers into SB who didn't understand what the department did and, as a result, they then made some terrible decisions. The worst offenders in this respect were those who came in with an agenda to make big changes, shake things up and get themselves promoted, leaving a trail of destruction in their wake. The argument for the tenure policy was that specialisms created an 'elitist culture' which needed to be stamped out. However, the reality was that, regardless of whether you liked the idea of an 'elitist culture', many of these established officers were extremely good at their jobs and it ultimately felt like they were being punished for this.

The period following the breakdown of the PIRA ceasefire was largely spent focusing on two key challenges: catching and convicting those responsible for the Docklands bomb and stopping the next attack from happening. The first task sat primarily with our colleagues in the Anti-Terrorism Branch and was led by the irrepressible Commander John Grieve, who eventually led an audacious mission with the British Army into the heart of South Armagh to try to arrest the bombers and bring them to justice.

Over the next two years, life on SO12 and in our sister department, SO13, was hectic. We all lurched from one high-tempo operation to another. In retrospect, I was pretty selfish during this period of my life. I had a wife and young daughter at home and I spent very long days at work, frequently spending up to sixteen hours a day on operational duties. I came home only to sleep and then would get up at 4 or 5 a.m. to drive across London to change time-lapse videotapes or sit in OPs with other similarly unshaven, sweaty, smelly detectives. We waited for our subjects to leave home to assist the surveillance teams out on the ground who would follow those subjects 24/7, gathering intelligence and evidence.

It is a strange life working on these operations. It's very intense and the bonds that you form with colleagues are powerful; perhaps stronger than any bonds I formed in the other policing I did in my career. I think it's the combination of long hours, the seriousness of what we were doing, the secrecy, and working with great people who were all completely committed to what we were doing. I have never laughed as much as I have laughed in some of those OPs or when I worked on surveillance teams as a photographer years later. I used to play a lot of sport in my younger years and working on such operations was a bit like being on tour with a sports team every day of your life: hard work and lots and lots of fun, piss-taking and laughter.

Although I cannot go into much detail about operational specifics, in 1996 and 1997 SO12 basically dismantled PIRA's mainland capabilities. We took out the PIRA 'A team' in Operation Airlines, which thwarted a plot to take out electricity substations around London and bring down the National Grid. It was estimated that had the attack been successful it would have taken a minimum of six months to restore full electricity coverage to the UK, crippling the economy. We then took out the 'B team' in Operation Tinnitus, which targeted an ASU that was sent to London to carry out an attack using a massive quantity of explosives kept in a storage unit in north London. It was at the conclusion of this operation that the Met firearms team, SO19, shot dead Diarmuid O'Neill, a member of the PIRA unit. O'Neill was born and bred in London to Irish parents and was the ideal local facilitator for the team as a classic 'cleanskin' who could move around without drawing attention to himself, mixing with locals who all knew him well, whilst simultaneously planning death and destruction on a massive scale. The police took no pleasure in his death. He was a young man with his future ahead of him and he got drawn into something that ended up costing him his life. Like so many before him, he had been groomed by extremists who had taught him how to cause carnage and kill innocent people. PIRA were responsible for a huge amount of death and misery over many years. It was all a pointless waste of life and it achieved absolutely nothing that could not have been brought about by purely political means. I once got into an argument about whether I considered myself to be British or Irish. I was born and brought up in Northern Ireland, I grew up in a Protestant community but I went to a Quaker school. I answered that question by saying that if I had to come down on one side of the fence and choose my nationality, I would say that I feel more Irish than British. This is based on my deep love for the island of Ireland and my love for the people of Ireland. However, I have lived in England since I was eighteen. I also love England and the British way of life. All four of my kids were born in England and I took an oath to serve Her Majesty the Queen. Right is right and wrong is wrong. PIRA were wrong in every way and I took great pride and pleasure in playing a part in their ultimate defeat on the mainland.

These operational successes helped to push the Republican movement back to the negotiating table with the British government. Shortly after this in 1998, the PIRA ceasefire was restored and the Good Friday Agreement was signed in Belfast, ending thirty years of PIRA terrorism in the UK. SO12 and SO13 had achieved great things in policing terms, had saved many lives and helped to change the course of British history.

A couple of years ago, the BBC made an excellent series called *Spotlight on the Troubles: A Secret History*. I would strongly recommend it to anyone who wants to know more about the Met's involvement in defeating Republican terrorism on the mainland during this period of time.

From 1999, my last three years in Special Branch were spent on a surveillance team, which were some of my most enjoyable years in the police. In this time, I worked on many highly sensitive national security operations as well as serious crime operations during periods of 'downtime' when our teams would be sub-contracted out to other Scotland Yard departments. However, this was another period in which I periodically spent a lot of time away from home. Still, I was fortunate because I was one of a small number of dedicated photographers, which meant that we could only work effectively during daylight hours and I therefore had more time at home than I'd had on B squad.

The years I spent on the surveillance team were intense but also great fun. We all did an initial four-week course: two weeks learning 'foot follows' and two weeks in cars. The approach and tradecraft of surveillance are very different depending on whether you are on foot or driving, and when on a proper operational team it is usually a mixture of both forms. Sometimes you might have to completely abandon your vehicle to follow a subject on foot and then get onto a train with them and travel to the other end of the country.

Instructors delivered the training from our sister unit SO11, which largely did surveillance against criminals – for example, bank robbers, drug dealers and paedophiles – whereas in SO12 we worked on operations against terrorists, foreign spies and political extremists. For reasons best known to themselves, SO11 instructors didn't like SO12 surveillance officers and they made it very clear that if they had their way they'd fail us all. I think in their heads they thought they were the only department that should be doing surveillance at all and they resented the fact that we wouldn't talk about what we did. I think that small-minded mentality has now changed, but back then there was a lot of rivalry between so-called elite departments.

The instructors were super-experienced but unforgiving of mistakes. Generally, students would be allowed one or two serious errors but more than that and they would immediately be binned from the course. Surveillance is conducted against some of the most challenging and frequently dangerous criminals. It is also incredibly expensive and obviously has a significant impact on the human rights of the individuals under surveillance and their families.

This was an interesting time in terms of photographic gear and processes. When I started in 1999, we used Nikon film cameras and wet film exclusively. We would shoot film and then drive to the Met Police photographic lab in Camberwell to get it developed. We would then drive back to the office in Vauxhall to put the images into albums and then drive over to Scotland Yard to hand the albums to a colleague. Not exactly the most efficient process! Three years later, we were using the first fully digital Nikon D1 SLRs and sending the images back directly into the operations room via a laptop and mobile phone, which allowed us to stay in the field longer and make the most of available light.

However, we continued to use fast black-and-white film from time to time because of its low-light capabilities, and we had our own darkroom where we developed the images. I loved to work in the darkroom, and it was here, in the small, dimly lit space, listening to BBC Radio 4, that I first heard about the events in New York on 11 September 2001 when Al-Qaeda terrorists launched multiple attacks on the United States, using passenger jets full of innocent passengers as missiles. I can remember leaving the darkroom and joining colleagues in the main office and we all stood there open-mouthed with disbelief watching Sky News.

Inevitably, our work changed overnight as the UK came to terms with a new reality of dealing with an enemy that was prepared to carry out the mass murder of men, women and children and who actively sought martyrdom. This was completely uncharted territory for Special Branch after many years of dealing with the IRA, which was an organisation whose members generally tried to avoid killing civilians if possible and who definitely didn't want to die on active service.

So, what makes an outstanding surveillance officer? There are several skills and qualities that are important. Firstly, the ability to feel comfortable and blend into almost any environment without drawing attention to yourself is paramount. This includes urban streets, leafy suburbia and rural locations, and inside pubs, shops, trains, buses, expensive hotels, grotty hotels and airports. This is something that comes with experience, but surveillance officers are taught how to avoid disturbing the environment that they are working in to prevent 'showing out' to the subjects under surveillance or, for that matter, the general public.

Bearing in mind that the whole point of surveillance is to gather intelligence and evidence to progress an investigation, a good surveillance officer also needs to have excellent powers of observation and awareness of their surroundings. They need to know instinctively when to get up really close to their subject and when to pull right back and use their instincts and experience to pre-empt what someone is going to do next or where they are going so that they can direct other members of the team to get ahead of the subject. When it all comes together it's a beautiful thing and it is a joy to be a part of an experienced team who have worked together a long time and who are all tuned in to each other. It's the best game of hide-and-seek ever invented.

Surveillance officers also need to be good drivers and navigators, as frequently a subject will leave home in the morning and end up hundreds of miles away by the end of the day. I can think of many times I had to frantically drive literally from one end of the country to the other whilst the subject sat relaxing on a train as we struggled to get ahead of him to provide an invisible welcoming committee as he arrived at his destination.

As a surveillance photographer, the three things that caused the most issues involved going to the toilet, running out of electrical power and dealing with the heat or the cold when stuck in the back of a vehicle for hours at a time.

If we needed a wee on a job, we used to use a Lenor fabric conditioner bottle that was an ideal shape and size. It had a nice wide neck so you didn't miss. However, if you were stuck in a van with another fellow photographer for a long time, the bottle could get pretty full, which wasn't great. There was also a strict code of conduct about not touching the neck of the bottle when sharing the piss bottle. That was definitely bad form. After every shift it was important that you made sure you emptied the Lenor bottle and washed it out. On one occasion I forgot to do this and left the bottle in my hot van for two weeks whilst I was on my summer holidays. When I got back, the bottle had been stewing nicely in the heat and I don't think it is possible to even describe the smell when I emptied it. If you needed a number two, you basically had to hold it in as long as you could and if that wasn't possible you would have to go and find a local loo. Murphy's Law dictated that the subject would almost certainly appear just after you left the van. If we were out in the countryside and there were no facilities around, we would call up on the radio and tell the team that we were going 'windsurfing'. This involved driving to a discreet location, winding the driver's window right down, getting out of the car and holding onto the open window of the door, then leaning back as far as you could as if it was the boom of a windsurfing sail. The leaning back as far as possible was an important skill that was learned from bitter experience. Not a pretty sight if some poor birdwatcher was looking on through his binoculars, but when you've got to go you've got to go!

Electrical power was always a challenge. Everything in the

surveillance van ran off a couple of leisure batteries and sometimes we would be deployed day after day and often in quite
remote locations. The SLR cameras and video cameras sucked
battery life, the comms radio also fed off the batteries and our
mobile phones also needed to be fully charged. This was always
worse in winter as batteries run out very quickly in the cold,
which brings me to the third surveillance problem.

When conducting surveillance in Britain, there was very little
of the year when it wasn't either too cold or too hot in the back
of the van. As well as basically being a metal box on wheels, all
the vehicles we used were sound-proofed, which made them
even warmer in the summer. In the winter, we would be bun-
dled up like Nanook of the North, trying desperately hard not
to breathe over the view-finder to avoid it getting steamed up. In
the summer, we would be stripped down to our pants with sweat
literally pouring off us.

We often spent long periods of time waiting for stuff to
happen. If a surveillance target settled down in the pub for
several hours or didn't come out of their house for a long time,
we would all be holed up discreetly nearby waiting for the 'off'.
It was weird because there would be hours and hours during
which nothing happened. Then, the radio would spring into life
as someone had theirs eyes on the subject: 'Standby, standby...
we have movement... subject is standing up... he's towards the
door... and he's out, out, turning left, left on foot back towards
the vehicle.' There might then be a period of manic activity when
the subject would meet with other co-conspirators and the team
would have to split to follow multiple subjects whose activities also needed to be documented, photographed or videoed.

Sometimes the most boring deployments quickly turned into the most manic and led to high-speed pursuits halfway across the country.

I've thought about those days on surveillance a lot over the years. It was the most fun I ever had in the police, and after reading about the psychology of addiction it ticked many of those boxes. Combining fast-moving surveillance and photography triggered continual dopamine hits of excitement, satisfaction and reward like no other job I have ever done. Perhaps that's why I also enjoy fishing so much: it brings out the primeval hunter-gatherer.

The boring periods of waiting were filled by talking complete bollocks to each other or by planning and executing cruel practical jokes on one another. On one occasion, we were holed up on a crappy industrial estate somewhere in the East End of London, waiting for a subject to move. There were three or four of our cars scattered around the site, and one of the bikers had jumped into my van with me to keep warm. We noticed that there were a couple of skips full of rotten food waste that were literally crawling with rats. We joked that if we had an air rifle and a telescopic sight we could have had great fun. Our sergeant team leader was horrified by the sight of the rats and stupidly told us that he was terrified of them.

After an hour or so, the team leader called up to say that he was leaving on foot to use the loo in a nearby pub. Whilst he was gone, we left the driver's door of his car wide open, got a couple of old manky sandwiches which we tore up into small pieces and laid a trail of scraps from the skips into his car, putting more scraps all over the seats. When he came back, we sat watching him, giggling like schoolgirls as the look on his face turned from confusion at seeing the driver's door of his car wide open to one of horror at seeing the trail of food from the rat-infested skips. He was not happy and outright refused to get back in his car. He asked us if any of the rats had gone inside and we told him that as far as we could see only one had gone in, which was nonsense. Eventually, the only way that we could persuade him to get in the car was to open all the doors and the boot for him and show him that there was nothing in there.

On another occasion, we were deployed on a terrorist job at a location in the north of England. I was up there for four days on and four days off for weeks on end and the surveillance teams and firearms teams were rotating across twelve-hour shifts day and night.

On one evening, it was our team's turn to do the night shift and given that I was the team photographer, and because you can't take photos in the dark, I snuck off to a lay-by in a rather remote spot to get my head down for a few hours in the back of my van. I laid out a camping mat in the back, climbed into my sleeping bag, pulled my woolly hat down over my eyes and went to sleep.

I woke up a couple of hours later to the sound of a dull metallic thud, but as I was half asleep I thought I was dreaming and attempted to go back to sleep. However, I then heard noises coming from the driver's compartment of the van, which was separated from where I was lying by a solid metal bulkhead. I lay there frozen still, listening intently, my heart pounding in my chest.

Then, suddenly, to my horror, I heard the engine start up and the van took off with me in the back wrapped in my sleeping bag like a cross between Captain Scott of the Antarctic and Tutankhamun.

I struggled out of my sleeping bag as the van started picking up speed and approached the driver's compartment. I unlocked one of the 4in. portholes in the bulkhead that I would normally use to take photographs through and peeped through to see what was going on. There was only the driver in the van, who was a young lad who looked about twenty years old. He was wearing a baseball cap and clearly had no idea that I was the van's cargo.

By this point, we were travelling along a quiet dual carriageway at some speed. I fully opened the porthole and shouted as loud as I could, 'What the fuck are you doing? Stop this van!' The effect was instantaneous. The thief absolutely shat himself and almost lost control of the van. He slammed the brakes on, jumped out and ran off, leaving the van in the middle of the road with the engine still running. I waited a few moments before opening the hatch in the bulkhead and climbing through into the front. The van had been hot-wired and the engine was still running, so I drove it back to our hotel and got the damage repaired the next day, sheepishly reporting the theft to one of the local Special Branch guys who then had to find a creative way of explaining it to the local police.

At this time, my kids were just about to start secondary school and infant school, respectively, and my wife and I had talked long and hard about getting away from London and moving to a part of the country for better schools and a quieter pace of life. I had qualified for promotion to sergeant so we decided to put the house on the market and move out of London. I applied to West Midlands Police to transfer as a sergeant and was successful, the house sold quickly and, before we knew it, we were on our way to a life in the Midlands.

I had my Special Branch leaving do in a pub in central London, and it was a predictably drunken affair. I had spent such a long time with my much-loved SB friends and we had become a close-knit family of brothers and sisters. We had done and achieved such a lot over the previous eight or nine years and had even helped to shape history. I got very drunk and, suddenly, it was all too much and I started crying. However, two days later, I was driving out of London behind a removal lorry containing all our worldly possessions.

CHAPTER 14

SENT TO COVENTRY

Joining the West Midlands Police in 2002 felt like a massive culture shock to me. I had been out of uniform in a specialist department for so long and, in many ways, what I had been doing since 1994 wasn't traditional police work at all; it was 95 per cent intelligence gathering.

I was sent to the force clothing stores and got measured up for my sergeant's uniform. Surprisingly, their stores were the complete opposite of the Met's. They were OK about uniform leaving their stores and didn't treat you as if they were paying for everything from their own pocket. I can remember standing looking at myself in the mirror in my new uniform with sergeants' stripes on my shoulders and thinking to myself, 'Oh shit, you idiot, you've really gone and done it now, haven't you?'

The West Midlands was the second biggest force in the UK after the Met. The force covered a large, mostly urban area of the Midlands, including Birmingham, Wolverhampton, Coventry, Sandwell, Dudley, Walsall and Solihull. They posted me to Coventry – a city I had never set foot in and knew nothing about whatsoever. All I knew was that the Luftwaffe had more or less flattened the place in the Second World War and that The Specials had written a rather depressing song about the city in the 1970s called 'Ghost Town'. After arriving, I was promptly told an apocryphal story about a German tourist approaching a cynical 'old sweat' police officer on the outskirts of Coventry. He asked him if he could direct him to Coventry city centre, only to be told, 'You lot were able to find it in the pitch-black from 10,000ft back in 1940, so I'm sure you can find it yourself in broad daylight now!'

At my new station, I was introduced to the most senior officer, Chief Superintendent Chris Duffield. He was charming and could not have made me feel more welcome, and this was pretty much how things continued over my first few days. Everyone was incredibly friendly and welcoming and any nervousness that I was feeling soon evaporated. Meeting my new team for the first time was a strange feeling. I had never had to supervise staff before, so this was entirely new for me, and I had twelve real human beings looking to me for guidance, leadership and support. Fortunately, as with everyone else I had already met, they were an excellent bunch. I soon realised why everyone was so nice. Coventry was a busy place and policing in the city could be a rough, tough business. The city had high levels of deprivation and therefore had problems with everything that typically accompanies urban poverty: drugs, violence and organised crime.

Initially, I had no idea what was going on. The radio communications all sounded so different from those at the Met. The policing language was completely new and force procedures were barely recognisable. I also had to find my way around, learn the new geography and conquer the West Midlands paperwork and

IT systems, which were also all alien to me. This is one of the odd eccentricities about policing in the UK. We don't have a national police force. We have this very fragmented system of forty-five individual forces servicing each county and the two police forces in Northern Ireland and Scotland. Each of these has its own chief constable, senior command team and different local procedures, HR processes, policies, IT systems and budgets. Every force enforces the same criminal laws, but they all do it in a slightly different way. It's incredibly inefficient and there is a lot of duplication of effort and waste of money. However, what the system does do well is it ensures that policing is carried out in a way that respects and understands local issues, history, culture and language. Generally speaking, moving large numbers of officers from one part of the country into another part of the country doesn't work very well for all sorts of reasons. This was demonstrated during the miners' strike in the 1980s. The Met caused a lot of problems in northern towns and they have never been forgiven to this day.

I was really fortunate to have a brilliant partner sergeant called Martin, who dug me out of the shit many times, and I learned quickly from him. He was Coventry born and bred and he knew the city and all the villains inside out. He was great fun to work with and we had a real laugh from day one. I realised very quickly that policing was policing and all of the skills that I had learned as a uniformed bobby in south London came back very quickly.

I think that the late 1990s to the early 2000s was the last period in which the British police were able to do their job without being shackled and hampered by pointless form-filling and key performance indicators (KPIs). This will be covered in more detail later, but it was also the period in which a new breed of police manager started to emerge. These were managers who could tell you everything about how to pass promotion-selection processes but almost nothing about how to catch criminals.

My team were a mixed bunch: we had a few old sweats, others with between three and seven years' service and a handful of brand-new probationers with less than two years on the job. I quickly got the hang of things and started to enjoy being a sergeant and doing real police work. We worked hard but had a lot of fun dealing with everything Coventry had to throw at us. Unlike in London, many of the people we dealt with had rarely been out of Coventry in their lives and lived in the bubble of their own council estates.

In Coventry, unlike London, local villains and likely lads rarely refused to tell you who they were simply because they knew that someone from the local police station would know them and everyone in their family already. What they didn't do, however, was come quietly when arrested and there would frequently be major punch-ups in the street that could get very lively very quickly in such situations. I was soon introduced to the quaint idea of a 'scuffle' in West Midlands Police jargon. A 'scuffle' could be anything from two women having a pushing and shoving competition outside Asda over the last shopping trolley, all the way through to a full-scale riot with petrol bombs, burning cars and police helicopters overhead, and anything in between.

Nonetheless, policing Coventry was great fun and also incredibly interesting as it had every policing challenge crammed into a very diverse city of 300,000 people. I don't know if there is any truth to this, but somebody once told me that government statisticians used to use Coventry as a kind of 'mini-UK' because the city had every aspect of typical UK life packed into a comparatively compact space. There were lots of deprived inner-city estates, middle-class suburbs and a few affluent neighbourhoods. It had a busy city centre with lots of shops, bars and nightlife and plenty of busy motorways, fast A-roads and semi-rural villages on the outskirts. In Coventry, it was perfectly possible to be dealing with drug-addicted prostitutes and violent gangsters one moment and a university professor living in one of the more affluent areas the next.

Early on, I had a particular problem with a group of five or six teenagers who were making life pretty intolerable for people living in the part of Coventry that I policed. They were a horrible bunch and were responsible for most of the crime in that area. They bullied all the friendly kids and caused an unbelievable amount of misery. I set out to turn the tables on them, and we hounded them mercilessly. At one point, my team arrested at least one of them almost every day and, eventually, we managed to get them all locked up and subject to anti-social behaviour orders when they were released from custody. I knew my approach was working when I found 'Sergeant Donnelly is a cunt' spray-painted in large letters on the side of a tower block. At that point I realised that we were definitely pissing off the right people.

In my first couple of years at Coventry, everyone was generally left to get on with things by a pretty supportive management team. However, slowly but surely there was a growing organisational obsession with performance metrics and KPIs. This was happening across the entire force and I knew from speaking to colleagues in London and elsewhere that it was a national obsession driven by the Home Office.

For me, with the benefit of nearly twenty years' hindsight, it was this period around 2004 that was the point where policing in the UK started to lose its way and from where I believe it has never really recovered.

The Labour government under Tony Blair did a lot of great things for policing. The funding of the British police increased by 26 per cent between 2001 and 2010. Indeed, this was a time when there were high numbers of police officers available to respond to emergencies, combined with the introduction of new neighbourhood policing teams across every part of the UK. These teams typically consisted of a sergeant, half a dozen uniformed constables and two or three police community support officers (PCSOs). Teams were permanently allocated to each council ward and they built close relationships with residents, businesses and local councillors to tackle local problems. It worked really well and these officers quickly became a font of knowledge as they knew every local criminal, who they associated with and where they could be found. These teams were also able to nip issues in the bud before they escalated into something much more severe. They also had an incredible intelligence-gathering ability not just around crime issues but also in matters relating to community tensions and terrorism. Crucially, they could spot the very young 'up-and-coming' criminals when they were in their early teens and divert them away from a criminal lifestyle and towards less destructive paths or get them the support that they needed from other agencies. There is a definite link between the demise of neighbourhood policing and government cuts decimating many front-line public services and the rise of the knife-crime epidemic and County Lines drug-dealing.

The neighbourhood policing teams dealt with local issues during daytime hours. In contrast, the 24/7 emergency policing was delivered by local response teams working across three shifts: the earlies (0700–1500), lates (1400–2300) and nights (2200–0700), which were on a 'six days on, four days off' pattern. It was one of these response teams that I was assigned to manage when I joined.

So, whilst everything in the police resourcing garden was rosy – at least for the time being – in life, every silver lining has a cloud and, in this case, it was a blizzard of New Labour performance measures that were introduced for every force in the country that started to cause problems. Initially, everyone pretty much ignored this new regime and carried on doing what they had always done – i.e. patrolling the streets, responding to emergencies, catching criminals and helping the decent people. Crucially, the organisation trusted us to use our common sense to focus on what was essential and ignore time-wasters. However, ever so gradually, senior police officers realised that if they wanted to progress their careers they would have to get with the Home Office programme and start cracking the whip on performance targets. And, believe me, there were targets for pretty much *everything*. Initial response times, time spent at the scene, dozens of data-quality targets, targets in the cellblock with detainees, quality standards for file preparation, the recording of crime, the detection of crime and on and on and on. The force published KPIs every month and individual command units were compared in league tables across the force and forces compared with each other nationally. No chief superintendent wanted to be at the bottom of the league table in their force and no chief constable wanted to be at the bottom of a national league table of forces.

The net result of this was that only the things that got measured got done well, and this meant that there was no longer anything to be gained organisationally from policing activities that had no tangible 'positive outcome'. So, for example, if a crime was assessed as too difficult or time-consuming to solve, it received very little attention, whereas crimes that were easier to solve received a gold standard of service because they would generate a Home Office approved 'detection', and points mean prizes. There were also lots of targets relating to crime reduction and this was where the most blatant practices took place to improve the statistics and make things appear to be better than they were. For example, there were lots of targets relating to burglary and vehicle crime reduction. As a result, officers often spent more time trying to show that something was *not* a burglary than if they had just recorded a burglary and investigated it properly. Every morning, tasking meetings were an exercise in statistical limbo dancing. New offences reported by members of the public in the previous twenty-four hours were subjected to a microscopic level of scrutiny, not necessarily to try to figure out who had committed them, perish the thought, but to try to re-classify them as something that didn't get measured. Damage caused to a rear patio door, almost certainly caused by a drug addict trying to commit a residential burglary, would be re-classified as 'criminal damage', which the Home Office didn't really care about. The owner of a car with a broken driver's side window would be persuaded that it had probably been caused by an errant stone from a passing car rather than the more obvious explanation that someone had been trying to steal the bloody thing.

However, if something couldn't be explained away as an accident or a less serious offence that wasn't going to be measured, the pressure was on to get it solved and 'detected'. Therefore, fairly trivial crimes like the theft of a car radio would receive a platinum-standard investigation. By contrast, a £10,000 fraud of a local business would receive virtually no investigative resources because it was too tricky and would take too long. Everybody at grass-roots level knew this was wrong, but to challenge this regime was pointless because pretty much every senior manager in policing across the UK was doing exactly the same things. Ambitious senior officers with an eye on their next promotion tolerated the practice because they knew perfectly well that they would be supported by chief officers further up the hierarchy. Every chief constable was trying to win the national beauty contest and didn't want to know too much about how the 'fantastic' results were actually being achieved. In the mid-2000s, the whole thing started to become a giant game of massaging statistics and finding ever more imaginative ways of making this possible. The primary purpose of policing (i.e. protecting the public) became almost secondary to chasing Home Office targets, and the rules were pushed to the absolute limit to hit those targets. I'm not proud of the fact that I, like most people, conspired in all this, even though I knew it was ridiculous.

However, this nonsense couldn't last for ever, and the Home

Office eventually got pissed off and clamped down by bringing in a whole raft of new performance measurements relating to the dreaded 'data quality' and new National Crime Recording Standard. This meant that all data collected by the police, particularly recorded crime data, had to be scrupulously transparent, with no possibility whatsoever that police officers were 'gaming the system'. From this time on, if someone reported a crime, *any crime*, it had to be responded to, investigated and faithfully recorded. Her Majesty's Inspectorate of Constabulary enthusiastically enforced this standard and would conduct audits and inspections of forces. Slow learners were put on the naughty step of shame with an 'inadequate' rating.

To explain what this means, I will describe how things were done before these targets were brought in and compare this with how policing looked afterwards.

POLICING BEFORE THE INTRODUCTION OF NEW LABOUR DATA-QUALITY TARGETS

A member of the public phones and reports a crime. The police attend the address of the caller and find no one at home. They leave a calling card for the occupier to get in touch if they still need assistance. The occupier does not re-contact the police. No crime is recorded and the police get on with their day dealing with victims who want to cooperate with them.

POLICING *AFTER* THE INTRODUCTION OF NEW LABOUR DATA-QUALITY TARGETS

A member of the public phones and reports a crime. The police attend the address of the caller and find no one at home. They leave a note for the occupier to get in touch if they still need assistance. The occupier does not re-contact the police. The police then keep going back again and again until the 'victim' either cooperates and reports the full details of the crime or tells the police to piss off and stop bothering them.

This is the equivalent of someone making a doctor's appointment and failing to turn up. The doctor then repeatedly goes to their house until they reluctantly let them in to treat them even though they are now feeling absolutely fine.

And, by the way, the second version of policing above is still how the Home Office expects policing to be done. In view of all this, there are a number of points that are worth making:

- Most Home Office recorded crime statistics in the UK have been nonsense for years.
- Setting targets in respect of crime-detection and crime-reduction creates the illusion of 'performance' but, in reality, all this does is encourage unusual and completely counter-productive behaviour across forces up and down the country.
- Imagine how many *proper* criminals could have been arrested and lives saved over the past twenty years if the police had been allowed to use their discretion, tell time-wasters to bugger off and concentrate on the most important things rather than chasing stupid targets.

It was around this time that several scathing exposés of contemporary policing were published. A lot of these books were written under pseudonyms because of the risks that the authors were taking, but they highlighted the collective madness that had infected UK law and order. Two of the better books to be re-leased were *Wasting Police Time* by David Copperfield (who was later identified as Stuart Davidson from Staffordshire Police) and *Perverting the Course of Justice* by 'Inspector Gadget' (who has remained anonymous).

It was also around this time that policing began to feel the full impact of two new pieces of Blair-era legislation: the Human Rights Act 1998 and the Freedom of Information Act 2000.

The Human Rights Act made, and continues to make, many police managers very nervous about taking risks or making difficult decisions that may potentially land them in court. Suddenly, the organisation became preoccupied with 'managing risk', and bureaucratic risk assessments for almost everything became the name of the game. This mindset gradually created a highly risk-averse culture where it was more comfortable, and certainly safer for a manager's career, to take the path of least resistance and avoid risky jobs rather than become the unhappy target of civil-liberties lawyers. It didn't help that some of the prominent cases that received publicity during this time involved lawyers championing the human rights of some thoroughly undeserving individuals – for example, criminals like Jeremy Bamber, who murdered his sister and his parents, and terrorists like Abu Qatada, who argued that they had had their human rights breached. I believe that we absolutely must safeguard the fundamental human rights of citizens and I have worked tirelessly to do that my whole career. However, I am more interested in the human rights of victims of crime than I am in the human rights of convicted terrorists and criminals. Certain well-paid lawyers don't appear to care one little bit about the innocent victims of crime who have had *their* human rights abused by their clients, and that can never be right.

The Freedom of Information Act spawned an industry of civil servants in every public body whose entire job was to respond to what would become a blizzard of freedom of information requests. The point of this legislation was to make public-sector decision-making more transparent and decision-makers more accountable. However, the result is that the legislation is now routinely abused by individuals making frivolous and time-wasting requests, journalists sniffing out a spicy story or commercial companies hoping to gather business intelligence and gain a competitive advantage. I had to personally deal with numerous freedom of information requests over the years, and some of these took me many, many hours to gather the necessary information. This was time that I would have much preferred to give to members of the public who needed our help.

After ten months as a newly promoted sergeant, I started to get a bit of a name for myself as a proactive officer with a pretty good arrest rate. I was asked if I would consider becoming a detective sergeant (DS) in the CID, by which I was naturally flattered. The DS role was highly sought after, and I had never been in the CID before and I was still quite new both to the rank and to the West Midlands.

I applied for the job and I was successful. Hindsight is a wonderful thing. If only we could spare ourselves the pain, disappointment and stress of poor decision-making. I realise now, of course, that when I was asked to consider applying for that job, I should have politely declined, pointing out that I had had a lot of significant change in my life over the previous twelve months already and some stability would have been good. However, my ego got in the way and I saw this as a great opportunity. Little did I know at the time it would turn into a complete nightmare.

The remit of the CID team was to deal with all serious crime that occurred in a specific geographical location, which in my case was a big chunk of the south of Coventry. We dealt with everything: burglaries, armed robberies, kidnaps, rapes, serious assaults, attempted murders and gang-related incidents. Our job was to pick these cases up from initial report and take them all the way through investigation and hopefully to court. Historically, there has always been tension between uniformed officers and detectives, with many of the former thinking the latter are prima donnas and a bit 'up themselves'. In turn, detectives can be quite critical of many uniformed officers, who might sometimes fail to do a thorough initial investigation, which causes a massive headache when detectives inherit the case, due to evidential gaps that should have been filled right at the start – for example, statements that should have been taken, evidence not exhibited properly and witnesses allowed to wander off without taking their details. Every morning, my small team would sit looking through the handover packages left for them by uniformed officers and grumble miserably about all the things that should have been done before they received them.

I've seen both sides and I think it's fair to say that both work very hard, it's just that the pressures are different for each role.

I was allocated a team of detectives based at a satellite station. This was geographically remote from where I had worked previously and I felt completely isolated with no one to turn to for help or advice. I had one or two very difficult, stroppy and obstructive people to manage, and the team had recently come under investigation due to the possibly corrupt activities of a detective who had resigned before I arrived. This had hit the morale of the rest of the team and I now realise that they probably didn't trust me, a complete unknown who had mysteriously appeared from another force. They probably thought that I was an anti-corruption officer planted on the team to look at everything that was going on. This was something that anti-corruption teams did do, but it wasn't the case with me. My team also had a very heavy caseload that I felt was out of balance compared with the other two CID teams. There were only about seven of us to do absolutely everything and the pressure was intense because of the seriousness of the cases we were dealing with. I was completely out of my depth. I quickly began to hate the job and the stress that came with it.

Before long, I started to get cold after cold and I ended up on courses of antibiotics for throat and chest infections. Obviously, this was my body telling me that I was stressed out and run down. I had taken on too much too soon after leaving London and perhaps I was a victim of my own success. I had gone over the top of my own performance curve and I was quickly burning out. Years after quitting, I began smoking again and I was drinking too much. Mentally, I was also becoming increasingly anxious about coping with the job and sometimes I would even have to stop my car on my way to work and throw up at the side of the road.

I had never experienced anything like this before in my life. I had always been pretty confident of my own internal emotional and psychological resources. It frightened me to feel so vulnerable and I was ashamed of what I saw as my own pathetic weakness. Sometimes I would look in a mirror and barely recognise myself. I saw a pale, anxious face looking back at me and I found this really troubling. This was my first experience of severe anxiety, but unfortunately it wasn't going to be the last.

I found myself bursting into tears for no obvious reason and I wasn't sleeping well. Eventually, after about eight months, I decided that I needed to swallow my pride and get away from the job. When I told my senior management team, they were very understanding and to my relief they told me that this was no problem and that I could go straight back onto my old team, which coincidentally didn't have a sergeant at that time. I felt a huge sense of relief going back to my old job and the smiling faces of my old colleagues. I was a bit embarrassed on my first day back, but to be honest nobody really cared and it taught me a valuable lesson about how we can often turn minor things into major things in our own minds. Ultimately, everyone should stop worrying about what other people think about them because they're usually too busy worrying about themselves.

I enjoyed my work as a sergeant in Coventry and, two years after joining the force, I studied for the inspectors' exams and passed them in 2004. My chief superintendent asked me to join the inspector team as a uniformed acting inspector and I gratefully accepted the offer. This would be a stepping stone to full promotion once I'd attended and passed a formal promotion-selection process.

I did this job for about a year and loved every minute of it.

In essence, rather than simply running one team of uniformed officers, I was responsible for everything whilst on duty, apart from the CID teams, who reported to the detective inspector. Becoming a uniformed inspector felt like a big step up in responsibility. Sometimes, I would be the most senior officer on duty in the entire city of Coventry, and I would have to make some big operational decisions from time to time. I also had to provide advice and guidance to lots of very experienced staff who would quickly identify bullshit if they heard it. I also started getting addressed as 'Sir' for the first time, which felt a bit weird, or sometimes, to my amusement, 'Serge' by one of my officers who had become so used to calling me 'Sarge' that they weren't quite sure what to do, so they fused the name into a kind of hybrid between the two.

Occasionally, in these roles, particularly in the early days, I would have moments when I would think 'Oh God! This is a proper grown-up job!' But on the whole it was an incredibly satisfying and rewarding position, and I had some great sergeants and experienced PCs that I leaned on and trusted 100 per cent. I loved the fact that I could continue to get involved in proper front-line policing when I wanted to, but that I was also part of a team that was sorting out complicated problems and managing lots of people. I could also delegate tasks that I had no interest in doing.

One of these tasks arose one evening when we were responding mob-handed to an address in Coventry where a notoriously violent career criminal lived. He was wanted for a recall to prison for breaking his parole conditions. We all knew that he would kick off as soon as he saw us, so I summoned five or six officers and a dog unit as part of a belt-and-braces approach. Leading from the front, I strode purposefully up to the door and knocked. I could hear voices inside and the door was then opened by a child of about ten years old. I asked him if his dad was at home, the kid turned and shouted, 'Dad!' and, almost simultaneously, our quarry appeared out of the downstairs toilet. He was a big hairy bloke in his forties wearing a string vest and yellow Marigold rubber gloves. In his hands he had a large plastic bowl containing what looked horribly like brown, shitty water with lumps of turd and toilet roll floating around in it. He then proceeded to tell us that he was trying to sort out his blocked toilet. I immediately assessed that very shortly that bowl of shitty water was going to get thrown over anyone who got any closer. Therefore, after taking several steps back, I summoned a couple of probationers and instructed them to explain to our toilet-unblocker that he was to be arrested and returned to prison. I then moved quickly and purposefully out of the firing range. Predictably enough, it then all kicked off and I winced at the sight of our gallant officers being showered with turd and soggy bog-roll as they tried to persuade our man to come quietly. The moral of the story is that rank has its privileges and that any idiot can get covered in shit.

On reflection, there are lots of unpleasant things that happened during my police career. Everyone reacts to certain events differently, and stuff that upset some people didn't bother me at all. One of the things that I struggled with was dealing with suicides, and for some reason I ended up responding to a lot of them. There was one period when I worked in Coventry when my team called me 'Dr Death' because I was always being sent to suicides both as a sergeant and as an inspector. It became a bit of a joke with the teams, only I wasn't laughing. There was one period when I went to three hangings in about four days and things definitely started to get to me. I never complained because it was my job as the supervisor to go and make sure there were no suspicious circumstances and that the scene was being managed properly, but I always struggled with these calls.

The worst night shift I ever had was one in which I had to sit for hours and hours in a grotty bedsit with a bloke who had killed himself earlier that evening. I was the sergeant, and it should really have been one of the PCs doing it, but there was literally no one available because they were all in the cellblock with prisoners, so it fell to me. The only place to sit was on the bed, and he was in the bed, so I had to stand because I couldn't bear to sit down. It was very sad because it was just before Christmas and I think he had recently split up from his wife and was living in this crappy one-room bedsit. He had put a big bag of presents for each of his kids at the foot of the bed and there was a letter on a piece of A4 addressed to each child. I still think about that now.

I have also always struggled with bad smells. Obviously, for someone who gags easily, some of the things that the police have to deal with could be a bit of a nightmare. I had to go to a lot of post-mortems over the years and I used to absolutely hate the smell. It used to make colleagues piss themselves laughing at me gagging all over the place. My wife also used to get really annoyed at me when I started gagging whilst changing nappies once the kids had moved onto proper food. I can look at anything, but bad smells finish me off.

On one occasion in London, when I was working as a paramedic, we were called to transfer a lady to hospital. She was dying and in her final hours. As we walked into the house we were hit with a dreadful stench and I started gagging before I even got into the room where her bed was located. I'm not going to describe that incident any further because it's simply too disturbing for me to write about.

I also got called to a council flat where the occupant hadn't been seen for a long time and, rather shamefully, the council only decided to do something about it after he hadn't paid his rent for several months. We got a locksmith to get us into the flat and everything seemed fine. No smell at all, which was usually the main sign. We checked every room in the house and found nothing. Finally, we tried to get into the bedroom but the door was stuck. I put my shoulder to it and it burst open to reveal a bit of a horror show. The occupant had obviously died some time before and the entire room was filled with millions of flies, both dead and alive, which all came flying at us out the open door. We both ran outside screaming like a pair of eight-year-old girls, flapping at our faces and hair to get the flies off us. Once we'd calmed ourselves down, we went back in to check the deceased properly to make sure there were no signs of foul play and I will never forget the horrible crunching sound as we walked through thousands of dead flies on the floor.

After about a year as an inspector, I started giving some thought to my next career move and for some stupid reason I let myself be persuaded that a spell in the chief constable's staff office might be a good idea. Some bright spark advised me that this was an excellent way to see the inner workings of the force and gain a better understanding of 'strategic thinking'.

I put myself forward, was interviewed with several other candidates and was successful. However, it would soon become clear that this was not going to be one of my career highlights.

CHAPTER 15

STAFF OFFICER

The role of a staff officer is to work directly with one of the chief officers in a force. In the case of the West Midlands, the most senior officers were the chief constable, the deputy chief constable and four assistant chief constables. All had individual staff officers, and each had a PA, who managed their diaries.

The staff office was, therefore, a weird little eco-system of senior officers, who were generally phenomenally busy, and us, their minions. It felt like a million miles from operational policing and I quickly realised that I was probably going to hate every minute. I had gone from being a largish fish in a small pond to a minnow in a large lake. I had lost my acting inspector rank to enter the staff office and was back to my rank of sergeant. I had also gone from a role where my opinions and experience were listened to and appreciated to one where I was completely invisible. On the rare occasions that I offered up my thoughts in a meeting, many senior officers would look at me with barely disguised disgust that I had opened my mouth.

It was my first proper exposure to chief officers. Such

officers are generally highly intelligent and most of them have a phenomenal work ethic. They usually started work early and finished late every day. They had a busy schedule of meetings covering an extensive range of complex issues and they were expected to grasp the details as well as the 'big picture'. However, many of them were quite one-dimensional in terms of their wider lives and rarely mentioned life outside work. Since that time, I've worked with a lot of other senior people from different parts of the public and private sector. Many of them are much the same; much happier to be at work than to be at home with their families. Each to their own I suppose, but it wouldn't be for me.

I can recall an amusing moment one Friday evening when I had drawn the short straw and was staying in the PA's office adjacent to the chief constable's suite until the chief decided to call it a day. Specific staff officer tasks had to be performed, such as letter writing, clearing away sensitive documents, locking all the safes and offices. It was about 7.30 p.m. when the chief popped his head around the corner from his office and said, 'Iain, could you be good enough to grab Mr Smith [the finance head] and ask him to come and see me?'

I advised him that Mr Smith had gone home. I knew that because I'd said goodbye to him myself at about 5.30 p.m.

He then said, 'Oh… right… in that case can you ask Mr Williams [the head of HR] to pop in?'

I advised him that this person had also gone home. The chief looked confused and irritated. 'What? Both of them? Is there *anyone* still here?' he asked.

I reminded him that it was Friday. I told him that everyone

had gone home and that it was just the two of us left. He looked a little bemused by this before saying, 'Oh… well, in that case, I suppose I'd better go home myself.'

It was a funny exchange but also a bit sad, really.

As well as being able to watch chief officers in their natural habitat, I was also introduced to the baffling language of senior officers in meetings. This was a particular spectacle when they were all in a meeting together as they would speak in a way that defied understanding by any normal person. The language they used was a weird concoction that I can only imagine was created by fusing the opaquest language from the civil service, local government, corporate life and some business master's jargon. More than anything, it had very little to do with rolling around in the gutter with drug addicts or chasing burglars over garden hedges in the early hours of the morning.

It was always amusing to sit and listen to officers having professional disagreements with senior partners from other government agencies. They all used such vague, coded language and nobody ever said what they were actually trying to say. Observing their professional disagreements was like watching two people trying to beat each other to death with a feather.

Terms like 'rather unhelpful' would be about as critical as it ever got. This was used when what that person really wanted to say was: 'I think you're a complete cock, and you're talking nonsense.' Many of these meetings with partners were usually wasted with a load of blue-sky thinking with no obvious policing progress or decisions made whatsoever. This probably explains a lot about how it is that the police now routinely have to deal with all sorts of issues that should be dealt with by other agencies;

it is a situation created over many years by a complete absence of plain speaking. In my opinion, chief officers across the UK should have been saying to their counterparts in the NHS, 'We are not a repository for mental health cases languishing for days in our cells. If you have funding issues you must address those issues to central government, but we cannot and will not pick up the pieces from a broken mental health system.'

However, interestingly, this odd, coded language soon became the approved way to get on in policing and was slavishly copied by every ambitious chief inspector, superintendent and chief super-intendent who had aspirations for the top. Their language became liberally peppered with impenetrable terminology that left most ordinary listeners completely mystified. Therefore, it soon became quite a painful task to write the minutes of all meetings I attend-ed as it was not at all obvious what someone had actually said as they concluded a five-minute-long, jargon-filled monologue that would have horrified the Plain English Campaign.

How did this happen? I really don't know, but I suspect that it was possibly another of the unexpected outcomes of those cash-rich Labour years where civil servants stuck their noses into every single aspect of policing and this language of 'lean sys-tems', 'customer journeys', 'performance metrics' and 'outcomes' infected the organisation, creating a generation of managers who seemed to have forgotten that they were police officers.

By the way, I started to see and hear slightly less of this sort of weird language as the resources began to disappear from po-licing after 2010. I guess that when everyone is running around with their hair on fire they're less inclined to talk in riddles.

One of the biggest problems in the 2000s was that these senior managers tended to promote in their own image. This created a growing culture where managers gradually bore less and less resemblance to the people who actually did the job, never mind the public who were receiving the services of the organisation. Those people actually doing the job of policing in turn mostly rolled their eyes when the boss walked out of the room. This generated an understanding that the only way to get on, in terms of getting promoted, was to 'swallow the corporate pill'. To be fair, there were plenty of examples of senior officers who were also operationally extremely competent but these were usually the ones who had cynically learned to 'turn it on' for the duration of the promotion process and then revert back to reality when doing their day job. Unfortunately, for every one of these, there were plenty who had bluffed their way up the promotion ladder. These people were seemingly divorced from reality and many of them unfortunately believed their own bullshit, which is always dangerous. In my later years in the force, the easiest way to identify them was to see who was most active on Twitter. With a few exceptions, there was a definite correlation between a lack of operational experience and Twitter activity, which was used as a vehicle for shameless self-promotion.

Many senior officers at this time had studiously avoided any job on the way up that had a large amount of risk attached to it because they knew that it could be career-threatening. Anything involving tackling serious criminality, child abuse or dealing with high-risk sex offenders would be the last thing that they wanted to get involved in. Much better to flit between projects or cushy strategic jobs rather than being exposed to that real policing stuff.

I suspect that this generation of performance-obsessed, corporate police types, who only ever asked 'how high?' when the Home Office told them to jump, left the service dreadfully ill-prepared for the horrible, cash-strapped years after the Tory Party were elected in 2010. This was a generation of senior officers who had never rocked the boat and who were deafeningly silent when police funding started drying up.

One of the reasons that I joined the police in the first place was that I couldn't bear the thought of being stuck in an office every day. An office environment can be so stifling and any little eccentricity or annoying mannerism on the part of your co-workers can quickly become completely infuriating.

The dynamics and office politics with the PAs in the staff office always amused me. Many of these women had been in their roles for a long time, working for several generations of senior officers who would come and go over the years, and this gave a few of them an inflated sense of their own power. It was funny to watch a superintendent or chief superintendent, who would have been treated like God in his or her own little fiefdom, grovelling and supplicating before the PAs, who would treat them like naughty children. These senior officers knew perfectly well that if they pissed the PA off they'd get nothing.

We had to write all sorts of reports and briefing papers for the bosses on a wide variety of subjects and the staff officers became pretty adept at hoovering up a lot of information quickly and making sense of it. We also had to write draft responses to letters from MPs, civil servants and members of the public on all sorts of things, but generally complaints. Many of these could be quite heart-rending, but some were just silly and annoying.

For example, a constituent would complain to their MP that they had not had their property returned to them after an arrest, but what they had neglected to explain to the MP was that the property in question had actually been stolen by them at gunpoint in an armed robbery. The chief constable would examine the responses to these letters to check he was happy before they were sent out.

Our chief at the time, Sir Paul Scott-Lee, was a genuinely lovely man. He had an almost supernatural ability to spot grammatical errors or typos within seconds of looking at a document. He was also able to instantly identify the one tiny flaw in a letter that would ensure that the matter would not be fully resolved. It took us all a while to get onto his wavelength, but he taught me skills that served me well for the rest of my career.

Ultimately, my heart wasn't in the role as a staff officer one tiny bit. Nonetheless, I stuck the posting out for just over a year and in the meantime I sat and passed the formal inspectors' promotion process. I had learned a lot about how the organisation worked, but I was itching to get back to operational policing. I made it known that I wanted out of the staff office and thankfully they found someone to take over from me. I then received my first proper inspector's posting and found out that I was going to Stechford in east Birmingham, or, as it was known at the time, D3 operational command unit.

CHAPTER 16

STECHFORD

I arrived at Stechford as an inspector in 2006 and was welcomed by my new chief superintendent, who I already knew from my time in the staff office. There were about eight uniformed inspectors at Stechford and they all had different day jobs. The inspectors were also required to take it in turns to act as the duty officer across three 24/7 shifts, which meant that they would generally be the senior operational officer on duty. My boss gave me my posting, which to my slight dismay was running the operations centre. This was the posting that the newest inspector was usually given.

The ops centre fulfilled many functions. Firstly, there were the communications staff who managed the deployment of officers to urgent and non-urgent jobs. Then, there were the staff who dealt with routine telephone and email enquiries from members of the public, and another team who worked in the front office dealing with members of the public attending the police station for all sorts of reasons. Finally, there was a team who dealt with a vast array of bureaucratic admin tasks connected to data inputting to different police IT systems, road traffic accidents, wanted people, warrants and God knows what else. In total, I had responsibility for about 120 police officers and civilian staff. Today, most of these functions have been pulled together into larger corporate teams servicing the entire force, but in those days, every operational command unit had its own ops centre.

It was an unpopular posting because every ops centre in every police station at that time was generally staffed by officers who could no longer carry out front-line operational duties. Many of these officers were classed as 'permanently restricted'. Many of them had genuine medical issues and they were often frustrated and angry that they couldn't work on the streets, which is completely understandable. Some, however, were either a bit work-shy or uncomfortable with confrontation and had therefore been given administrative roles. They should probably never have been police officers in the first place and the organisation would probably have been better off without them. So, on the one hand, you had officers who bitterly resented being in the ops centre because they wanted to be operational and, on the other hand, you had officers who would rather have been at home watching daytime TV. The latter group were quite happy to take their wages and do as little as possible. The net result was that, with some notable exceptions, the get up and go of the ops centre police officers had got up and gone. Ultimately, the centre was a massive moan-fest for the inspector and sergeants who had the unfortunate task of trying to motivate the staff. I admit that I do not suffer fools gladly, and it was not long before my patience started to wear thin with some of them.

As well as being staffed by a mixed bag of police officers, at least two-thirds of the ops staff were civilians, and this was a new challenge to me. I'd worked closely with civilian police staff for many years but I had never actually managed them before, so this was a bit of an eye-opener. Managing police officers is very different from managing civilian staff. Generally speaking, police officers understand that they are in a disciplined service and when a sergeant or inspector asks them to do something they know that they're not really *asking* them, they're *telling* them. It's very, very rare in the police to have to order someone to do something because cops understand that when there is a job to do, regardless of how unpleasant it is, they have to do it. In my thirty-year career, I think I only had to say the words, 'I am ordering you to do this' two or three times, and that was only as a last resort when dealing with a particularly stroppy and unco-operative officer.

Civilian police staff were a different kettle of fish altogether. Most of them were great fun to work with, but I had to draw on every ounce of my sometimes-limited reserves of patience and good humour with some of them. They were an altogether more fragile bunch than the police officers I was used to managing. In the ops centre, there was a drama of some sort or other almost every day. Some of these issues were work-related but most concerned something going on at home that had spilt over into work. Sometimes, I would be dealing with things that made me want to weep. Here is an example exchange:

Employee: 'Excuse me, Sir, Julie keeps looking at me, and it's making me feel anxious.'

Me: 'Why don't you sit over there where she can't see you?'

Employee: 'No, I don't want to sit near Barry because he picks his nose, and it makes me feel sick.'

Or:

Employee: 'Sorry, Sir, can I leave early today? I need to take the cat to the vet. His glands are blocked and he needs them cleared.'

Or:

Employee: 'Sir, have you got a minute? It's about Sandra. I don't want to work with Sandra because she keeps turning the air conditioning on and I'm freezing, and I didn't bring my cardie to work today. I like it nice and warm but then she gets all snarky, and when I leave the room, she turns the temperature down again.'

There was a particular group of individuals who, when I saw them making their way towards my office, I wanted to hide inside my filing cabinet or climb out the window to avoid them. They were the Olympic-standard complainers who took it in turns to raise real or imagined grievances on a daily basis.

Employee: 'Sir, I'm sorry to bother you, but the new chair I've been given is giving me terrible neck pain.'

Me: 'Oh, really? There's nothing worse than having a pain in the neck is there? But I'm confused, isn't that the special, very expensive orthopaedic chair that you asked for and were measured up for by occupational health?'

Employee: 'Yes, it is, Sir, but I don't like it, and I want my old chair back, please.'

And so it went on. At least 20 per cent of my time was spent dealing with intractable HR issues, occupational health referrals, health and safety assessments and refereeing childish disagreements between staff members. The poor old sergeants had a hell of a time trying to work out the staff-duty rotas. It became like

one of those puzzles you get in a Christmas cracker where you
have to move all the pieces in the right order to make the picture
because certain people refused to work or sit near certain other
people.

It was a relief to be able to get out and about operationally with
the response cops, and I was able to do this when it was my turn
to be duty officer and I was therefore in charge of everything
that went on during one of the 24/7 shifts.

Stechford was the busiest operational command unit in the
West Midlands Police, and statistically one of the busiest in the
UK. It covered multiple areas of urban deprivation and very diverse communities: from large Pakistani Muslim communities
of Small Heath and Alum Rock to mostly white neighbourhoods
in Shard End and Sheldon. I had never policed Birmingham
before, and I had never patrolled majority-Muslim areas, so
it was a pretty steep learning curve for me. It took me a long
time to get used to driving a police car around Small Heath and
feeling very much in the minority from an ethnic and cultural perspective. Communities like Small Heath were incredibly
different to the places I had worked before. Thankfully, we had
quite a few Asian officers who spoke Urdu, Punjabi or Farsi on
our team, and I even had some of them on speed-dial when I got
into a pickle.

Policing in the UK is an unbelievably challenging occupation, but the cultural diversity of the UK creates very specific
challenges. It is not the same policing a largely rural or affluent
Oxfordshire community as it is policing a deprived inner-city
part of London, Birmingham or Manchester. Yet, every police
officer in the UK receives broadly the same training regardless

of whether they're going to be working in Bourton-on-the-Water or Brixton. Some parts of the UK are definitely harder to police, and perhaps there needs to be more recognition of that in terms of the skills, training and even the remuneration for officers working in places like Small Heath.

Small Heath was a challenging area to work. There were very high levels of crime and violence, much of which was linked to fallouts between rival drugs gangs. It was hard to communicate effectively with many people who lived in Small Heath because their English was poor or non-existent, and there was also a very male-dominated culture that made it difficult to speak freely with women and children, who would usually defer to the male head of the household. Quite frequently, there would be an outburst of violence between large groups of men carrying improvised weapons, baseball bats and samurai swords. We would get there and find complete carnage, with cars ramming each other, blood everywhere, and everyone would immediately scatter. No one ever wanted to talk to the police, and we would have no idea what on earth the fighting had been about. Gradually, we would get calls from different hospitals where the injured participants had been deposited, often with serious injuries or bits of them missing. We would go there and try to find out who had done what to whom but, once again, it was rare that anyone would want to talk to us. We would later find out that it had all kicked off because of something like a disputed sale of a building plot thousands of miles away. Within minutes of receiving an angry phone call from Kashmir, the men from two rival families were out on the streets in Birmingham going at it hammer and tongs.

The issues we dealt with in the predominantly white communities were somewhat different, and included a lot of anti-social behaviour, drink-related violence and petty property crime. Many of these areas were pretty grim, and riding unregistered, usually stolen, scrambler bikes and quad bikes dangerously to piss everyone off was a local speciality. Some of the pubs on these estates were dens of iniquity; about as far removed from a suburban gastropub as Alcatraz is from Chatsworth House. Picture a single-storey boozer with a flat roof and razor wire around the heavily graffitied walls, one or two shady characters standing outside smoking joints and the obligatory Staffordshire Bull Terrier/Pitbull cross with studded collar standing guard. Some of these pubs were generally the venue of choice in which drug addicts would offload their stolen gear. Such individuals were particularly good at nicking joints of meat, packs of bacon, jars of coffee and Gillette razors. I imagine this was similar to other parts of the country as such products are easy to offload in these kinds of pubs.

We also had Birmingham City Football Club on our patch, so Saturday afternoons and evenings could get quite lively as the Blues seemed to attract more than their fair share of knuckle-dragging football hooligans from rival clubs around the country. The local derby between the Blues and Aston Villa frequently turned into a pitched battle outside the ground. It always amused me that otherwise law-abiding, sensible family men would go completely loopy and try to fight everyone after their team had lost and they had drunk eight pints of lager. We used to have a small team of detectives whose full-time job was basically reviewing CCTV footage and identifying the worst troublemakers after every game and, in due course, they would be named and shamed in the *Birmingham Mail* after their court appearances.

Late shifts and the early evenings were always relentlessly busy. Serious incidents happened more or less every day and often several cracked off simultaneously, so you had to be switched on, be able to think quickly and keep a calm head. Most of the inspectors at Stechford were super-experienced and very helpful, and I learned a lot from them. If you can work at a place like Stechford in the police I think you can work anywhere. A lot of ex-Stechford people later moved to some of the most difficult and challenging roles in the force as they were experienced with dealing with serious criminality, including murders and firearms incidents. Many years later, towards the end of my career as a superintendent, it was often ex-colleagues from my Stechford days who would be asking me for surveillance authorities to investigate major criminals and organised crime gangs.

My day job, when I wasn't dealing with constant moaning, was new to me, and there was a lot to learn regarding control room procedures and all the different IT systems. There were also tons of performance indicators that my department was responsible for delivering on behalf of the command unit. Every month, there was an audit of incident logs and crime records carried out by a department at HQ to ensure that we were compliant with the Home Office crime-recording and data-quality standards. These bizarre rules were clearly dreamt up by someone high on drugs as they seem to be designed to force every police officer in England and Wales to waste as much time and public money as humanly possible. If we failed this audit, the command unit automatically failed *every other* performance metric for the entire month as a punishment, and every unit was competing with each other. In my first month at Stechford, I was blissfully unaware of this regime because my predecessor had failed to give me a proper handover. My temporary state of ignorance came to an abrupt end when one day the very, very pissed-off superintendent barged into my office when he was told we'd failed the monthly audit. He let me know in no uncertain terms that I needed to get my shit together.

The reality, of course, was that many of these police performance measurements were completely counter-productive, and they created a catch-22 situation where hitting one target would almost certainly guarantee that you'd fail another.

One day, about six months into my new job, my chief superintendent popped into my office and told me that we were going to be visited by Sir Ronnie Flanagan, the ex-chief constable of the Royal Ulster Constabulary. My boss told me that Sir Ronnie had been tasked with looking at police bureaucracy to make recommendations to the government as to how things could be improved and streamlined. When the day of his arrival came, I had prepared an extensive dossier of examples of the madness of wasted time and resources, uncooperative 'victims' and pointless bureaucracy. Sir Ronnie was charming and when I showed him this stuff he sat and shook his head in disbelief and said that, unfortunately, it was the same everywhere he had gone in the UK. He seemed genuinely determined to try to get the Home Office to see sense and I felt hopeful that something might change. But, of course, nothing changed. It just got worse and worse.

Since that time, I have had quite a lot of dealings with the Home Office and I now completely understand why nothing ever improves for policing. They have very little understanding of the reality of real-world policing and far too many of them operate in a realm of Excel spreadsheets, pointless policy documents and politically correct initiatives.

I worked in the ops centre for about eighteen months until, eventually, we got the news that a new inspector would be arriving at Stechford. I made it clear that I'd done my bit and wanted a change. It was at about this time that the force announced that it was going to be creating new multi-disciplinary teams on every command unit to deal with child abuse, domestic abuse and vulnerable adult abuse and to manage sex offenders. These disciplines had always existed individually but there was a need to professionalise and improve the quality of investigations. This development was in response to the recommendations from public inquiries into the deaths of Victoria Climbié in 2000 and Peter Connelly (Baby P) in 2007. In these cases there had generally been poor communication between partner agencies, a lack of relevant and timely data sharing and a tendency to give abusive carers the benefit of the doubt rather than removing and thus safeguarding children at risk.

Each of these new units was to be managed by a newly created detective inspector. I put myself forward for selection for this position, sat the interview and was successful. Most of my peers thought I was insane. This was going to be a highly pressurised job. Many of the police managers who had been caught up in inquiries into high-profile child deaths had been dragged through hostile judicial investigations for many years afterwards. Not only that, but Stechford had very high levels of deprivation and all the ingredients for a dozen similar tragedies involving vulnerable members of the community. If such crimes were going to happen anywhere, they were going to happen in Stechford. I knew all this, but I was genuinely interested in this area of policing, and I believe that putting yourself into uncomfortable situations is often the best way to learn. I would also be trained as a senior investigating officer, which meant that I would be nationally accredited to investigate the most serious crimes, including murders.

After a few weeks, I passed the ops centre over to the new inspector and I scarpered off to my new job. As I was leaving the office, I saw one of the centre's serial complainers making a bee-line for my replacement, and I heaved a huge sigh of relief as I closed the door behind me.

CHAPTER 17

PPU

M y new team was called the public protection unit (PPU), and I went from having over a hundred staff reporting to me to about twenty. They were a great bunch of officers and all very experienced in their own fields of expertise, but part of my job was to mould them into a cohesive team where they could assist one another if one part of the team was busy and another part was quiet. In reality, this never happened because everyone was always stupidly busy, and each discipline was quite specialised in terms of how they worked and their own areas of knowledge.

I had a lot to learn about all four disciplines, but I tended to focus most of my time working on child abuse investigations because these were the most serious and complex and always required an immediate response. They were the cases that were also most likely to end your career.

I spent most of my first few weeks on training courses of one sort or another. I started my senior investigating officer course and then I did my specialist child abuse investigation course, both awarding nationally recognised qualifications. I then had to meet and get to know a whole raft of professionals from other partner organisations, mainly managers from children's social services, NHS paediatricians and other medical professionals involved in child welfare. Inevitably, there were a lot of well-established protocols that we all needed to understand and adhere to. Out of all of the different types of policing I have ever done, this was the one where we needed to work most closely with partner organisations.

This was all new to me, and it came as a bit of a shock to find out about the sheer volume of cases my new department would deal with.

I had two sex-offender managers (SOMs) on my team, and their job was to ensure that all of the registered sex offenders living on our patch were being managed according to national guidelines. All sex offenders are required to register their addresses with the police and probation services. There were also a whole range of different conditions that they would have to adhere to, depending on the nature of their offending, prison licence conditions and level of risk. They would also have to permit access to their premises by police at any reasonable time without prior notice. I was fortunate to have brilliant SOMs who knew their business inside out and exactly who they needed to be worried about or keep an extra-close eye on. Sex offenders, particularly those who offend against children, are notoriously manipulative and usually take great pains to hide their offending from the authorities. They are also prepared to 'play the long game' and will take their time in identifying and grooming new victims and the families of the targeted victim. However, a good SOM knows all the right questions to ask and they are eagle-eyed when they visit offenders and will quickly spot any-thing in the house that gives them cause for concern. Each SOM was responsible for supervising and monitoring about eighty sex offenders on our patch alone, which was a huge workload.

The internet massively increased the number of people on the sex-offenders register and there was barely a week that went by without a new name being added to the list. The UK was ex-periencing an explosion of people being arrested for possession of child sexual abuse images from the internet and, from time to time, once the computers belonging to such individuals were analysed, intra-familial sexual abuse or sexual abuse of children connected to the family would be exposed. The child abuse units would then pick these cases up.

I attended some brilliant courses on investigating child sex offenders run by the Child Exploitation and Online Protection (CEOP) unit in London. It proved to be a massive eye-opener. The courses were run by Dr Joe Sullivan, one of the most expe-rienced forensic psychologists in the world, who has spent his entire career working with and investigating child sex offenders. Joe was entertaining and fascinating in equal measure. What he didn't know about child sex offenders wasn't worth knowing. He had worked in prisons for many years, interviewing some of the most serious offenders and learning about how they thought and behaved. He showed us videos of interviews that he had conducted with lots of child sex offenders explaining how they had gained the trust of the people around the victims and the different methods they used to gain the compliance of the child. There were various tactics that they consciously employed with victims and carers and there was a lot of consistency across offenders, almost as if they had all gone to the same school to learn about child sex offending. Joe gave us a taxonomy of about five or six typical types of offender and explained how we could use this knowledge in planning arrests, the conversations we should have with suspects generally, how to treat them in custody and the interview techniques we should employ to get the best outcome. It was disturbing and alarming but brilliant stuff and my team used these tactics in every investigation. We would study the victim's account, analysing it to establish the mindset of the offender and their particular grooming techniques, and when we then came to the arrest we would put Joe's advice into action. By doing this, my team had one of the highest detection rates for serious sexual offences against children in the force. We were so 'sold' on this approach that my amazing, wonderful detective sergeant Josie eventually studied to become a forensic psychologist in her spare time. Josie was a force of nature and incredibly committed to her job. She was one of the best detectives I have ever worked with and she achieved stellar results. Hundreds of dangerous people went to prison because of her and thousands of children were protected as a result of her professionalism and dogged determination.

The child abuse detectives dealt with the physical and sexual abuse of children as well as serious neglect. They also investigated the sudden or unexplained death of any child under the age of eighteen. I was the senior investigating officer in the event of child death but, ultimately, I was responsible for defining the investigative strategy for every serious case. I also had responsibility for deciding which cases we should discontinue, usually on the basis that we had done everything reasonably possible, and such cases would then be handed back to social services.

The job was extremely stressful at times because we all knew that if we missed something or made a wrong call the consequences were serious, and we would probably be hung out to dry by the courts and the media. The volume of referrals was unmanageable, and each detective was carrying many serious cases simultaneously. We all knew that any one of these cases could easily end in the death of a child at the hands of a parent or a dangerous individual, like a new boyfriend coming into the home. Many of the parents we dealt with led chaotic lives blighted by physical abuse, drugs, alcohol and mental illness. The biological fathers were usually absent or uninterested, and the mothers would often have a succession of different sexual partners who had no biological tie to the child and no interest in their welfare. It was a toxic and dangerous mix for children.

Most of our referrals would come from social services or from A&E when a child was presented with injuries that were believed to be non-accidental. Investigating such incidents was never straightforward because very young children can't tell you what happened and the carers stay tight-lipped, so it usually comes down to expert medical evidence and identifying inconsistencies in the accounts given by carers. Frequently, however, it was tough to prove guilt to a criminal standard. If this was the case, we would go back to social services, who would put in place a protective regime. Children would very often be removed and placed with a foster family until social services were happy that the child was no longer at risk, and part of our job was to help make that decision to remove a child. I had to authorise those removals, which was often at the point of birth. I knew what a big responsibility this was, and it was traumatic to see the distress caused to a mother by removing their baby as soon as it was born.

I dealt with a lot of child deaths during the three years I spent in this role. These were always incredibly sad and difficult to deal with, but we had to get on with the job and try to remain as professional and emotionally detached as possible whilst at the same time treating bereaved parents with compassion. Every death of a child is a possible murder. However, it was more likely to be an accident or a catastrophic medical issue, so it was vital to keep an open mind and follow the evidence. As a father of four kids, I know how hard parenting can sometimes be, and how desperate a parent can feel as a result of sleeplessness, frustration and stress. Many of these deaths occurred in the early hours of the morning, and I was on a force-wide on-call rota for sudden or unexplained deaths of children, so I would quite regularly get called out in the middle of the night and have to drive to some far-flung part of Birmingham to deal with them. Many of these had been accidental as a result of parents sharing a bed with their baby and then rolling on top of them during the night or the baby overheating and dying. Babies find it difficult to regulate their own body temperature, so this is a big risk factor, particularly when combined with other factors, such as cigarette smoke in the house.

I also had to investigate a few child suicides, and these were definitely the worst things I had to deal with in my entire career.

They were often the result of bullying at school or in the local neighbourhood and they were desperately sad. The youngest suicide I dealt with was that of a ten-year-old. At that time, my own son was ten years old, which made it even more traumatic. I will spare you the details of what happened, but it was terrible. I still occasionally have very bad memories about that incident and others like it more than ten years later. In this particular case, I had to go to the hospital in the early hours of the morning and help the paediatrician remove the dead child's pyjamas as potential forensic evidence. It was a really dreadful thing to have to deal with, and I can't begin to imagine how that child's parents coped with such a senseless tragedy.

We were required to attend forensic post-mortems and I also found this very difficult. The paediatric pathologists were brilliant and they did their job with the utmost sensitivity. I have no idea how they could keep on coming to work every day to do their jobs. Thank God we have people who can do this stuff, because they were frequently able to say with confidence that a death was caused as a result of a medical issue and this would then allow parents to grieve the loss of their child without having any cloud of suspicion hanging over them.

Despite the grim nature of our work, we had a lot of laughs on the team too, and I tried to maintain a very light-hearted atmosphere as much as possible. Police officers tend to have quite a dark sense of humour and this was particularly the case on my team. It was not uncommon, however, to have staff in tears over something they had just dealt with and it was important to give them the space they needed. One of the requirements of the job was that all staff had psychological assessments roughly every six months. These were a bit of a joke, however, because every time the psychiatric nurse came and spoke to the staff individually she would say, 'Your staff are all suffering from high levels of stress and burnout, and you are too.'

'Yes, I know,' I would respond, 'but the referrals aren't going to go away or stop coming in, and we've been told we won't get any more staff, so what do you suggest we do?'

There was never a realistic answer to this question, so we just carried on and everyone made the best of it. I do not doubt that many people who did this job went on to develop long-term psychological problems, not so much because of what they saw and dealt with, but because of the constant fear of being blamed if something bad happened that was outside their control and they were not supported. Officers who work on these teams deserve great respect and recognition. Sadly, the only time they seem to receive any attention is when something goes wrong.

Today, there are very high levels of stress, anxiety and depression in UK policing, and the government has made a half-hearted attempt to address this on a national scale by providing dedicated 'support'. However, this situation has been created by a policing and criminal justice system that is so unbelievably broken in so many ways that treating the symptoms without addressing the causes will achieve nothing.

During this period, I went through a very unexpected and traumatic marital breakdown, followed by a divorce. I can remember sitting in my office with my head in my hands crying as I tried to make sense of what had happened. We had two kids and a mortgage and everything in my life was suddenly such a terrible mess emotionally and financially. I didn't know where to start with it all. The team were all amazing. They really looked after me and showed me great love, but I was pretty hopeless for a few months as I tried to get myself back onto an even emotional keel. In the meantime, I was going out and dealing with child deaths, and I was also on the on-call murder rota at weekends, so I was having to try to deal with adult murders and other very serious incidents too. I wasn't sleeping well, and I was probably teetering on the verge of a serious nervous breakdown. But I carried on. I look back on it all now and realise that I should have taken some time out to recharge, but I never took a single day off work.

At one point, I hadn't slept a single wink for four days and I genuinely thought that I was going mad. I don't mind admitting that at one point I even called the Samaritans in the middle of the night because I was feeling so desperate and I was worried that I might do something stupid.

During this period, I had to go to an awards ceremony one evening for members of my team who were receiving awards and afterwards the command unit business manager, Terry, came up to me and asked if I was OK. I lied and said I was fine even though I actually felt like I was having some sort of out-of-body experience. She told me that I looked really terrible, and I broke down and told her that I hadn't slept for four days and that I thought I was cracking up. She got me a lift home and the next day I went to see my doctor, who immediately gave me medication to calm me down and help me sleep. I think that doctor possibly saved my life because I had started to feel really desperate and was having some very dark thoughts.

Our colleagues in the domestic abuse team were also cracking under the pressure of completely unrealistic workloads. Occasionally, I would go into their little office and see the teetering piles of referrals all over their desks. These were graded according to risk: medium, high or very high, and they were then managed and prioritised based on this risk score. The score was worked out using a questionnaire that officers attending the original incident would fill out, which was based on academic research that assessed the behaviours exhibited by a perpetrator that was indicative of the future likelihood of a domestic homicide or a serious assault.

The problem with assessing risk in this way is that it can produce very inconsistent results and often depends on the way a question is asked, the thoroughness or inquisitiveness of the officer, the truthfulness of the victim and all sorts of other variables. Also, like every risk assessment, it will only ever provide a snapshot of a moment in time. Thus, a risk assessment carried out on a Thursday that comes back as 'medium' could easily escalate to 'high risk' on a Friday for all sorts of random reasons. It really was a game of Russian roulette for the domestic abuse team and they would come into work every day half-expecting to learn that one of their abuse victims had been murdered.

Domestic abuse is such a complex issue and victims can fail to disclose their abuse for a very long time until they call the police for the first time. It has become such an epidemic in UK society and the police have to respond to all domestic abuse calls. Indeed, a typical response officer will spend an inordinate amount of time sorting out domestics. The problem, however, is that the definition of what constitutes 'domestic abuse' has become broader and broader over time. According to the Crown Prosecution Service, the current definition is: 'Any incident or pattern of incidents of controlling, coercive or threatening behaviour, violence or abuse between those aged sixteen or over who are or have been intimate partners or family members regardless of gender or sexuality.'

Therefore, it is not unusual for the police to get called to an incident in which a teenage brother and sister are squabbling over the remote control, or a silly argument between a father and their teenage son that has escalated. Strictly speaking, these types of incident fall into the official definition of what constitutes domestic abuse and investigating them requires a lot of additional work. The police have been criticised so many times for failing to protect domestic abuse victims, but the simple truth is that they are often too busy dealing with trivial incidents that would be better resolved with words of advice, which would free them up to focus on the victims who are genuinely at risk.

Right at the end of my service in 2019, dealing with domestic abuse was the single biggest demand on front-line police officers, probably followed by dealing with serious mental health issues in the community as a result of government funding cuts for those services.

Besides dealing with child abuse, the other part of my PPU team were the officers who managed allegations relating to vulnerable adults. Typically, these involved elderly residents of care homes or adults with learning difficulties who had received unexplained injuries or who were subject to some sort of abuse. There were only two officers at Stechford working on these kinds of cases: Bev and Martin, who were both extremely good at their jobs. They had also become very experienced at dealing with dysfunctional teenagers from local children's homes who frequently went missing, and it was this issue that grew into one of the most significant developments of my time in the PPU and probably my entire career.

CHAPTER 18

SEXUAL EXPLOITATION

B etween 2008 and 2009, we started seeing a recurring pattern on the PPU whereby teenage girls were regularly going
missing from children's homes in Birmingham and staying away
for long periods, often up to three or four days. Sometimes they
would come back of their own accord, usually heavily intoxicated through drink or drugs, and other times they would be found
by patrolling officers in a car with an adult male.

Nearly all these girls had very troubled backgrounds. They
had been in and out of the care system most of their lives. The
children's homes seemed uninterested in where they were or
who they were with and defaulted to picking up the phone and
calling the police to report them missing.

We had many children's homes on our patch, and Bev and
Martin began spending an increasing amount of time trying
to track these girls down and returning them, only for them to
walk out the next day and disappear for another two or three
days. The girls were not making any allegations on their return
and there was no obvious evidence of anything untoward going
on. Initially, this was dismissed as teenage girls being defiant and

choosing to spend time with their unknown friends at locations that they were unwilling to tell us about.

However, gradually a picture began to emerge of children's homes being deliberately targeted by a group of Asian men who would 'befriend' the girls, pick them up in their cars and take them away somewhere. Initially, no one was making any allegations, and the girls' behaviour was viewed as attention-seeking nonsense. I must admit that despite Bev and Martin's protests, initially, I too was sceptical that the situation deserved any time or effort from the police. I told them that we had quite enough to do without being distracted by a few attention-seeking teenagers.

It was only after one particular incident when one of the girls was admitted to hospital with injuries consistent with a severe sexual assault that alarm bells started to ring. She refused to tell us what had happened and she declined a forensic medical examination. Gradually, this type of incident became more and more regular, and it became evident that these girls were being groomed, raped and sexually abused by people whose identities we were unaware of and at locations that we didn't know about. But no one was making any allegations and the prevailing culture at that time was that if nobody told us that a crime had been committed, then no crime had been committed. The reality was that the PPU was inundated by other serious allegations and referrals from social services that were prioritised, so these vague and unsubstantiated rumours of serious sexual assaults were passed over.

There was also a real reluctance to acknowledge the uncomfortable fact that the majority of this grooming was being

carried out by Asian men. Managers from all agencies were terrified of being accused of racism by pursuing unfounded allegations against one specific ethnic group, so it was just easier to
stick their heads in the sand and ignore it. I tried to raise these
concerns with senior officers, managers from social services and
the managers of the children's homes, but we were more or less
ignored. They argued that these were teenage girls who were
somewhat out of control, acting promiscuously and making
poor relationship choices. They justified this on the basis that
we hadn't received a single criminal allegation of a sexual nature
and therefore all of these activities were clearly 'consensual' and
that these girls were basically 'prostituting themselves'.

Bev and Martin were relentless in their determination to
expose what they knew was serious sexual abuse of very vulnerable children who were only fourteen or fifteen years old. We
spoke to our counterparts in neighbouring command units and,
sure enough, there were identical incidents across the rest of
Birmingham.

It's easy to ignore one or two people who are saying something. But it is much harder to ignore a dozen people from different places who are all saying the same thing. The DCI crime
managers from four or five of the worst-affected command units
in Birmingham commissioned an investigation into what was
going on. We were given dedicated intelligence analysts and
resources to pull together an intelligence assessment of victims,
suspected offenders and key locations. Crucially, we also managed to gain the trust of one or two of the girls. They still refused
to make any criminal allegations but they did give us accounts of
what was going on.

The intelligence assessments made for grim and depressing reading. A typical scenario was as follows:

Girls were being approached and befriended by Asian men in the general vicinity of the care homes. They would be offered alcohol or cannabis, taken for a drive around the city and then they would 'chill' without anything of a sexual nature taking place. This would go on for a while, and the girl would then introduce one of her fellow care home residents to her new 'boyfriend', who would, in turn, introduce the girls to his friends. Gradually, there would be an expectation from the men that the girls exchange minor sexual favours for the alcohol and drugs and they might be given little presents or taken shopping for new trainers. The girls thought very little of this and saw these men, who were generally in their twenties, as their boyfriends. They were being given the male attention that they craved and they described themselves as being 'in love'. Generally, a gift of a new mobile phone would follow and then the men would use these phones to contact and control the girls at all hours of the day and night.

After some time, the girls would then be asked to provide sexual favours to one or more of her 'boyfriend's' mates and over time this would feel quite normal to her. Eventually, she and other girls would be invited to a party, either in a flat somewhere or in a cheap hotel room, where they would be plied with alcohol and made to have sex with multiple men. It would not be unusual for many adult men, who the girls had never even met, to turn up at these parties and queue up to have sex with them. The girls would be so drunk that they had no ability to give true consent and the older men outnumbered them so they were too scared to say no.

We had discovered that we were dealing with very serious sexual offences being committed against some of the most vulnerable children in society. However, the biggest challenge we faced was that the girls didn't see themselves as victims at all and they were generally very distrustful of the authorities. They were the product of chaotic, dysfunctional homes and many had been physically or sexually abused for much of their lives. They craved positive affirmation and they had never had positive male role models at any point in time, so this behaviour had simply become a 'new normal'. The men had groomed them so thoroughly and successfully that they felt complete loyalty to them. We knew that it was going to be fantastically difficult to build a successful prosecution against our suspects in the absence of a formal complaint and if the girls refused to submit themselves to physical examinations for forensic evidence. We also knew that it would be easy for defence barristers to tie the victims up in knots and portray them as being promiscuous, willing participants in these activities.

We had a pretty good idea who the victims were, even if they had not all come forward. The victim profile was quite clear: female, resident at a children's home, mid-teens, regularly going missing and staying missing for long periods of time. What wasn't so clear was the identity of the perpetrators or where the girls were being taken to. The perpetrators were almost exclusively Asian men in their twenties or thirties but they had been careful never to use their actual names with the girls. They were known by street nicknames that didn't mean anything to us and returned nothing when searched against police intelligence systems.

My team started to brief the response teams and neighbour-hood teams and encourage them to submit intelligence on who these girls were associating with. We made it clear that if the girls were seen out and about with men matching this description, we needed as much information and intelligence about them as possible. Many of the front-line officers were sceptical – some of them knew the girls and described them as being foul-mouthed and gobby from previous encounters they had had with them. They struggled to see them as victims, but we tried to explain that these girls had been groomed and brainwashed and that they needed our help.

We made very slow progress, and the number of missing episodes across care homes started increasing as more girls were clearly being drawn into this activity. The care homes themselves were hopeless about protecting the girls and this helped make the situation worse. They did very little to try to stop the girls from leaving and made no attempt to find out who they were leaving with. We tried to persuade them that in the eyes of the law they had parental responsibility for these girls and, on that basis, they needed to show more interest in what was going on and if necessary physically prevent the girls from leaving. They made the rather spurious argument that to do this would consti-tute 'an assault' on the girls and, on that basis, they were unwill-ing to put themselves in that situation. It was very frustrating, and we told them that most of the girls were going to be raped, pick up sexually transmitted infections and goodness knows what else, but our pleas fell on deaf ears.

Eventually, however, in November 2009, we got our first real opportunity to mount a credible criminal investigation. Two girls from a children's home in Telford had been kept captive in a flat and a hotel in Birmingham over a weekend and both were subjected to a horrific ordeal at the hands of many different men. My team got involved in the initial investigation and we contacted our counterparts in West Mercia Police to inform them of what we were dealing with. As luck would have it, they were already involved with the girls in Telford and one particular female detective had established a good relationship with them.

She agreed to travel to Birmingham and help us interview the girls and she persuaded them to submit to a forensic medical examination. Everything went to plan and both girls cooperated with us because of the trust that had already been built up with the officer. The girls were video interviewed and they provided us with a very detailed and disturbing account of what had taken place. Gradually, a case was built against a number of local men who were already known to police for other serious criminal matters.

It took over two years for this case to come to court but, in April 2012, Shamrez Rashid was jailed for eleven years for child abduction, two rapes, attempted rape and attempted sexual assault.

Amar Hussain was sentenced to ten years after he was found guilty of child abduction, three rapes and attempted sexual assault. Jahbar Rafiq was found guilty of rape and sexual assault and was jailed for eight years. Adil Saleem was found guilty of rape and sentenced to eight years. And Amer Islam Choudhrey was convicted of child abduction and sexual assault and received a jail term of fifteen months.

Those two girls deserve great credit for their bravery in giving evidence. They should feel very proud of themselves and I sincerely hope that they have been able to move on with their lives to some extent.

This, I believe, was one of the earliest successful multi-defendant investigations into what came to be known as child sexual exploitation (CSE) in the UK. It was followed by a great many high-profile criminal trials across the country in Derby (Operation Retriever), Telford (Operation Chalice), Oxford (Operation Bullfinch) and Rochdale (Operation Span). Thanks to courageous and dogged investigations by *Times* journalist Andrew Norfolk in 2011, the scandal of widespread child sexual grooming of vulnerable girls was exposed in the press. For the first time, he shone a spotlight on this most despicable of crimes. He rightly shamed police forces and local authorities into facing up to the uncomfortable truth that fears of accusations of racism had created a collective paralysis that had condemned hundreds of our most vulnerable children to systematic sexual abuse and psychological trauma.

Many people have asked me over the years why I think it was specifically Asian men who had been responsible for this sexual exploitation. Quite frankly, I have no idea why this is the case. I will leave that question to the psychologists and sociologists to answer because I could only guess. What I do know is that it has been an incendiary issue and a culture of political correctness across the public sector allowed such exploitation to flourish and go unchallenged for so long. The police service was also culpable in this regard. During this period, many senior officers were too focused on burnishing their politically correct credentials, whilst eyeing up their next promotion. I have always tried to do what I believe to be the right thing in the eyes of the law, regardless of the race, ethnicity, colour or religion of the people who are involved. Ultimately, in such cases I will refuse to tiptoe around an issue for fear of upsetting someone.

At the start of 2010, I was starting to get itchy feet. As you've probably guessed by now, I have quite a low threshold when it comes to boredom. Whilst some people are happy to spend up to ten years in one particular role, I start to feel the need for a change after two to three years. One of the great joys of policing is that it's an incredibly diverse organisation, and the big forces like the Met and West Midlands have a variety of opportunities for enthusiastic people. My advice to anyone who wants a long career in policing is to spend enough time in each role to become competent and gain credibility, but keep moving and keep challenging yourself.

I was asked by an ex-colleague if I would consider transferring to the West Midlands counter-terrorism unit. This was a difficult decision for me because I had enjoyed the PPU, but the pull of a return to counter-terrorism, where I had spent so many years in London, was strong. Ultimately, I agreed, and within a few weeks I had said goodbye to my lovely team, handed over the department to my replacement and said goodbye to Stechford.

CHAPTER 19

CTU

I was excited to be returning to counter-terrorism. It had been eight years since I had left Special Branch in London and in that time I had done a lot of different things. But, in my heart of hearts, I felt that counter-terrorism was still my policing 'home' because it was where I had spent so many years and done so much.

However, I quickly realised that a lot had changed in those years, and the entire national counter-terrorism community had been put on steroids after the catastrophic attacks in London in 2005. The entire network had been given a massive cash injection over the previous five years and, rather than things being done on a relatively local level, a national network of counter-terrorism units (CTUs) and counter-terrorism intelligence units had been created. These units worked alongside MI5 and genuine joint working was now the name of the game.

My new workplace was a large, modern and rather swanky new facility in Birmingham. It was a world away from my previous experience of CT when we were working in rather low-tech, tired and dilapidated buildings in London. Someone had obviously been splashing the cash.

My new job was to be the manager of the counter-terrorism police operations rooms. This is where the live operations were conducted from, and my staff would manage and oversee the deployment of all of the covert resources on the ground in real-time. I'm not going to talk about what these resources were or what they did because of my ongoing obligations under the Official Secrets Act. There have been a lot of books and TV programmes created that in my view have disclosed far too much about this world and the only people this really helps are criminals and terrorists. All I will say is that in a live terrorism investigation there is a wide range of sensitive human and technical capabilities deployed to gather evidence and intelligence to progress investigative priorities. These activities then drive the overall strategy set by the senior investigating officer.

As well as swanky new accommodation housing many hundreds of staff, the technology had come on leaps and bounds in the years that I had been away from this world, and nowhere was more tech-focused than the department I was responsible for. It had more gleaming boxes of technological tricks than I had ever seen before, with humming server rooms and a room with walls full of screens dominated by one enormous screen about 15ft wide by 6ft high. The staff worked in pairs: one to listen to the surveillance commentary on the radio and to pass instructions to the team; and the other to carry out fast-time enquiries on people, places, vehicles and anything else that needed to be researched.

I had a team of about fifteen staff, who were a mixture of police officers and civilians, which included two sergeants. This was quite a small core team; however, we would bring in trained staff from other parts of the UK during busy periods and the team could swell to somewhere between twenty-five and thirty operators. I had a lot to get my head around, not least the technology and the new ways of working. I had been on a CT surveillance team before, so that element was very familiar to me. However, the kit that the teams had access to had evolved and the ability to send and receive images and video had really improved.

When we had conducted CT operations back in the 1990s, it was all straightforward and very low-tech. Someone would sit in the ops room in Scotland Yard wearing a headset and listen to the surveillance team out on the ground and they would use a big paper map book, sticky labels and a finger. They would write a summary of what was going on: where the subjects were going, who they met and what they did. This was all recorded longhand on carbon forms. One copy was ripped off and handed to a DS controller who would raise 'actions' from the narrative. These actions would be allocated to intelligence officers like me to go away and do some digging and find out what we thought was going on. So, for example, if the surveillance team were watching a subject who drove to a block of garages, opened one of the garages and disappeared inside out of sight, the action would be something like: 'Research ownership and current occupancy of all garages at the rear of flats in Acacia Avenue, Ilford, Essex with a focus on the third garage from the left, visited by subject X at 13.45hrs on 12/07/99.' I would then find out who owned or rented that garage and the garages adjacent. How long had they been using it? How was it being paid for? Can we obtain spare keys? Everything that a subject under surveillance did would be researched and, from this research, a picture would start to emerge as to what was going on, and then we would try to make sure that we were one step ahead of the conspiracy.

The way we had done this in the 1990s was very simple, but it was incredibly effective and we caught and convicted a lot of terrorists that way. So, my initial thoughts when I saw all these new gadgets and gizmos was, 'Have they over-complicated all this?' Whilst technology can be great, it also means that there are a lot more things to go wrong. In the end, however, I had no cause to worry because the teams were drilled to revert to old-school pen and paper in the event of technology failure.

I soon settled into life in the CTU, but I quickly realised that operationally it was going to be either 'famine or feast' and most of the time it felt tranquil compared with the frenetic pace of life back in the PPU. I also realised that I was now a tiny cog in the massive machine that was the national CT network. It felt like after 2005 the CT world, for very understandable reasons, had had buckets of cash lavished on it and hundreds of people allocated to huge teams. However, for quite a lot of the time, these people didn't really have enough to do, which didn't seem quite right when front-line policing was becoming so strapped for resources and where many people, mainly children, were starting to die as a result of gun and knife crime.

I worked with lots of great people and they were all very good at their jobs. Relationships with MI5 were generally excellent too, which was a marked change since my days in Special Branch when relations with them were strained. They had evidently recruited a lot more 'normal' people in recent years who just wanted to do the right thing and didn't have a massive superiority complex towards stupid old Plod. We all worked together very seamlessly and happily most of the time. Differences were resolved amicably and professionally, and we rubbed along together well.

The biggest difference between dealing with the IRA and dealing with Islamist extremists was that ultimately members of the IRA didn't want to die, and they generally didn't set out to indiscriminately murder as many people as possible. When I joined the CTU in 2010, the people that we were dealing with had no such scruples. They positively welcomed death, saw Westerners as evil and decadent and they wanted to kill as many people as possible. Men, women and children were all fair game.

This meant that terrorist conspiracies would now need to be interrupted at a much earlier stage. In the old days, we would let IRA active service units run, gathering more and more evidence as we went along, right up to the point when they were preparing to launch the attack and then we would scoop them up. Dealing with this lot was a whole different ball game. They could go very quickly from being radicalised to launching a deadly attack. This then created a difficult balancing act of judging when we had enough evidence to support a successful conviction at court, but not allowing the targets to progress their plot to the point where the public was put at risk. In a totalitarian state, they would have been arrested immediately and sent off to some awful internment camp. If we were in the United States, we would lure naïve half-wits into conspiracies using sting operations to incriminate them and send them to prison. Many of the terrorist cases that US authorities prosecute would never be permitted in the UK because of the rules of 'agent provocateur'. In other words, they entice people to commit an illegal act. If these people were left alone, many of them wouldn't have the ability or the wherewithal to mount a terrorist attack. Thankfully, this isn't the British way, and we played by the rules of the UK courts.

One of the most important responsibilities of our team was to help train lots of the staff who could be brought in to work in the operations room during a crisis that required a significant uplift in resources. A terrorist investigation tends to move very quickly. It can start small, but once the full extent and seriousness of what we are dealing with becomes obvious, the operation can grow rapidly, and the resources must grow too to manage multiple surveillance subjects in multiple locations. The job of my team was to manage the covert assets on the ground. We also had to learn how to work and communicate with teams from other organisations, including MI5, military special forces, police firearms teams and all sorts of other resources, depending on what was going on. The staff from these organisations also needed to be familiar with our operating protocols, so we hosted lots of different people in the ops room almost daily.

Senior officers also needed to be trained, and we held regular CT commander courses organised at a national level. These were incredibly realistic and lasted a week with several days devoted to live exercises involving the full range of covert resources out on the ground, following actors who played the part of the terrorists. It was all made as realistic as possible, and every course was mentally exhausting with multiple subjects being followed by multiple teams simultaneously. My job was to run the ops room and provide regular briefings to the senior officer in charge, who was normally an assistant chief constable. These courses became essential after the tragic shooting of Jean Charles de Menezes on 22 July 2005. During a counter-terrorism surveillance operation, de Menezes was mistaken for a suicide bomber and shot dead by firearms officers in Stockwell Tube Station in London.

The courses were designed to ensure that senior officers running high-tempo terrorist operations understood exactly what resources they had available to them, what those resources were capable of doing and the frequently ambiguous behaviour of live terrorists under surveillance. This meant that if they needed to authorise police firearms officers to kill terrorists before they killed members of the public, they would be able to justify that based on sound evidence and intelligence, which could also be used later in court if required.

These courses would often end in 'executive action' being taken, which involved police firearms teams working with military special forces. The scenarios would test the ability of police to hand over operational control to the military, who would take over and resolve the situation if deemed operationally necessary. However, this was never a given, and the CT commander would be kept guessing to simulate as closely as possible the often slightly chaotic behaviour of real terrorists.

We also used to help run regular large-scale multi-agency exercises designed to simulate 'Mumbai-style' mass-casualty attacks on soft civilian targets. These exercises became incredibly important after the Islamist Lashkar-e-Taiba attack on multiple targets in Mumbai in 2008, culminating in a bloody siege at the Taj Hotel. Over 170 people were killed in these attacks. Similar tactics were used in the attack on the Westgate shopping centre in 2013 in Nairobi, Kenya, by al-Shabaab extremists, killing seventy and wounding 175 people, and in Paris in the deadly attack on the Bataclan theatre in 2015, in which eighty-nine people were killed.

These large-scale exercises were incredibly realistic and would involve the full range of police and military resources and dozens of actors playing terrorists and hostages. They would usually culminate in a full-scale assault by special forces to release the hostages and neutralise the terrorists. Today, these critical incidents are just as likely to be resolved by highly trained and heavily armed police counter-terrorism specialist firearms officers (CTSFOs), who are trained in many of the offensive tactics and weaponry used by military special forces, such as the SAS. These teams were created for a couple of reasons. Firstly, there was a realisation that an attack of this nature was likely to happen very suddenly, requiring a rapid response. CTSFO teams can be scrambled in minutes, whereas special forces require a little more time to make their way from their standby locations. Secondly, traditional police firearms tactics tended to focus on containing the threat from a gunman and then moving to a negotiating position. Traditionally, an armed suspect would only be directly engaged if they posed an immediate threat to the officer or a member of the public. However, recent mass-casualty attacks demonstrated that these tactics had to change and become much more offensive so that officers could move towards a threat and neutralise them more quickly. Many of these tactics are now also taught to the crews of police armed response vehicles because they are likely to be first on scene in such incidents. The London Bridge attack in 2017 showed how effective this training can be as an armed response vehicle crew quickly neutralised all three terrorists within seconds of arriving.

During my time in the CTU, I was fortunate to be closely involved in some very successful Al-Qaeda operations that resulted in murderous attacks being prevented and lives undoubtedly saved. For example, Operation Guava was an investigation into a terrorist conspiracy involving nine men who planned to bomb targets in London and cause mass casualties. Operation Pitsford was an investigation into eleven men who also planned mass-casualty attacks. These operations were fantastically successful, but they were also intense and we all spent very long hours at work and rarely had a day off for many weeks.

After the Operation Pitsford arrests, I was asked to manage the detention of the eleven conspirators at a secure CT detention facility. I had never done this before so it was a bit nerve-wracking. I had to become very knowledgeable about counter-terrorism detention legislation very quickly because the detainees were represented by lawyers who had been defending the interests of terrorists for many, many years. These lawyers had also represented IRA terrorists throughout their long campaign so they knew their stuff and would quickly spot anything that they knew might help get their clients off at court.

When I actually met them, I thought that the detainees were a rather sorry-looking bunch. However, I was comparing them in my mind to the IRA, who were on a whole different playing field in terms of their operational competence. Having said that, these people were clearly incredibly dangerous maniacs who were determined to try to kill and maim as many innocent British civilians as possible. Prison was definitely the best place for them.

At the end of seven days' detention, charges were authorised by the Crown Prosecution Service and we took them down to the magistrates' court in London in an armed convoy that didn't stop from the moment it left the detention facility to the moment it pulled into the secure compound of the court. They were all quickly remanded in custody and put back into the armoured vans. We then took them across London, again escorted by the Met Special Escort Group, who are amazing at what they do, on a blue-light run all the way to Belmarsh prison, where they'd be kept on remand. I must say that I've done a lot of impressive blue-light runs in the police over the years, but this was definitely the best ever. It was fast and smooth as the Special Escort Group blocked every junction right across London to allow the convoy to pass through unimpeded. It was poetry in motion.

When we arrived at Belmarsh, the giant metal gates slid open to allow our convoy into the reception yard. HMP Belmarsh is a category-A prison, which means that it's one of several facilities around the UK that are designed to hold the most dangerous prisoners: usually a mixture of terrorists, armed robbers, gang members with a history of extreme violence and murderers. It is an unbelievably grim place and almost impossible to either get into or escape from.

We got them out of the van and they were ushered through several more sets of steel doors into the internal reception desk, which looked very similar to a police custody centre. The key difference was that this place was staffed by prison officers, who took this in their stride as they'd seen it all a hundred times before. By now, our prisoners were looking thoroughly gloomy as they stood waiting in their handcuffs, standard police-issue tracksuits and plimsolls.

Working on such big jobs was great, and I was lucky to be involved in a number of them, but I wasn't enjoying working on the CTU. I was starting to feel stifled and really fed up. I realised that it had probably been naïve of me to think that everything would be the same as it had been when I left Special Branch, but it was *completely* different. What had previously felt like a small, close-knit family where everyone was trusted, respected and treated as equals, regardless of rank, had changed into a much larger, more impersonal organisation where I didn't feel at home at all. There was also a bit of a toxic culture at that time where the long periods of inactivity between big operations meant that many senior managers defaulted to micromanaging and fault-finding. It was certainly the unhappiest inspector team that I had ever experienced. Many of us used to secretly meet for coffee and plan our escapes out of the unit like we were in a Second World War prisoner of war camp. I recently had a conversation with an ex-colleague, who I used to work with in those days, who got so fed up that he resigned from the police and moved into another industry after twenty-eight years' service, despite the fact he was only two years away from retirement. That says a lot to me and not in a good way.

God moves in mysterious ways sometimes, and just as I was thinking I needed to find a new job, after three years in the CTU, I received an email from a friend, who pointed out that the College of Policing was looking for a detective inspector to run a national project driving the new child sexual exploitation action plan. This job had my name all over it so, without further ado, I submitted my application and went down to London for an interview with Peter Davies, who was a deputy chief constable and the head of CEOP. To my absolute delight, I was successful.

CHAPTER 20

CSE PROJECT

———————————————

When I left the suffocating environment of the CTU and started my new job in London, I felt lighter and happier than I had done for a long time.

My experience dealing with child sexual exploitation in Stechford became incredibly important in my new role. In the three years that I had been in the CTU, several things had happened nationally. Firstly, Andrew Norfolk of *The Times* had continued to unearth shocking stories of sexual abuse that had been going on for many years in Rotherham and other northern towns. Secondly, there had been further high-profile investigations across the UK that had identified a very similar pattern of offending to what we had seen in Birmingham. There was a growing clamour by the government and the media to put a stop to this disgusting crime that was becoming an international embarrassment to Britain, as well as a personal and professional embarrassment to the people who should have been doing a lot more to stop it.

I hit it off with my new boss Peter Davies straight away. As the leader of the CEOP, he was hugely experienced in all things related to child exploitation. He had been charged with delivering a national action plan for UK policing to tackle CSE more effectively with a range of partners, including Barnardo's, The Children's Society, the NSPCC, the National Working Group for Sexually Exploited Children and Young People, the Department of Education, the NHS and others.

I was working directly with Peter, but I also reported to the College of Policing, who were paying my wages. I had never worked with the college before so this was all new to me, and I had to try to get my head around this rather byzantine organisation that seemed to embody some of the most confusing and dysfunctional aspects of both policing and academia. I had a lovely College of Policing manager, Jo, who helped me navigate her organisation and equipped me with everything I needed to do my job.

The challenge was a daunting one. I had to work with all forty-five police forces in the UK to embed the national action plan to significantly improve the policing response to CSE, and I had twelve months to do it. No pressure. It was not going to be easy because even though CSE was now regularly in the headlines, there were still significant barriers to overcome.

The single biggest barrier was the inconvenient reality that police funding had fallen off a cliff in 2010 when David Cameron became Prime Minister. When elected, Cameron had the police service well and truly in his cross-hairs, and he and his new Home Secretary, Theresa May, set about a brutal schedule of highly unpopular reforms and cost-cutting that decimated police numbers and eventually more or less dismantled neighbourhood policing in the UK. Cameron had been a special advisor in the Tory government way back in 1993 when Home Secretary Ken Clarke had tried to impose unpopular reforms on police pay and terms and conditions of employment via Sir Patrick Sheehy. These were rejected outright by policing, causing frustration in Tory ranks, so it was not necessarily a surprise that he had them in his sights when he became Prime Minister.

As a result of the budget cuts, every chief constable was running around desperately trying to find costs to cut and ways to balance their books. The wider police workforce nationally was also in something of a government-induced state of meltdown following the Winsor review of police pay and conditions. The Tories clearly didn't agree with the idea that people should spend their entire working life in the organisation. Suddenly, Theresa May and Tom Winsor had pulled the career rug from under the feet of police officers nationally, who now found that they would be working for longer and for less money than they had signed up for. This led to a growing exodus of some of the best talent and most experienced officers from the police to the private sector in the years following the review and morale hit rock-bottom for those who stayed. It was a further kick in the teeth for police officers when Tom Winsor was appointed Chief Inspector of Constabulary, which was rather like making Miss Trunchbull from *Matilda* head of Ofsted. Winsor not only became a hated figure in policing but also a figure of some ridicule when he turned up at the 2013 National Police Memorial Day ceremony in a uniform that looked like he had been let loose in a dressing-up box. Winsor has never been a police officer or a member of the armed forces, which made his ludicrous choice of uniform even more bizarre.

The service was therefore trying to find ways of reducing demand on its ever-diminishing resources, so people were probably not going to be too happy about someone like me rocking up and asking them to take on a load more work with CSE.

The other barrier was the fact that CSE is largely a hidden crime, and there was a perception amongst many senior officers in certain parts of the country that it was a 'northern problem' that they didn't need to worry about. Whilst it's true that CSE definitely manifested itself in some places more than others, the sexual exploitation of young, vulnerable girls and boys by older men took on many different forms and no force in the UK was immune.

I decided that the best way forward was to create a tool for all forces to assess themselves against the elements of the action plan. I would then travel to every force and spend some time with them, talk to key people and see if I could help in any way. So this is what I did, and within weeks I had set off on what turned into a road trip that lasted many months, travelling backwards and forwards across the whole of the UK. It was tiring but enjoyable, and I would frequently visit five or six different forces in a three-day period. Part of my job was also to identify those forces that were doing an excellent job and ensuring that I captured all that knowledge and experience so that we could share it with forces that were struggling.

As I travelled the country, it became clear that every force was really starting to feel the squeeze from government cuts. This was also at a time when more and more was being expected of each force, particularly on what came to be known as the 'vulnerability agenda'. This was basically a new and growing focus on the importance of all the issues that public protection units had traditionally dealt with. Domestic abuse, child abuse, mental health, CSE and now modern slavery had previously been seen as the narrow preserve of these units, but there was now an expectation from the government, Home Office and the police inspectorate that these issues should be the responsibility of *all* police officers and staff. Whilst this is a very noble aspiration, the government were simultaneously taking a chainsaw to police budgets at this time. In addition, they were conspicuously *not* saying, 'Oh, by the way, because we now want you to focus more on all these vulnerability issues, here is a list of all the things that you no longer need to do.' The expectations around all other policing activities didn't change, which put every force under growing and unreasonable levels of stress.

The thing I enjoyed most about my crazy road trip was seeing the incredible diversity of policing across the UK: from the big city forces like the Met, Greater Manchester and Merseyside, with many thousands of officers, to the little shire forces, with barely more than a thousand. I loved hearing all the different accents and meeting some real characters. I was made to feel very welcome everywhere I went. In the police, we might all speak differently and wear slightly different uniforms and cap badges, but there is definitely one big overarching policing family. Another thing that united everyone was a deep dislike of the policies of Theresa May.

It was around this time that May delivered her much-derided speech to the Police Federation annual conference, during which she poured scorn on the warnings that the body had given her about the severity of the cuts to police budgets:

Today, you've said that neighbourhood police officers are an 'endangered species'. I have to tell you that this kind of scaremongering does nobody any good – it doesn't serve you, it doesn't serve the officers you represent, and it doesn't serve the public … this crying wolf has to stop.

You can choose to work with me. Or you can choose to shout from the sidelines. What I offer is a positive vision for policing, one in which it is an exciting time to be a police officer, where you have the freedom to get on with your job, where you are rewarded for your skills and hard work, and where policing is fit for the future. What I have set out today will help transform policing for the better. If you want British policing to be the best it can be, join with me to make that happen.

How right they were, and how wrong she was.

Shortly before this, I had received my Police Long Service and Good Conduct Medal, which was given at twenty-two years' service. This was quite an emotional milestone for me because when I first joined in 1989, someone with twenty-two years' service seemed to me to be so old and I was often in awe of how experienced they were. I realised that I had come a long way from being that green, fresh-faced 23-year-old looking at myself in the mirror in Hendon all those years ago in my first uniform. I was given the choice of getting my medal in London by the Met or in the West Midlands, and I decided that it would be nice to go back to London and join my classmates, or at least those who hadn't died, been sacked or been sent to prison. I was pleased to find that none of them fell into any of those categories and it was fantastic to see so many people that I hadn't seen in such a long time. Some had aged better than others, but everyone had so many funny stories to tell. Some had gone on to very senior ranks in the police, moving from force to force on promotion, and others had stayed as uniformed constables at the same police station their entire career.

It was around this time that my home force, West Midlands, announced a selection process for promotion to chief inspector, and I decided to apply. After jumping through lots of hoops, sitting an assessment centre and then an interview, I was told that I had been successful. This was a big relief because I had gone for it twice before and been unsuccessful and had promised myself that if I were again unsuccessful I would give up any aspirations for further promotion. It's worth expanding on the promotion system a bit more because I think that this is another factor that has contributed to the demise of British policing.

Over thirty years, I was blessed beyond words to work for some really amazing and inspirational police managers. I also worked for some truly dreadful people with no emotional intelligence or humanity who had been promoted way above their competence by cynically 'playing the game'.

There are so many brilliant, capable managers and leaders in the police service who are also brilliant police officers, but the promotion system prevented them from being appointed to the most senior roles. This is because the selection criteria – usually dreamt up by the College of Policing – doesn't value or acknowledge operational experience, which gives an advantage to the corporate types and the bullshitters. This is most frequently seen at the promotion process for chief inspector; many brilliant officers get 'stuck' at the rank of inspector.

There is general agreement in policing that promotion processes are chaotic, inconsistent, fickle and, generally, have almost nothing to do with whether anyone is any good at doing the job. They are also completely different according to where you are in the UK. The process takes minimal account of what a candidate has done in their career and favours those who are good at self-promotion and parroting buzzwords. The 'evidence' of suitability that many candidates put forward is at best greatly embellished and at worst completely fabricated, but no one ever gets challenged or called out for fibbing.

I have seen so many different versions of the promotion process at four different ranks, and the one common denominator was that they were all hopeless. It seemed as if the organisation couldn't manage to devise a process that had the confidence of the people who put themselves forward for promotion. It also spawned some truly terrible leaders, who turned passing promotion processes into an art form by dedicating themselves almost exclusively to understanding the rules of the game. They would then network enthusiastically and shamelessly suck up to anyone who they thought might be able to give them an advantage. Certain individuals going for promotion would disappear for months beforehand to refine their application form and seek out 'mentoring' opportunities from senior officers who were also experts at playing the game. Lots of outstanding people with many years of operational experience, who would have been fantastic leaders, just gave up in complete frustration. They were too busy doing the job well by running teams and protecting the public to waste their time learning the ridiculous jargon that would light up the eyes of the new breed of senior officers and HR managers.

The process that I found most baffling was the chief inspector's selection, which, as mentioned above, I went through three times before I was eventually successful. These processes bore no relationship whatsoever to real-world policing, a candidate's operational competence or how they were perceived by their peers or staff. It really was simply a cynical exercise in learning the weird, ultra-politically correct rules of the game. The most bizarre part of the process was the lengthy application form, which was based on a range of competencies drawn from the College of Policing competency and values framework. Candidates would have to frame their evidence for promotion in terms of each of these competencies and *every single word* written on the application would be scrutinised and scored by a team of assessors, who had clearly had their brains removed and rinsed under a cold tap before they were allowed to participate in this dehumanising pantomime of a process. Candidates literally spent weeks upon weeks crafting and polishing these application forms, and anyone who naïvely thought that they could get through the process by 'being themselves' or by relying on their widely acknowledged professionalism and experience was doomed to instant failure.

So, how do I think policing promotion processes should be done? I think there is a fairly simple solution, which probably means there is zero chance it would ever actually be adopted in policing.

Firstly, there needs to be some element of staff, peer and manager feedback about a candidate. And not just from a current manager because, as I found throughout my career, that person might hate you and you probably hate them in return.

The feedback needs to come from a range of different managers who know and have worked with the applicant. Equally, if the applicant is already a manager, their own staff and peers will have a view of whether they are any good or not. The reality is that everyone on a team knows who the good people are and who would be good in the next rank. They also know who the bullshitters are, or the people who would make them want to instantly throw themselves under a bus if they found out that they were going to be their next manager. If the applicant gets a thumbs up here then they proceed to the next stage.

For certain ranks, e.g. sergeant and inspector, there is a requirement to learn a great deal of legislation. There are no shortcuts in this regard; you either know it or you don't. If you don't know the legislation, you are a liability to yourself, your staff, to the public and the organisation. Therefore, applicants should sit a knowledge-based exam that tests their understanding of the necessary legislation. This is what currently happens; however, the questions are frequently ambiguous and designed to trip people up, which means that you can know the legislation inside out and still get the questions wrong. So, exam people, don't be dicks. Design the questions to be crystal clear, and if you must use multiple choice answers, make the answers sufficiently different to give candidates a sporting chance.

The final stage in the process should replicate how the actual job works in the real world and assess the applicant's abilities in that situation. However, it needs to be as close to the *actual* job in the *actual* world, not some horrible, dystopian, imaginary world in which you can get nothing right. So, give applicants a load of documents to read and absorb quickly, and then ask them to decide how and why they are going to prioritise their tasks. Using meaningless corporate buzzwords should lead to an instant fail because that nonsense is of no utility or relevance whatsoever at a firearms incident or after an industrial accident where some poor bloke has had his arm ripped off by a piece of machinery.

I would completely skip the entire interview stage because this is the ficklest part of the promotion process in policing. It encourages nepotism and suck-upism. Interviews also allow senior officers to completely ignore everything that has happened in the process up to that point and fail someone because they don't like their accent, haircut, shoes or breath or because that particular member of the panel is just having a bad day.

Back on the project, things had been going really well. Everything that I had set out to do had been accomplished, and I felt reasonably confident that the policing community nationally would now be in a better place to tackle CSE. After my year on the CSE project, I was given a chief constable's commendation by Simon Bailey, the national lead for child abuse investigation and protection. I asked to stay on and do another twelve months in the role, but my force told me that they wanted me back. So, with a heavy heart but lots of happy memories, I returned to Birmingham to take up my first chief inspector job.

CHAPTER 21

CHIEF INSPECTOR

Coming back to the West Midlands as a newly promoted chief inspector in June 2014 was quite a nerve-racking experience. I had been away from the mainstream force for four years, and lots of things had changed. Like every other force in the country, it was in the midst of trying to cut costs and many difficult decisions were going to have to be made. PCSO redundancies, the closure and sale of police stations and other real estate and a wholesale transformation of the organisation were on the cards. It wasn't a comfortable or happy time to be in policing.

The rank of chief inspector is a big jump from inspector. It's the lowest rung on the senior management ladder so chief inspectors are generally at the beck and call of everyone above them in the hierarchy as well as having a large number of people to manage and motivate. It's also a stepping stone to the rank of superintendent, which is quite a big pay jump. However, chief inspectors get paid more or less the same as inspectors, which is a bit of a nonsense considering how much more responsibility they have.

I found out that my specific posting was to be a detective chief inspector in the intelligence department, colloquially referred to as 'DCI Intel'. This came as something of a surprise to me because I had never been in an intelligence department before and I had no idea whatsoever what I was supposed to be doing.

They sent me on a week-long 'strategic intelligence managers' course' with the College of Policing and, as with many courses in policing, it bore almost no relevance or resemblance to the job that I ended up doing. It was a generic course to be delivered to managers from lots of different forces across the UK. As every force is entirely different they all do things differently, thus making the course a bit pointless.

I landed back at HQ and met the rest of the management team in the intelligence department, who were more or less a good bunch. I was told that I would be running the homicide intelligence team and the local intelligence teams on the eastern side of the force, so it was going to be a bit of a mixed bag.

So, what does an intelligence officer actually do? Well, according to the College of Policing,

The intelligence officer develops and evaluates intelligence, making an assessment of the threat, risk, harm, vulnerabilities and opportunities which exist and identifying gaps. They manage the dissemination of the assessment or intelligence product, support reactive, proactive operations and/or crimes in action and provide advice on appropriate tactical options to support policing priorities.

That is a bit of a mouthful so I tend to describe it as 'gathering, assessing and sharing information that helps people make better decisions about what to do'.

The homicide intelligence team, unsurprisingly, supported murder investigations from the moment the organisation responded to a new murder, all the way through to (hopefully) a conviction of a defendant at court. After a murder was committed, the team would immediately start to pull together an intelligence document that would answer many questions common to every murder. For example: What has happened as far as we know? Who is the victim? What do we know about them? Where did it happen, and what do we know about these locations? Were there any witnesses, and what are they saying? Is there any obvious suspect and what do we know about them? Why do we think this murder happened?

As the investigation progresses, the intelligence requirement changes according to the needs of the senior investigating officer, and the intelligence team would serve the needs of that officer. So, for example, if the investigation identified some potential suspects, we might acquire data relating to their current mobile phones. The intelligence officers and analysts would use clever software to see if there had been any contact with the victim or other suspects. They would try to find out when that contact took place, and where they were before, during and after the time of the murder. They might overlay this phone-usage data with the movement of vehicles that were known or suspected as being used by the perpetrators at that time.

The intelligence team would build up an excellent understanding of what had happened, and when, where and who was involved. This would become an evidential product that could be used to justify the arrest and charge of suspects, and when added to other evidence, such as fingerprints, DNA, CCTV and eyewitness testimony, all these pieces of the jigsaw would form the basis of the prosecution case at court.

It was a super-interesting job, and the people who do it are very good at it. My team were incredibly busy because the West Midlands had one of the highest murder rates in the UK, and they were usually juggling a great many cases simultaneously at various stages of investigation. Many of these murders were linked to drugs and organised crime in some way, and there were often overlaps between several different murder investigations over a longer period of time, so it could get very complicated and confusing very quickly.

The other bit of my job was quite different and involved running two local intelligence teams on the eastern side of the force. These teams were based on a particular police command unit, and they provided the intelligence support for all day-to-day policing activities. They would support the daily and monthly tasking and coordinating processes chaired by the local superintendent, and they would prepare briefing documents on a wide range of local issues. Many of the intelligence officers had been on these command units for a long time, so they knew the area and the local villains very well. A big part of my job was to work closely with my senior counterparts in these places to make sure that they had what they needed and that everyone was happy. Often, it was as much about managing their unrealistic expectations because they had asked for something unnecessary or something that should be done by someone else.

I soon realised that the intelligence department got involved in literally everything going on in the force; from some of the most trivial issues to the most serious and everything in between. It was a good place for someone like me who had done a lot of different jobs over the years, and there was very little that I hadn't dealt with at some point. However, as front-line resources became more and more squeezed, the force began to become more stressed and every department started to feel the pinch.

I described earlier how the entirety of the police intelligence function was conducted by the old-style collators with their thousands of little cards when I first joined.

Over the following years, and right up to when I retired in 2019, I never saw any intelligence system or team that was even remotely as effective as a good collator's office, despite (or maybe because of) all the new computerised intelligence systems. So, why was this the case?

I think the main reason for this subsequent lack of efficiency was that the intelligence process back then was really, really simple. There was none of the fancy jargon that later came to dominate the intelligence world. For me, it all started to go a bit wrong with the National Intelligence Model (NIM). NIM was brought into policing nationally in 1999 and it sought to professionalise what until that time had been a rather vague 'make it up as you go along' approach to police intelligence. This was great in theory, but the problem with NIM was that it over-complicated everything and confused many people. Rather than a couple of super-knowledgeable, crusty old cops who'd been on the job for decades, you now had an office full of people who lacked that knowledge and experience and whose job was largely to administer a computer system and maintain Excel spreadsheets. The process for submitting intelligence became time-consuming and bureaucratic, and the net result was that officers just didn't bother. They found that when they did bother, they would invariably have things sent back to them because they hadn't filled in a particular field on the computer system, or they'd got someone's date of birth wrong.

Policing language soon became filled with all sorts of weird and wonderful terminology relating to NIM that no one understood or really cared about. Terms like 'strategic assessments' and 'problem profiles', 'subject profiles' and 'market profiles' were used everywhere. Like any new discipline, the system attracted more than its fair share of evangelical zealots, who insisted that everyone stick slavishly to NIM doctrine. Very quickly, local intelligence teams became the unloved members of the police family. Most operational officers and detectives accused them of 'eating like an elephant and shitting like a mouse'. In other words, they demanded a hell of a lot from everyone and didn't give much back.

By the time I took charge of the local intelligence teams in the West Midlands, common sense had returned to some extent. We produced only one type of document for decision-makers: an 'intelligence assessment'. This could be an assessment of anything, depending on what the requirement was. It might be a local gang issue, a spike in burglaries, a shooting or a problem nightclub. It was written in a standard way, regardless of what the subject was, and the document was created in such a way that it could be given to someone who knew nothing whatsoever about that issue, and very quickly they would have all the information that they needed to plan the next course of action.

However, the damage had already been done to the police intelligence world. Ultimately, all operational cops want to know the following information: 'Is the person standing in front of me, or driving the car that I've stopped, believed to be involved in crime or a potential risk to me? If they are, what sort of crime or violence have they committed? Who do they hang about with? And where do they currently live if I need to get hold of them again?' It's really not complicated, but in my opinion NIM over-complicated everything.

One very good thing that did come out of NIM, however, was the monthly tactical tasking and coordinating group process where the local superintendent would meet with key sergeants and inspectors to set priorities for the coming month and review progress against the previous month's priorities. This was always a very business-like meeting, usually lasting a couple of hours, which would look at key issues and identify the most prolific offenders to be vigorously targeted by patrolling officers and proactive crime teams over the following days and weeks. A vast amount of crime is driven by drug addiction and committed by a relatively small number of people. These 'prolific and priority offenders' became the focus of a great deal of policing activity. The aim was to either divert them into substance-abuse treatment or arrest them and have them remanded in custody and convicted. We were under no illusion that putting someone in prison was going to change them, but when a criminal is in prison, at least they're not creating new victims.

Anyway, what I mean to say is that I missed those wads of little collator index cards.

Following an internal reorganisation, our department lost

several posts at all ranks, and I found myself being responsible for all ten geographical intelligence teams across the force. I had four teams in Birmingham alongside units in Coventry, Solihull, Wolverhampton, Walsall, Sandwell and Dudley, which meant that I was responsible for ten inspectors, twenty sergeants and about 120 intelligence officers and analysts. In hindsight, this period in my career is a bit of a blur, and I spent a lot of time shuttling all over the force sorting out problems and working with ten different local senior management teams. Still, it was exciting, and I got to know a lot of people across the entire police force.

My life was incredibly busy at this time. Happily, I had remarried, and my wife Kay and I had two babies in quick succession. Well, more accurately, she had them and I watched her have them. I was therefore juggling ten geographically dispersed teams before coming home to two children under three years old who were still in nappies. My teenage son was doing his GCSEs and I was also driving up and down to Sheffield helping my daughter with university life.

Then, one day, I realised that I had less than five years to go until I reached thirty years' service and was entitled to retire. Whilst five years is still quite a long time, everyone I knew who had been in this situation had told me that it would go quickly. So, I started to give some thought to life after the police, and I decided that I needed to pick up some new skills that would help me make that transition. I'd always been interested in technology, and my time in the CTU had exposed me to a lot of innovative technology that the cash-rich CT community had had access to. However, mainstream policing had been badly neglected and left behind. One of our chief officers had a national responsibility for internet investigations and another had responsibility for cyber-crime, so I offered to do all their work for them. Gradually, I became very knowledgeable about using technology to investigate crime. I did a lot of work building up a strong network of people like me in other forces around the country.

This is an issue for policing that's worth spending some time talking about because I think it's one of the reasons the crime detection rate is so abysmally low. When I joined the police, and for the first twenty years, crime investigation didn't change that much. We established what had happened, how it had happened and to whom it had happened and then tried to find out who we thought was responsible. We took witness statements and examined the scene of crime for forensic material that may have been left behind. For a long time, the only vaguely technical evidence we may have been interested in was CCTV footage or maybe call records from landlines or mobile phones. We would gather intelligence, identify a suspect and arrest them. We would search their home, business or car for evidence linked to the crime and take fingerprints or saliva to compare with marks or bodily fluids found at the scene or on the victim. It was a very predictable, standard process that we followed for pretty much every crime – the only difference being the degree of thoroughness, depending on the seriousness of the investigation. For example, if your car got broken into, we would swab it for DNA and recover samples of broken glass to compare with shards recovered from a suspect's clothing, and that would be it. However, for a murder, we would spend a full week exhaustively examining every aspect of the crime scene in minute detail and taking hundreds of forensic samples from dozens of places.

Gradually, over time, technology in common usage began to accelerate in scale, speed and complexity. Mobile phones morphed into smartphones holding vast amounts of data with complex security denying easy access. Home computers that previously had the disk memory of a few hundred megabytes of data quickly began to hold many gigabytes and now routinely store several terabytes. The types of data, apps and documents contained on PCs, laptops, tablet computers and smartphones exploded in terms of variety and complexity. In addition, today, very little data is stored on a physical device. It is more likely to be stored somewhere in a cloud computing data centre based in the United States or Ireland. The internet created an almost infinite number of opportunities for committing crime whilst sat in the comfort of your own home without ever seeing your victim. Social media platforms, gaming platforms and dating sites became the hunting grounds of choice for rapists and child molesters, whilst eBay and Gumtree made selling stolen goods or committing fraud child's play. Data privacy issues drove the adoption of end-to-end encryption, and criminals and terrorists quickly embraced these technologies, which made it much harder for law enforcement to understand and infiltrate criminal conspiracies. Technology is now a key facilitator for almost every type of crime. The days of having to feed your drug habit by breaking into someone's home and stealing their telly are becoming a distant memory. Drug dealers use encrypted apps to run their business, and use young kids to deliver drugs to punters with very little chance of being caught.

Knowing where to find evidence is challenging enough, but extracting it from a device, analysing it to make sense if it and presenting it in a way that tells a story to a lawyer or a jury is an entirely different matter. Each of these stages now requires fairly specialist knowledge, software and hardware – all of which were and still are in short supply in the policing world.

Complex crime, murders and terrorist investigations now hoover up a staggering volume and variety of digital evidence from hundreds of devices and sources, and the number of those sources and amount of data is growing almost every month. That's the bad news. The good news is that it's nearly impossible to commit a serious crime without leaving some sort of electronic trail that skilled and dogged investigators can follow. It has become a rapidly evolving arms race as the police try to keep pace with new tech. For example, the explosion of household devices which are now connected to the internet (known as the Internet of Things) can tell a story to an investigation. Investigators now routinely build up an evidential case from GPS watches, satnavs, Wi-Fi routers, dashcams, fancy doorbells and even fridges. Remote-controlled home-heating systems can even be interrogated for information that may be useful.

Sadly, the police service in the UK has failed to properly keep up with the technology that is necessary to investigate crime and has relied for too long on a small number of in-house experts, who quickly find themselves overwhelmed and can usually only support the most serious investigations. Many of these experts then get lured away from policing by banks or private companies offering much better pay. Fundamentally, the service hasn't made enough progress in helping the average front-line officer investigate digital crime in the past ten years – another unhappy outcome of cuts to police budgets.

In fairness, however, the service itself and the Home Office have been very wasteful. Vast amounts of money have been squandered on national digital programmes that have delivered very little. The 43-force structure in England and Wales has also made things even messier as everyone is doing things different-ly and buying systems that don't work with existing systems or with neighbouring forces. This has created a horribly tangled ball of technological wires that will take years to unravel. Flag-ship programmes designed to create a new national intelligence database for policing and a new emergency services communi-cations network are now years overdue and many millions of pounds over budget, and there are still very few signs that they will be successfully delivered anytime soon.

In 2018, the Home Affairs Select Committee released a report entitled 'Policing for the future'. In compiling the report, the committee took evidence from a wide range of witnesses, in-cluding the commissioner of the Metropolitan Police, Cressida Dick, who told them that the service could not 'go on dealing with rising demand and greater complexity for ever without having to make some hard choices. You make choices either about reducing the scope of the mission or taking more risk about what you do.' Nearly three years on, the mission (i.e. to try to do anything and everything) remains the same, whilst demand and complexity has continued to grow.

The report went on to state:

Police forces' investment in and adoption of new technology is, quite frankly, a complete and utter mess ... Forces are facing rapidly-evolving threats from criminals who exploit new technology in advanced and innovative ways, yet their own technological solutions are not always up to the task. There are enormous opportunities for policing, including greater use of artificial intelligence and the exploitation of data, but the service is often failing to take advantage of them.

We believe that the biggest failing in this area is not the level of funding, but rather the complete lack of coordination and leadership on upgrading technology over very many years. This is badly letting down police officers, who are struggling to do their jobs effectively with out-of-date technology. It is astonishing that, in 2018, police forces are still struggling to get crucial real-time information from each other, and that officers are facing frustration and delays on a daily basis.

Almost nothing has changed since 2018 and, arguably, the situation is a lot worse because of the need for the police to operate in a more complex environment.

Whilst the technology to investigate digitally enabled crime is still poor, some new kit has made life a bit better for police officers. Nationally, there has been the widespread adoption of body-worn video for front-line officers, and this had made a big difference in terms of protecting officers from false claims of assault or misconduct. In fact, a study by Cambridge University in 2016 found that complaints against officers had fallen by 93 per cent since the adoption of body-worn video, which says a lot about the merit of many of the complaints made against officers previously. In the past, it was always the word of people being arrested against the word of officers, which made it difficult to prove or disprove either version of events.

However, there have been increasing calls by rank-and-file officers for police video footage to be released to the media in order to refute biased and selectively edited footage from mobile phones claiming to show the police acting oppressively. There have been a number of high-profile instances recently where such footage has made its way onto national TV and the officers concerned have been unable to respond or show the full context of the incident. This is deeply demoralising for front-line police officers, who now worry that getting into a confrontational situation in a public place will result in them being splashed all over social media and the TV – with all the vile intimidation, trolling and risk that this creates for officers and their families. It's unacceptable and unreasonable to expect people to go to work to do a difficult job only to find themselves in that situation. People wouldn't be allowed to start filming nurses and doctors trying to do their job, or social workers trying to engage with a family in crisis, so why is it acceptable for police officers to have to put up with it?

Try to imagine for a moment how it would feel if when you went to work *everything* you did was video recorded, everything you said in a car was recorded and every time you got into a difficult situation or conversation someone got out their mobile phone and started filming you?

It should be a civil or criminal offence to film a police officer in such a situation and then publicly display the footage anywhere other than in the context of making a formal complaint or inside a civil or criminal court. This would ensure that police officers can be held accountable, but at the same time their privacy and human rights are respected.

Another significant development in 2018 was the introduction of mobile devices that could access most of the police systems used by operational officers. Typically, this includes command and control logs, which officers can now update immediately rather than having to wait and pass details across the radio, which would then have to be typed up by a control room operator. Officers can access all of the criminal intelligence that they need if they're going to arrest someone at an address or if they stop someone in a car who's refusing to cooperate. The handheld devices in the West Midlands were pretty good, and they included software that alerted officers to high-risk issues, wanted people or gang activity if their device had detected, via GPS, that the officer had moved into a particular location.

The introduction of Skype video conferencing in 2016 also made a big difference to the working lives of the police. It massively reduced the amount of time spent travelling to meetings and it enabled us to discuss critical incidents by pulling together the key people into a call very quickly. Prior to that, everyone would have been dragged away from their jobs and made to travel up to HQ from all over the force to have face-to-face strategic meetings with assistant chief constables. As a mission support superintendent, I chaired the daily force tasking meeting via Skype. Senior managers would join that meeting from every department and geographic command unit in the force.

Meanwhile, West Midlands Police was still on a 5/2 diet thanks to ever-deeper cuts to police budgets. At this time, Theresa May, by some horrible twist of fate, and just when police officers thought it couldn't get any worse, became our new Prime Minister. Barely a week went by without news arriving about the latest 'efficiency saving' that would mean the loss of jobs, more police stations closed and the British public put at an increased risk of violence and criminality. Ultimately, trying to police Britain during the years of austerity had become very bleak indeed.

CHAPTER 22

OPERATIONAL
SUPERINTENDENT

The chief constable set a date for another massive reorganisation that would fundamentally change the way that policing was delivered for the West Midlands. He did a good job of selling it as a positive development. Still, no one was under any illusion that it was anything other than another money-saving exercise devised to urgently reduce costs in response to government cuts to police budgets. By this stage, I had been DCI Intel for about two years and I had therefore been exposed to most of what life across every part of the West Midlands could throw at me.

In January 2017, as part of the force reorganisation, all my intelligence teams were disbanded and two new, much larger, teams were created: one at HQ in Birmingham city centre and the other in Bournville in the suburbs. I was given the job of managing the teams at Bournville, and these teams would focus on what was happening across the force 24/7, providing intelligence support to front-line officers and investigators. We would support the response to critical incidents, high-risk missing people, firearms incidents and all sorts of other live issues. The people providing the 'slower burn' intelligence support and the analysts would be based at HQ.

I did this for about a year and enjoyed it most of the time. It was hectic and there was always something interesting or serious going on somewhere across the force. I became the force lead for 'threats to life' because of the sheer number of these that we were dealing with on our team. Before the reorganisation, these had been dealt with across all ten police command units, spreading the load, but now they all came to my teams and it was part of my job to assess them and decide if we had done enough to reduce the threat. In police jargon, a 'threat to life' is recorded and managed when the police become aware via intelligence that person 'A' intends to cause serious harm to or kill person 'B'. Frequently, the threat can be against multiple individuals. The police deal with a lot of these, particularly the big urban forces like West Midlands, the Met and Greater Manchester. It was not unusual to have three or four new threats coming in every day in my old force. Almost all of these cases involved fallouts between or within serious and organised crime gangs and typically resulted from unpaid drug debts, theft of drugs or suspicions that someone was a police informer. Often, they could be about a trivial 'disrespect' issue: revenge for a previous attack on a gang member by a rival gang or a gang member finding out that his girlfriend was sleeping with another gang member when he was in prison. The one thing that they all had in common was that none of the people involved were nice people, so they were taken seriously.

You might think, 'Who cares if two drug dealers want to kill each other? Let them get on with it.' Well, apart from the small matter of the right to life under Article 2 of the Human Rights Act, there is also the genuine risk that some poor innocent person will get shot in the crossfire in the process. Remember, drug dealers and criminals are usually not the sharpest knives in the box, so there is always the risk that they will fire a shotgun or spray an Uzi through the wrong person's front window just as they were settling down to watch *Coronation Street*. There is also a significant financial burden that comes with arresting criminals – a single murder costs the taxpayer about £2 million to investigate, prosecute and incarcerate the guilty party. Better all round to try to stop such crimes from happening in the first place.

The police do a lot of work behind the scenes to try to prevent people from getting murdered. I won't go into the sort of things that the force does, because a lot of it is sensitive, but these preventative actions often have to be done very quickly. When I was in the police, there was always the possibility of something going wrong and us getting blamed, which now seems to be the default response by the media when anything bad happens.

By this stage in early 2017, I only had about two years to go before I retired, and most days I would think that I was an absolute idiot because I was still managing a lot of risky stuff. I knew that any one of the threats to life that I was dealing with could go really badly pear-shaped through no fault of mine and then the much-distrusted Independent Office for Police Conduct (IOPC) would descend like a ton of bricks and find some poor bastard like me to hang out to dry. Fortunately, none of the cases did go pear-shaped, and that's definitely a testament to the professionalism of our staff and their thoroughness in managing high-risk issues.

At this time, the force ran a selection process for several temporary superintendent jobs. I applied and was successful. The new operating model included a small team of uniformed superintendents who took it in turns to have overall responsibility for the entire force, seven days a week. I was very fortunate to be asked to take on one of these roles. After being offered the position, I went off to get my uniform sorted out because it had been nearly ten years since I had been in uniform. When it arrived later that week, I put it on and stood looking at myself in the mirror with a superintendent crown on my shoulders. It was a very proud moment because I, like many people in the police, had had many disappointments and frustrations with various promotion processes. It was great to be finishing my career at the senior rank of superintendent.

The title of my new job was 'mission support superintendent'. Alongside the other new support superintendents, I was responsible for running the force during a particular shift. We would have to make decisions regarding where to put resources to manage the biggest risks and chair the daily force threat and risk management meetings that took place every morning at 9 a.m. and again at 3 p.m. We would look back over the previous twenty-four hours and then look ahead to allocate resources and make sure that serious incidents were being managed properly. Most days, there would be shootings, stabbings, high-risk missing people to track down or other serious incidents that would require an enhanced response. We also gave the legal authorisations for various things that needed the permission of a superintendent, such as urgently accessing telecoms data in life-threatening situations, and I was also trained to authorise covert surveillance deployments.

One of the tasks I was required to carry out was to authorise the detention of suspects beyond the normal limit of twenty-four hours. If an offence is serious and complex, and there are good reasons that the suspect needs to be kept in for longer to conduct the investigation effectively, a superintendent can extend their detention for a maximum of a further twelve hours. If we needed more time than this we would have to apply for that in a magistrates' court, but those cases were quite rare. I would therefore travel to one of a number of cell blocks around the force to speak to the investigators for a specific case, consult with the suspect's solicitor and speak to the detainee to explain their rights. This brings me to another reason that I think arrest and prosecution rates have plummeted nationally.

Years ago, most police stations had their own cell block or 'custody suite'. Generally, the custody sergeants were drawn from that local station and they knew the officers well. If you arrested someone, it was a fairly simple matter of returning them to the nick, booking them in with the custody sergeant and handing them over to local investigators, who would also be based in the same building. It was a pretty straightforward process that ensured that the arresting officer could be back out on the street sniffing out more criminality and responding to urgent calls in less than an hour: ten minutes to get the prisoner to the station, twenty minutes to get them booked in and another thirty minutes to write up their statement of the arrest.

The years of austerity from 2010 changed all that. Lots of

police stations were sold off or closed and much bigger cell blocks were built to accommodate large numbers of detainees, but a force that previously had ten local cell blocks might now only have two or three at most. Arresting someone now requires the arresting officers to travel much longer distances, often in heavy traffic, and get in a queue before they can book them in. It is not unusual for officers to have to wait a couple of hours before they get to the front of the queue. Furthermore, the investigators are usually not based in the local stations and they too may have to drive some distance to deal with the suspect. It is now quite normal for a very simple arrest, that would previously have taken only an hour to deal with, to take a couple of officers off the street for an entire shift. So, unsurprisingly, lots of officers will now avoid arresting people unless it's absolutely unavoidable, and this leads to fewer cases being investigated and fewer people being charged and taken to court.

Another explanation for the reduction in charges and prosecutions is all about police numbers. This is not only about how many officers there are on duty, but also what you do with them. It's important to explain here how to increase the likelihood of catching someone who has committed a serious crime, which then leads to a successful investigation and prosecution. Much of the academic research into this question is crystal clear and my own experience points to the same conclusions. Solving a crime is all about responding quickly and arriving quickly, ideally when the suspect is still there or nearby. As well as having a fighting chance of catching someone, the police are also then in a position to swiftly identify witnesses who are still physically at the scene, secure vital physical and forensic evidence that would otherwise be lost or contaminated, find items discarded or dropped by the suspect and contain the area to stop them escaping. This will also allow a police dog to track the suspect or a helicopter to find them using thermal imaging. As well as all of those things, the police also need to attend the scene as soon as possible to give the victim a high standard of care and support because if this happens they are more likely to cooperate with an investigation – this is particularly important in instances of domestic violence or with sexual offences.

However, and here's the thing, the police can only do this properly if two conditions apply. Firstly, there needs to be enough officers available on duty to respond in sufficient numbers. Secondly, these valuable resources cannot be tied up dealing with trivial rubbish. In light of this assessment, it is very obvious why arrest, charge and conviction rates have been so woefully poor in recent years. The rapid response detailed above was the bread-and-butter approach to policing back in the 1990s. There were plenty of us on duty and we prioritised the most serious stuff, meaning that when someone dialled 999 and told us that they were being burgled or beaten up, we got there super-fast and we arrested people a lot of the time. That now happens quite rarely.

Solicitors and barristers often complain about how their court work is drying up and how the public are now being 'denied justice'. I totally agree that the public are being denied justice for all sorts of reasons, but ironically much of this tiresome bureaucracy was created in response to complaints by lawyers. For the past twenty years, in many of the cases that I have been involved in, lawyers have routinely portrayed the police as being corrupt in court to throw sand in the eyes of juries and create doubt in their minds. Lawyers still routinely advise 99 per cent of their clients to make 'no comment' in every police interview, even if they know that their clients are guilty of a serious crime. This has made many officers more reluctant to arrest people unless they know they have an absolutely cast-iron case, which is very rare. It is also one of the reasons that so many officers are reluctant to conduct stop and search because they know that this will be portrayed in court in a very negative way by defence barristers.

Lawyers have also complained about how little they earn from the criminal justice system since the big changes to legal aid provisions in 2013. These changes were made by Chris Grayling when he was Lord Chancellor and, in short, restricted the eligibility criteria for legal aid generally and meant that criminal lawyers would be paid fixed fees for each case – in 2011, it was reported that the UK was spending £39 per head of the population on legal aid compared with £8 in New Zealand and £5 in France and Germany. I feel quite sorry for the current generation of younger lawyers because they are now paying for the sins of a generation of lawyers before them who shamelessly pillaged the legal aid system for many years.

I can remember those years very well indeed and the frustration of seeing defence lawyers blatantly gaming the system to maximise their earnings. The standard tactic was for them to advise their clients to make 'no comment' to police when it definitely wasn't in their interest to do so. They would then advise them to plead not guilty even when the evidence overwhelmingly showed their guilt. Then, they would seek adjournment after adjournment at court to rack up their billing, and when they really couldn't string it out any longer they would advise their client to change their plea to guilty at the very last moment. It was a monumental piss-take and it resulted in huge legal aid bills, a waste of court time and stress for victims and witnesses. Crucially, it also took police officers off the streets as they would be forced to hang around courts for days waiting to give evidence, knowing that the case would probably be adjourned yet again. It was a bit like the MPs' expenses scandal in that things had become so blatant that something had to change.

When the rules changed, guess what? Many more lawyers started advising their clients to plead guilty early in the process so that they could get paid quickly. The lawyers have helped to create this situation, so they can't be too surprised that court cases have dried up and many police officers have somewhat lost their appetite for getting involved in confrontations on the streets that might lead to a contentious arrest and then a torrid time in the witness box.

Another big change that I saw over the last ten or fifteen years of my service was how what are known as 'constant watches' became a massive drain on police officers' time. 'Constant watches' are where a police officer has to physically sit and watch a detainee in a cell who has either stated that they are feeling suicidal or has a 'suicidal' marker on their profile on the Police National Computer. This means that at some stage in the past the detainee had expressed suicidal thinking whilst in custody or had tried to take their own life other than in a police station. The police deal with a lot of people like this, and the collapse of community mental health provisions in the UK has created a crisis in police custody centres, which often become the only places available to take someone in who is experiencing a severe mental health crisis.

The other type of constant watch is in a hospital where a member of the public is admitted either because they are a victim of serious crime or because they are suspected of committing a serious crime. For example, if someone has fallen off a roof whilst running away from a crime and broken their leg, the police would have to babysit them in hospital until they are released.

It would not be unusual for fifteen or twenty uniformed officers across a single force to be tied up for entire shifts doing constant watches at any one time. That's forty-five to sixty officers across a 24-hour period who are not dealing with the public or preventing crime. This is another example of the risk-averse culture that has consumed policing. Only a few years ago, we would have left both victims and offenders in hospital in the hands of medical staff, and we would have only sat there keeping watch for days and days if the suspect was extremely dangerous. I have a very good friend who loved being a police officer but she resigned after about five years because she was sick and tired of having to sit for entire shifts, bored out of her mind several times a week, with 'vulnerable' prisoners in the cell block.

If someone is that vulnerable the very last place that they should be is in a police cell. If the offence that they are in custody for is a minor offence they should be released immediately, sign-posted to their doctor or social services and dealt with in a different way. There are few crimes that a genuinely suicidal person can commit that are so serious that they justify keeping such a person in a police cell. The obvious flip side to this is that if the police did start releasing suicidal individuals for committing petty crimes, very quickly everyone coming into custody would soon claim to be suicidal, knowing that this will earn them a 'get out of jail free' card.

I really enjoyed working as a mission support superintendent, but it could be quite stressful. This was not necessarily because of the operational decisions. I was fine with that pressure; it was more about the stress of arbitrating between lots of senior people across the organisation who all felt that their need for resources was more urgent than anyone else's. Most of the people I was dealing with were very experienced superintendents, and none of them were shrinking violets. They were a hard-headed, feisty bunch, and you had to be on the ball. They only really cared about their particular problem, but I had to worry about everything going on across the force 24/7.

It was a massive eye-opener to see just how horribly stretched the force had become. When I had been a uniformed inspector back in Stechford eight or nine years before, we were able to patrol the streets and respond to most calls quite quickly. We were also able to provide a neighbourhood policing presence in every community seven days a week.

But now it was a very different story. Many things received little, or no, police attention and response teams were run ragged. Far too many officers were getting tied up with dealing with things that should have been nothing to do with the police, simply because other front-line services providing support to people with mental health, or drug- and alcohol-related problems, had also been cut. Victims of quite serious crime, who previously would have been seen within an hour or two, frequently had to wait a week or more to see a police officer. I knew things were bad, but it was shocking to see just how bad. It was hardly surprising that so many officers were experiencing mental health problems or thinking of leaving the force. Nonetheless, they were doing a heroic job and there were regularly stunning examples of great bravery and commitment. Still, I couldn't help but wonder how long this situation could last before something really bad happened. As well as working long hours in stressful conditions, officers were frequently having their shifts changed and rest days cancelled to plug gaps in resourcing, and I knew that this would be putting them under even more pressure at home with their families.

After 2010, there was another big change that was made to the police organisation. In addition to the loss of 20,000 police officers nationally, there was a loss of 23,500 members of police staff who carried out all sorts of essential back-office duties. This has had a terrible impact on the ability of the organisation to provide a good service to members of the public.

However, during this time, there seemed to me to be a corresponding increase in the number of senior civilian managers and project managers across many forces who were earning quite a lot of money. What then happened as an unwelcome by-product of all this was that lots of decisions that would ultimately go on to have a significant operational impact were being made by civilians who had no understanding of how they would play out in the real world. There was also a tendency to bring in lots of overpaid external consultants, who also had no experience whatsoever of policing, and these consultants were taking their advice from police officers who had been handpicked for their intellect rather than their operational experience. It would then be down to the cops on the beat to try to make things work. This often meant completely re-engineering systems and process-es on the fly that had been put in place and were totally unfit for purpose. This bred a lot of cynicism amongst rank-and-file police officers. On the one hand, resources were being slashed across front-line services. On the other, millions of pounds were simultaneously being lavished on clueless consultants and senior police civilian managers who added very little value to front-line policing.

When Boris Johnson replaced Theresa May as Prime Minister, one of his first major pledges was to replace the 20,000 officers that had been removed since 2010. This was very welcome news. However, in reality, this means that the service will actually have to recruit about 50,000 new officers to replace the 30,000 who will leave during that period due to the fact that there was a large influx of people (like me) that joined thirty years ago. In addition to this, research has shown that there needs to be roughly ten people to apply to be a police officer in order to get one success-ful recruit. Many applicants fail the vetting process, fail the med-ical, change their minds or simply aren't suitable. The net result of this is that the police service in England and Wales will need about half a million people to apply in order to get 50,000 police officers onto the streets. There is a huge challenge to recruit and train enough suitable people of good character, whilst ensuring that those people are supported and supervised effectively in the future. This also means that in three years' time, roughly one in three officers nationally will have less than three years' service and most of them will be on the front line, which means that in the near future at least 50 per cent of our front-line officers will be rookies. It takes most officers three years on the job to gain the skills that make them any good at policing. Until this point, they are simply learning how to be a police officer.

This level of inexperience is not good for anyone, and it's likely to lead to very poor standards of investigation and a situation where you have the blind leading the blind. It will also create a major shortage further down the line of the deep skills and experience required to investigate the most complex crimes like terrorism, murder, rape and serious and organised crime. If the police service finds itself overwhelmed by an influx of inexperienced officers, it almost guarantees future miscarriages of justice and potentially higher instances of misconduct and corruption.

I was right in the thick of it when working on mission support because at this time Birmingham had earned the unfortunate reputation as the murder and gun crime capital of the UK, and it was certainly a busy time for us as we tried to keep a lid on the constantly simmering tensions between crime gangs. If it wasn't going off in Birmingham, it was bubbling away in Coventry or Wolverhampton, and it was all driven by the drug markets. I'd seen the horrible effect of drugs my entire police career, and it was definitely getting worse. I think we have to accept that the war on drugs was lost a long time ago. We need to start treating drug addiction as an illness and safely prescribe what people need in certain situations. This would take millions of pounds of revenue away from criminals, reduce crime that is carried out to feed drug habits, improve public health and massively reduce murders. However, I would also like to see much tougher police enforcement against dealers and against so-called recreational drug users who fuel enormous misery, violent crime and the exploitation of vulnerable children.

Will anything change? Probably not. I won't hold my breath because hardly any politician supports the provision of free drugs to drug addicts.

After a year of working as a mission support superintendent, I had assumed that I would stay in the role right to the end of my career after another twelve months, but then an unexpected opportunity presented itself. The force was looking for a superintendent to project-manage a hi-tech data analytics project. This would be a global first for law enforcement, and it involved building an artificial intelligence capability to try to prevent gun and knife crime.

I'd done a lot of work on the technology side of things by this stage, so I knew that I was in with a good chance. So I applied, had an interview and was offered the job.

CHAPTER 23

LAST TWELVE MONTHS

A s I reached what would be my last twelve months of service, it's worth just spending a moment describing what
this felt like.

As you'll now appreciate, a thirty-year police career is full of
ups and downs, laughter, sadness, fear and excitement. It also
takes its toll on your family and your physical and mental health.

As I approached the end of my career, I had very mixed emotions. I felt a huge sense of relief flooding over me that I would
no longer have to deal with things that I knew could go badly
wrong through no real fault of mine, but which could put me
and others in criminal or civil courts for many years. I've always
been a bit of a worrier, and I've seen so many outstanding officers caught up in messy issues and then treated in a way that
they didn't deserve. Often, they were just in the wrong place at
the wrong time or maybe made a decision in good faith that
ended up going horribly wrong. They became victims of an unforgiving 'blame culture' that had infected UK public services.

Over a number of years, I had periodically struggled with
quite severe anxiety. It's hard to know how much of this was

about what I did and saw in the police and how much of it was just me being me. In reality, it was probably a bit of both. I think that, on balance, the things that made me feel particularly anxious were caused by the worry and fear that modern policing generates. Fear of blame. Worrying about complaints. I had never taken any time out because of my anxiety; I had just gone to see the doctor, got sorted out with medication, got on with it and put on a brave face. I never told anyone about this at work, and it's only now that I feel more comfortable admitting it. It was something that I had always felt a bit ashamed of. But now that I'm no longer in the police, I feel that it's important to be more honest. Thankfully, the stigma that goes with struggling with mental health is a lot less of an issue today than it used to be. I know a lot of police officers who have struggled with their mental health, so I'm in good company.

That's what people don't understand about the police. It's generally not the things that you have to deal with that stress you out. It's trying to deal with an atmosphere where you know that if something goes wrong, you'll be hung out to dry by the media, by the courts and by chief officers who will cave into political pressure and won't have your back.

As well as feeling relieved and excited about leaving the force, I was starting to feel quite uncertain about the future. I was planning to start my own business as an advisor to technology companies working with law enforcement, but I had some self-doubt about whether I would be able to make that transition to life in the private sector. Would I be able to run my own business and manage all the financial, contractual and administrative things that I'd never had to do before? Deep down, I think I knew that

I'd be fine and that I'd figure it all out. But, even so, the gremlin of self-doubt was pretty persistent.

In the end, I had very little time to think about it because my new position was going to be very intense and I certainly wasn't going to have the chance to put my feet up for my final twelve months.

The West Midlands Police was, and still is, leading the country in terms of its use of new technology, and in particular its approach to data analytics. This is all about using the most modern data science methods to make sense of the vast quantities of data that all large organisations gather on a day-to-day basis. Historically, this data just sat there stored on some server somewhere doing nothing. People might have dipped into it on a case-by-case basis to find something out or to make a query to answer a single question, but data scientists bring all of that data that has been gathered over many years into one place. They use it to extract a new and better understanding of a particular problem. They will find lots of statistical correlations between different datasets, and they test different theories about what can be inferred. Ultimately, this means that by using data we can now answer questions that would have been impossible to resolve only a few years ago.

In a police context, some of this was about allowing our staff to search every dataset from a single query and thus save a lot of time – for example, pulling out everything we knew as an organisation about a person, a vehicle, an address or a phone number. This was incredibly helpful for intelligence officers and investigators, particularly in the early stages of an investigation when it was unclear what had happened and there were a lot of intelligence gaps that needed filling in. Before having this capability, the police would have had to query ten or twelve different systems, and each would provide part of the answer. It was slow, inefficient, time-consuming and very inconsistent in terms of the results.

However, we had an aspiration to start using this data to build an artificial intelligence capability nationally that would be used to quickly answer all sorts of problems that policing routinely grapples with. The terms 'AI' or 'machine learning' are much bandied about and provoke all sorts of fevered speculation about evil robots or some master computer that will become so intelligent and malign that it will learn to murder us all as we sleep. The reality, of course, is a lot more mundane.

Machine learning is just a new way of understanding the vast quantities of data that our society gathers routinely by automating and accelerating tasks that many human analysts would have worked on previously. These new systems will churn through many terabytes of data and produce answers in seconds rather than days or weeks of human effort. Data scientists will often set out to address a particular problem that an organisation is interested in answering, in an attempt to make that organisation more efficient or improve customer satisfaction. The private sector has been using these techniques for years, but it was all new to policing.

The West Midlands Police made a successful bid for funding to the Home Office to build a 'proof of concept' artificial intelligence capability by using data from multiple partner forces to answer a number of questions. These questions are referred to as 'use cases', and the primary use case was the following:

Can we predict those individuals who are most likely to

commit their first offence of serious violence using a gun or a knife within a short window of time?

The UK was in the midst of an epidemic of knife crime and gun crime, and both Birmingham and London were suffering particularly badly. The loss of dozens of young lives was catastrophic, and those in deprived parts of the inner city were suffering the most. There was an urgent need to try to find innovative solutions. We felt that if we could quickly identify those most at risk as both perpetrators and potential victims, we would be able to save lives by diverting those young men away from this lifestyle by getting other agencies involved. It wasn't about locking them up before they'd done anything; it was about offering them an enhanced level of help and support.

My project was called the 'National Data Analytics Solution', and we were working with a bunch of very clever data scientists from Accenture. I had previously been a bit sceptical about Accenture's involvement with the West Midlands Police, and I tended to regard them as being in the same category as other management consultants that we had dealt with over the years. These companies tended to parachute in a load of kids who were barely out of university. They would then spend weeks creating fancy PowerPoint presentations that either stated the bleeding obvious or completely confused everyone. Finally, they would produce an invoice for an eye-watering amount of money before buggering off, leaving a trail of destruction behind them.

This team, however, were a super-bright, great bunch. I enjoyed working with them, and I was able to teach them a lot about policing in exchange for them teaching me a lot about data analytics. It was a real eye-opener watching them gradually building a capability that we then began to test against over 500 million lines of data going back over twenty years to start extracting some fascinating insights.

I also had the great pleasure of working directly with Deputy Chief Constable Louisa Rolfe, who shortly afterwards was promoted to assistant commissioner in the Met. She was a fantastic boss, and a lovely person to work for.

The project was dogged with headaches that unsurprisingly highlighted many of the things that are currently wrong with policing.

First of all, the Home Office took an age to decide whether the project was going to be funded, delaying everything for months. Once they had allocated the funding, they then insisted that the project needed to be completed by the end of the financial year, which meant that we had only eight months left to complete a massively complex, twelve-month project. The Home Office was insistent that no funding could be carried over to the following year. This is typical of the inflexible culture in the civil service. The Home Office was allocating £4.5 million of taxpayers' money to this project, but they seemed unable to grasp that giving us only eight months to do it, because of their own glacially slow bureaucracy, risked dooming it to failure.

Having finally secured the funding, we got to work, only to find that most of the police forces that signed up to partner on the project refused to give us any data. So, to be clear, this was a publicly funded project to tackle gun and knife crime – the two biggest risks to the public in a generation – and there were police forces refusing to give another police force their data, even though their own chief constables had agreed to join the project. It was unbelievable. One of our partners was the Met, a force that was experiencing a knife-crime epidemic, and yet it too refused point-blank. So why was this?

It was the institutional fear of making a mistake and being held responsible that was to blame – something that has been a recurring theme in this book. The forces were terrified of getting fined for a data breach by the Information Commissioner's Office – the public body that had been set up to enforce data protection legislation, including the new European General Data Protection Regulation legislation that had become law in the UK in 2018. They also refused to provide data to us because we were going to be storing it in a cloud-computing environment, which was something that every corporation and financial institution in the UK had been doing for many years. This proved to be just too much for those forces that had IT policies that were still stuck in the Dark Ages.

Another reason that I suspect the partner forces refused to provide their data was that other curse of UK policing: the 45-force structure in which every force is doing things differently. A kind of sibling rivalry between forces was often a major barrier to cooperation, and there was a mentality that 'if we're not in charge of the game, then we're not playing with you at all'. I'd seen this time and time again in my career when perverse or selfish decisions were made rather than doing what was best for the public. At one point, we had six or seven data protection officers from individual forces in the room and they all had a different understanding of what the law allowed them to do. It was very frustrating, and I wanted to go round the room banging heads together and shout: 'This is people's bloody lives we're talking about here, you bloody idiots!' But I bit my lip and took a deep breath instead.

The next big frustration was the way that the project was misrepresented by the media. Certain outlets were very critical about it and argued that the police would simply use the technology to target and discriminate against certain ethnic groups. Nonetheless, the same journalists were simultaneously wringing their hands about the number of young men killing each other with knives on the streets of our cities. Other publications preferred a different sort of misleading sensationalism and portrayed the project as akin to 'evil police robots' wanting to arrest everyone before they'd even committed a crime. To be fair, there have been some examples of police using technology in a way that had an adverse impact on human rights. A notable example of this happened in 2010 when the counter-terrorism network installed a series of CCTV cameras in predominantly Muslim communities in Birmingham to tackle Islamist extremism. So I can understand that technology has to be used in an appropriate and sensitive way by the authorities. However, law enforcement needs to have the space and the confidence to innovate, and some media commentators have a tendency to see every technical innovation as an attack on human rights rather than an honest effort to protect the wider public from serious harm.

The year absolutely flew by as I found myself travelling all over the UK and was up and down to London for meetings, press interviews and speaking at all sorts of events. Eventually, my final week in policing arrived. I was taken out for a very boozy evening by the Accenture team to say goodbye. However,

I realised that trying to keep up the drinking pace with a bunch of 25-year-olds probably wasn't going to end well, so I made sure that I caught the last train home.

The project had maintained a fairly hectic pace right up to my final day, and I was frantically trying to finish off some reports to the Home Office even in the very last minutes on my last day at work. Then, just before 5 p.m. on Friday 29 March 2019, I logged off my computer for the very last time and sat very quietly for a few moments' reflection. I got up, walked past the reception staff on the ground floor of HQ, said goodbye to them and walked out the door to my wife, who was waiting to take me for dinner.

After thirty years in the police force, I was done.

CHAPTER 24

CAN WE TURN IT AROUND?

It is difficult to describe how it felt to leave the police service after a very intense thirty-year career. I had an extraordinary mixture of emotions.

There was a sense of excitement at starting a new chapter in my life and having the time to do some of the things that I had been looking forward to for years. There was also a sense of exhilaration at no longer being 'owned' by this massive organisation that had routinely controlled everything that I did, and when I did it, encroaching into many aspects of my private life. The police discipline code holds police officers, both on and off duty, to much higher standards of behaviour than arguably any other profession. Police officers regularly lose their jobs and livelihoods as a result of relatively trivial incidents or lapses in judgement that would barely raise an eyebrow in other walks of life. Individual officers and the wider organisation are routinely scapegoated by the media, politicians and the public when things go wrong – which of course they regularly do.

Police officers are also subjected to intense and often unreasonable levels of scrutiny over difficult decisions they made in a split second by teams of lawyers many years after the event. I found that in policing there were many occasions when it was a case of 'heads you lose, tails you lose'. This is the main reason I didn't stay on after I had done my contracted thirty years. I could easily have remained in the force because I was only fifty-three, I was fit and healthy and I was very experienced. However, it had become a fairly thankless occupation and one full of worry that I would find myself blamed for something bad that had happened. I often used to think, 'Why the hell do you keep putting yourself into these risky jobs that stress you out and where you get no thanks for doing it?' I think the answer to that is simple. I took an oath to do just that on 13 February 1989. And I'm proud that I carried on taking those risks right to the end.

Despite this, leaving the police felt like a bereavement. The job is endlessly challenging and fascinating. The camaraderie is incredible and there's frequently a lot of laughter and piss-taking. I also got to do things that were exciting, great fun and sometimes terrifying. The sheer breadth of things that the modern police officer gets involved in is astonishing, and I would challenge any other organisation to offer the same range of career opportunities.

Writing this book has been incredibly cathartic and it has helped me make sense of some of the madness of the past thirty years. Emotionally, I've had some real highs and lows since leaving and perhaps this is all part of the way that the human brain sifts and sorts through everything to help you reset and move forward in life.

So, how do I think we can return the police to something

more like the organisation that I joined without sacrificing all the really positive things that changed for the better over that time and which definitely needed to change?

My first wish would be for our police to be able to exercise a lot more discretion about what they have to deal with. Currently, officers adopt a 'just in case' mindset. They fear that a very trivial issue might escalate into a much more serious one if they don't get involved, and if that happens they worry they'll be blamed. Fear of blame and frivolous litigation affects policing behaviour; however, a lot of this behaviour is also driven by rigid Home Office rules. It is then reinforced by weak senior officers and the police complaints organisation, the IOPC, which is far too keen to throw good people under the bus if they make a mistake.

We need to adopt a much more supportive regime that starts from the understanding that life is messy and often bad things happen for no reason other than the fact that one person has decided to do something bad to someone else. If this happens, it should not automatically be assumed that it was the fault of the police or another public servant. The police are currently expected to intervene in *everything*, which means that they're unable to deal with anything properly. We don't blame GPs or other medical professionals as soon as someone dies because they made a poor lifestyle decision, so why are we so quick to blame the police when someone dies as a result of making a poor life choice or doing something stupid?

The way to make this a reality, rather than a vague aspiration, is to change the Home Office crime recording and incident reporting regime to focus on and prioritise only those offences that cause the greatest harm. Also, if a complainant fails to cooperate with the police, officers should be allowed to disengage quickly rather than waste their time chasing around after them for days on end. I regularly reviewed command and control logs where the police had gone back over ten times to try to track down an uncooperative caller without success. The only exception to this proposal should be if the offence that they are reporting is very serious, or if there is credible evidence to suggest that the victim is exceptionally vulnerable.

The truth is that nobody knows what to believe any more regarding crime statistics. The rather baffling and opaque Crime Survey for England and Wales (CSEW) routinely contradicts the official statistics of recorded crime published by the Home Office. According to the CSEW, crime has steadily dropped since 2011; however, according to Home Office statistics, crime has steadily risen. To further complicate things, the Cambridge Crime Harm Index, created by Professor Larry Sherman of Cambridge University, has adopted a third way of calculating crime by assigning a score to every incident based on the harm that it causes individuals. Using this methodology, Sherman's team calculated that the harm caused by crime in the UK was roughly three times more than either the CSEW or the Home Office statistics in 2019.

So, what are the public meant to make of all this? Are crime levels increasing or decreasing? I don't understand it and I was in the police for thirty years!

The Police Foundation review of policing in 2020 placed a greater emphasis on the Crime Survey for England and Wales data, rather than Home Office data, as a more accurate measurement. This inevitably raises the question as to why such an unbelievable amount of police time and energy is devoted to slavishly adhering to Home Office data rules when it seems that no one (apart from the Home Office) actually believes that the government's figures are accurate.

Traditional types of crime, such as burglary and car crime, have significantly fallen, but they haven't gone away. This means that investigators now need to understand how to investigate those crimes as well as crimes facilitated and enabled by technology. Much violent crime also requires the same old-fashioned investigative skills that I and others learned twenty years ago, but which appear to have been somewhat lost in the modern police force.

The fall in traditional types of crime, such as burglary and car crime, is largely a result of better home and car security devices. However, burglary is now frequently a much more serious and traumatic event for the victims due to the rise in car-key burglaries where criminals will smash their way into a home, threaten or assault the occupants to gain access to their car keys, before stealing the vehicle. Such cars are also stolen by criminals who drag the victims out of their vehicles and assault them when they are stopped at traffic lights or in a supermarket car park. Frequently these high-performance cars are then used by those same criminals in other serious crimes, such as armed robbery, or quickly taken out of the country and sold on by organised crime groups.

It is generally agreed that whilst the volume of less serious 'traditional' crime has fallen, the volume of the most serious crime types has increased. Thus, if you are a victim of crime now it is likely to be a very much more traumatic experience for you.

There has been a 50 per cent increase in crimes involving knives since 2011 and murders have risen by 24 per cent since 2015. Meanwhile, certain chief constables have their poor officers driving around in rainbow-liveried police cars to promote their latest hate-crime initiative and encourage reporting of the dystopian-sounding 'non-crime hate incidents'. Would it be too much to suggest that the police focus on dealing with serious crime before worrying about 'non-crime' incidents?

Interestingly, anti-social behaviour, or 'yobs, yobbing' as it was known in Coventry, has dropped off significantly in the past eight years – aside from in the most deprived neighbourhoods where it still remains a problem. My suspicion is that the internet, and all its distractions, now offers anti-social teenagers something to do rather than hanging around the streets. I also believe that online gaming is a factor in the reduction of low-level crime types, such as criminal damage and public order offences, that went hand-in-hand with anti-social behaviour incidents. I also suspect that the explosion in the availability of cheap and powerful new strains of cannabis and synthetic drugs means that the teenagers, who would previously have been causing these annoying anti-social problems on the streets, are now doing one of three things: they're online playing *Grand Theft Auto* with their mates; they're on Pornhub; or they're completely out of it on skunk cannabis.

So, in terms of crime recording levels, I think we need to start again with a blank sheet of paper. It confuses everyone and the whole process ties the hands of the police up in doing things that no one really cares about.

Secondly, we need to have a grown-up conversation about

what we mean when we talk about 'vulnerability'. The police have become too tied up in dealing with low-level vulnerability in the community and this has created a situation where they no longer have the resources or time to investigate crime. The perception of there being 'vulnerability everywhere' has created a police service that is terrified of failing to protect every single vulnerable person in society. This is just unrealistic. The problem is just too big, and the burden is too heavy to be carried by the police in this way. These problems need to be shared by every public-sector body, which need to be funded properly. We need a long-term strategy to prevent families and communities falling into despair and kids ending up feeling that they have no option other than to join criminal gangs.

Next, from my many years in the police and seeing the impact of a relentless increase in demand on the organisation, I believe that we urgently need a calm, rational, evidence-based, national debate on policing and a rethink on what the role of the British police service is in the twenty-first century. This needs to be completely taken away from the political realm because politicians on both sides of the divide got us into this mess in the first place. Critically, respected figures from within policing itself need to be listened to, because everyone seems to think that they know better than the people who are actually doing the policing on our streets.

What do the public actually want the police to do? Fight crime? Look after mentally ill people? Police the roads? Deal with social-media squabbles? Stop terrorist attacks? Tackle drug dealing and organised crime? Deal with alcoholics and drug addicts sleeping in doorways? What are the priorities for policing?

The answer to this question cannot be 'All of the above' because that's not possible or reasonable.

Next, we need a commitment, that is enshrined in law, to keep politics completely out of policing. Policing should not be treated like a political football that gets kicked all over the place every four years based on whatever a few misguided and uninformed politicians with no understanding of public safety happen to believe. It's far too important for that, and it does nobody any good.

The Labour government created a policing train set and tried to micromanage every tiny detail of what the force did. Dictating the size and colour of every train, the length and width of every piece of track, when the trains were allowed to run, who was allowed to play with the trains and a train timetable that made no sense to anyone. In 2010, the Conservative government came in wearing their size-eleven hobnail boots and took half the train set away, put Tom Winsor in charge of everything and then kicked the trains all over the room.

One of the most basic responsibilities of good government is to keep citizens safe, and Theresa May and the Conservatives failed on that front spectacularly. The irony of it was almost unbearable. There we were in the police, like a bunch of complete mugs, working day and night for years to try to keep the country safe from criminals and terrorists. Putting ourselves in harm's way, submitting ourselves to intrusive vetting procedures to make sure that we were trustworthy, and all the while the government succeeded in damaging Britain's security more than any organised crime group could ever conceive.

Theresa May and her clueless advisors will undoubtedly go to their graves in denial that their unbelievably reckless behaviour ruined policing in the UK and, more importantly, cost the lives of dozens of young men in the inner cities. But every police officer knows the truth of what they did. Will anyone ever hold them accountable? Will they get dragged through the courts for years like police officers do when they make a mistake or they are involved in an incident that ends badly? No.

A de-politicisation of policing would require the abolition of police and crime commissioners, who are aligned to political parties, and the return of some sort of independent body made from a truly representative cross-section of society. Membership of any political party or a criminal record should render an individual ineligible to ensure political independence.

These oversight authorities should be local or regional and, in turn, have their priorities defined by an apolitical national body made up of knowledgeable, non-partisan, experienced professionals, working with senior police representatives, who would set national priorities and allocate budgets according to fact-based assessments of risk. The Chief Inspector of Constabulary would not necessarily need to be a police officer, but without a doubt they would need to be wholly independent of government and unafraid to challenge political interference.

Next, one of my real bugbears. We need to sort out police uniforms and address increasingly lax standards generally. This is a big issue for me, and I think that there must be an improvement in this regard.

There was an image widely circulated in the media recently of several officers from a force in the north of England standing in front of a location where the police had been called to keep the peace. They all looked incredibly scruffy. None of them were wearing a hat, several of them had their hands in pockets, and this, combined with those awful hi-vis jackets, made them look 'like a bunch of security guards on a building site' (in the words of an ex-officer who commented on the thread). It is difficult to understand why this is acceptable, particularly as the place was swarming with journalists and cameras, which guaranteed that they would end up in newspapers and on websites across the world. My own experience of the past ten to fifteen years was that gradually, ever so gradually, police uniforms have become more paramilitary in appearance, and this more casual look has created an increasingly casual and lax attitude amongst officers.

As I have already highlighted, I think that scrapping the height restriction for police officers and adopting almost non-existent fitness requirements for existing officers have conspired, together with the sloppy-looking uniforms, to erode the gravitas and credibility of uniformed police officers in Britain, and thus the respect that they are able to command in the eyes of the public.

A scruffy police officer who hasn't shaved for two days isn't going to command any respect on the street. It is all about projecting a smart, professional appearance to people of every age and social background.

I believe that as the police have adopted a more casual appearance, public respect and trust has declined in response. This increasingly casual appearance has also been accompanied by increasingly casual attitudes amongst PCs towards police supervisors and amongst supervisors towards PCs. Many years ago, the only place you would have called a sergeant by his or her first name was in the pub, and even then I found that hard. For inspectors and above, it was totally unacceptable to call them by their first name. This is no longer the case. This over-familiarity has made it much harder for supervisors to challenge unacceptable behaviour or under-performance. Thus, the cycle of lax standards spirals downwards. I once sent a slovenly PC packing when he came into my office when I was a detective inspector asking to get something signed, when he said to me, 'Excuse me, mate, can you sign this?' I went completely ballistic.

I have no desire to see officers put back in old-style serge trousers that swelled up like cotton wool when they got wet or long greatcoats that made it almost impossible to run. However, there must be a greater balance between practicality and a smart appearance if the police service wants to be taken seriously by the public. If police officers look the part and present a confident, smart, professional appearance, then they can expect greater levels of public respect and trust. However, if they walk about looking (as my father would have said) like eight pounds of shit in a ten-pound bag, then no one is going to respect them.

In my opinion, there needs to be a mandated national police uniform. By all means each force can have its own local badge, but if you see a police officer patrolling in Devon they should look exactly like a police officer patrolling in Newcastle. The organisation is fragmented enough with every force using different systems and with different ways of doing everything. At least if everyone looked the same there would be the appearance of national consistency. It would also enable the service to procure uniforms in one go and get better value for money from suppliers. It can't be that hard.

We also need to have a serious conversation about those

dreadful hi-vis jackets. They look absolutely awful, particularly once they get grimy. The only exception should be for officers on traffic duty or maintaining public order. They're pointless if you want to do any proactive policing – something that seems to have been another casualty of austerity. I will say it again: you can't sneak up on someone when you are wearing a hi-vis jacket!

In addition, traditional custodian helmets should be worn outside at all times. They may not be the most practical thing in the world, but they are the most iconic and reassuring symbol of British policing.

Male officers should either be clean-shaven or have full beards. If they want to grow a beard, they should grow it when they're on holiday. I know that tattoos are a very sensitive subject, and very common in this day and age, but I do think that they should be covered up.

My message to sergeants is this: the PCs are not your mates. You can be friendly and approachable, but when the time comes to give someone a bollocking, you need to be able to do that with confidence. The police is a disciplined service. Allowing officers to wander around with their hands in their pockets and without their hats on is no good for anyone. If the police want the respect of the public, they need to show that they deserve that respect, and with a smart appearance they are halfway there. Finally, let's lose the rainbow lanyards, shoelaces and car liveries. It's patronising and it doesn't build trust in anyone.

Next, the service needs to find much less bureaucratic ways of getting rid of lazy or incompetent officers. Sadly, the culture of entitlement and grievance that is now seen across wider society can also be found in a minority of police officers. This means that challenging bad behaviour, sloppy work or laziness almost inevitably results in some sort of formal grievance procedure, allegations of bullying or repeated periods of sickness and absenteeism.

The systems currently in place for getting rid of lazy or unprofessional police officers are unbelievably bureaucratic, time-consuming and ineffectual. My own experience of trying to put officers through that process resulted in nothing but wasted time, frustration and massive stress. This emboldens other lazy officers, who see that there is almost nothing that the organisation can do to get rid of them. Such officers just get moved on to another department and become someone else's problem. On one occasion, when I was a chief inspector, two of my sergeants became so overwhelmed and worn down by trying to get rid of one particularly disruptive and lazy officer that they ended up getting ill with stress and going off sick. You couldn't make it up.

I have heard rather alarming stories that the long-overdue and fantastically positive mental health message of 'It's OK not to be OK' is now being abused by lazy officers who are basically saying, 'I'm feeling a bit sad today, so, if it's alright, I'm going to have a few days off.' This just heaps more work and pressure onto those who refuse to play this cynical game and consequently *they* end up getting ill.

Speaking as someone who has struggled periodically with severe anxiety when I was a police officer, I completely get it and I'm very relieved that the police are much more aware of mental health issues, and there is definitely more that can be done in this regard. However, managers need to be savvy enough to try to explore the difference between someone who is genuinely in distress and someone who's trying it on. Policing just isn't going to be for everyone. If someone is continually finding it too up-setting and stressful, they definitely need to find a different job more suited to them. There's a contract here. If you do the job and do it well, you'll be fine. However, if you can't or won't do the job, then you probably need to leave the police, otherwise you will become a burden on the organisation and a liability to the public. As anyone who has been diagnosed with a clinical mental health condition will affirm, there's a big difference be-tween feeling unhappy or fed up because of something that's going on in your life and having a clinical mental health prob-lem. Having said this, the police service definitely needs to get a grip of the perennial problem of lazy and work-shy staff. These people are unprofessional and dishonest, and unprofessional and dishonest people shouldn't be in the police.

The next item on my list of suggestions to improve policing would be the abolition of the archaic structure of forty-three forces in England and Wales all doing things differently. At the very most, there should be five or six regional forces with shared resources and common support structures. The police need IT systems that allow them all to work together and exchange in-formation and intelligence instantly, and front-line officers and investigators need to be equipped to deal with digitally enabled crime and internet offending.

Every company that I have worked for as an advisor in the past two years has told me the same thing. They have all com-plained that the police service is the most difficult and frustrat-ing customer imaginable, and many of them have just given up and chosen to work with less troublesome organisations. The service is incredibly bureaucratic and slow and procurement is a nightmare. There is also a worrying tendency for many senior officers to refuse help. Perhaps this is because they think that they should have all the answers. Perhaps they're just too busy to take a step back and think about how they might do things differently. Perhaps they just don't understand what it is that external companies can offer them. What I do know is that the police force is facing a number of genuine challenges that must be overcome. Many of the solutions to these challenges already exist, but senior police decision-makers need to take time out of their busy schedules to think about what can be done to fix the issues in policing once and for all. They need to work out how they can turn the tap off rather than keep mopping the floor.

What tends to happen in most big forces is that they bring in extremely expensive consultancies to try to solve multiple problems in one go and they end up paying far too much money and hardly any of the problems ever get solved. These companies 'land and expand' and before you know it they've parachuted in a small army of inexperienced consultants who know absolutely nothing about policing.

In truth, it would be much better to embrace smaller, innovative suppliers who can quickly solve a specific problem for a fraction of the price using agile methods. Durham and Cumbria police forces demonstrated how this could be done with the 'Red Sigma' crime-fighting platform. Durham cemented its reputation as the most innovative and disruptive force in the UK under its iconoclastic chief constable, Mike Barton. Durham was the only force in the UK that achieved an 'outstanding' grade for effectiveness four years in a row from the Inspectorate of Constabulary. Other forces would do well to swallow their pride and replicate what Durham are doing right.

Next, we need to put an end to the damaging myth that all police officers are racists. As someone who has spent thirty years in the force, it's not true, it's self-defeating and it's not helping to protect our most deprived communities.

Are there some racists in the police? Yes. As is the case in every profession and amongst people from all walks of life. However, my experience is that the overwhelming majority of police officers are good people and they try to treat everyone properly.

As I have explored, in 2020, Professor Larry Sherman showed that young black men are twenty-four times more likely than young white men to be murdered, and they are quite usually murdered by other young black men.

The 2020 'Homicide in England and Wales' report by the Office for National Statistics stated:

> For the three-year period year ending March 2018 to the year ending March 2020, when looking at the principal suspect of a homicide offence, around two-thirds (67 per cent) of suspects convicted of homicide were identified as White. This is a lower representation than in the general population (around 85 per cent). Around one in five (21 per cent) suspects were identified as Black, seven times higher than the general population (3 per cent).

In this desperately sad and depressing scenario, you have a situation where police officers are routinely condemned for 'disproportionately' stopping and searching young black men in the inner cities. What are the police to do?

Accusing the Metropolitan Police of 'institutional racism' has, I believe, condemned many, many young men to an early death in the past twenty years because it has made police officers think twice before intervening in impossibly difficult situations as they know they will probably not be supported by politicians or their own leaders and they will be vilified by the press if something goes wrong.

Rather than blaming the police, we need to start talking about how we can combat crime by helping young people in certain parts of Britain to live positive, fulfilling lives that do not leave them feeling that their only option is to turn to a life of crime and violence. To blame the police for all this is like blaming umbrellas for heavy rain. The police are trying to stop bad things from happening; they need to be supported rather than condemned. Therefore, we need to rebuild the neighbourhood policing structures that were dismantled by Theresa May. We need to start funding youth provision, provide mentors to kids that are going off the rails and return schools-based police officers to support teachers and nip issues in the bud before stabbings make that impossible.

The horrible statistics above arise from a multitude of complex social issues. These include (but are not limited to) long-standing poverty and deprivation, low levels of aspiration and educational attainment, childhood trauma, mental health issues, addiction, a lack of positive family role models, the removal of funding for many front-line youth services and many, many other factors that I am not qualified to talk about.

I believe that parts of the media and certain politicians declared 'open season' on the UK police after the force was branded 'institutionally racist' by Macpherson in 1999. The British police were the best in the world, but the British establishment, with the reckless way in which they have attacked policing, and the media, with their dishonest and selective coverage of events, really don't deserve them.

So, this is what I think needs to change, but what do the typical rank-and-file officers think needs to happen to turn things around in policing?

I am part of a large Metropolitan Police online community group that has over 10,000 members made up of retired and currently serving officers. I asked them what they thought about the current UK policing situation. I do not pretend that this was in any way an academically rigorous survey or that the results would be statistically significant, and I am aware that online community groups do not provide objective or representative opinions, but I was curious what people would say in this most unfiltered of environments. The questions that I asked were:

> Do you actually believe that the job *is* currently fucked? Or do you think that this is just something that the police have always said?

> For those who are still serving or served until recently, what are the two or three things that you would change about policing today to prevent the job becoming totally fucked?

I received hundreds of comments, many of which were sent as private messages, and they were fascinating. There were lots of thoughtful responses as well as dozens of visceral, angry, sweary responses that came as no surprise. I have distilled the comments that I received into the following key recurring themes:

- The police are not in a good place after ten years of cuts with desperately weak leadership and no operational focus.
- Keep politics and politicians out of policing.
- Rebuild community policing teams because they worked.
- Police leaders need to stop trying to appease the 'woke' vociferous minority. They do not speak for the majority of citizens in the UK.
- The police are now unable to deal properly with crime because they are too busy dealing with trivia and things that should not be the responsibility of the police, like issues relating to mental illness and the protection of the vulnerable.
- Basic investigative skills and proactive street policing skills have been lost. We need to get basic policing skills right.
- Serving officers are fearful and have little confidence that they will be supported by the organisation or by the media.
- The changes that Theresa May made to terms and conditions of employment will ensure that people do not stay in policing for very long, and this will gradually erode the deep skills and experience necessary to deal with the most complex and serious types of crime.
- The promotion process at every rank is seen as favouring only those who can talk the talk, and operational competence, or experience, is not required or recognised.
- There is a deep sense of weariness at constant internal change, much of which is perceived to be done to enhance someone's

promotion prospects, and anyone who challenges unnecessary change is dismissed as being 'negative'.

- Senior officers should stop apologising when officers have done nothing wrong and publicly speak up for them.
- Local officers should work from local police stations and be deployed to jobs by local control room staff who know the area and the local problems.
- Deviating from policy or making a mistake should not always be treated as a disciplinary issue. It should be treated as an opportunity for learning.
- Operational discipline and behavioural standards should be restored. There is far too much familiarity shown towards sergeants and inspectors.
- Uniforms are scruffy and do not inspire respect.
- Make it easier to get rid of lazy or ineffectual officers at all ranks, including senior officers.
- Bring back police canteens. These were seen as a welcome oasis of rest, banter, team spirit and camaraderie.
- Bring back proper police training schools and physical street duties tutoring. Online and distance learning does not prepare people for the rigours of the job.
- Stop treating stop and search as a political issue. It's a common-sense policing tactic that deters people from carrying drugs, weapons and articles used to commit crime in public.
- Senior officers should cease their virtue-signalling on social media. Social media should only be used for community reassurance and for operational purposes and not shameless self-promotion and sucking up to senior managers.

There was an approximate 60/40 split between the majority who felt that the job was now properly fucked and those who thought that this was just something that had always been said.

*   *   *

The Metropolitan Police Service was founded by Sir Robert Peel in 1829 as the world's first-ever professional police force. Ever since that time, the Peelian principles have guided the style and ethos of British policing. In an attempt to highlight the underlying issues that the UK police force faces today, I have taken those nine original Peelian principles and re-written them to reflect the depressing reality of policing in Britain in 2021.

PEELIAN PRINCIPLES 1829 VS 2021

1829
The basic mission for which the police exist is to prevent crime and disorder.

2021
The basic mission for which the police exist is to gather data for the Home Office and to run around after time-wasters who can't sort their lives out.

1829
The ability of the police to perform their duties is dependent upon public approval of police existence, actions and behaviour.

2021

The ability of the police to perform their duties is dependent upon the approval of a small minority of noisy activists, self-appointed 'community leaders' and the media.

1829

The police must secure the willing cooperation of the public in voluntary observance of the law to be able to secure and maintain the respect of the public.

2021

The police must secure the willing cooperation of the public once they figure out all the terrible legislation that has been dreamt up by politicians, which means that no one has the foggiest idea of what they are or what they are not allowed to do.

1829

The degree of cooperation of the public that can be secured diminishes proportionately to the necessity of the use of physical force.

2021

The degree of cooperation of the public diminishes proportionately to the use of micro-aggressions by the police or failing to ask nicely.

1829

The police seek and preserve public favour not by pandering to public opinion but by constantly demonstrating absolute impartial service to the law and by ready offering of individual service and friendship to all members of the public without regard to their wealth or social standing.

2021

The police must ignore public opinion by constantly pandering to whoever shouts the loudest and by offering friendship to everyone, including criminals, who are misunderstood and sometimes just need a hug.

1829

The police use physical force to the extent necessary to secure observance of the law or to restore order only when the exercise of persuasion, advice and warning is found to be insufficient.

2021

The police use physical force to the extent necessary to guarantee they go viral on YouTube and are then publicly shamed by all news outlets.

1829

The police, at all times, should maintain a relationship with the public that gives reality to the historic tradition that the police are the public and the public are the police; the police being only members of the public who are paid to give full time attention to duties which are incumbent on every citizen in the interests of community welfare and existence.

2021

The police, at all times, should maintain a relationship with the public that gives reality to the fact that the police are now exactly the same as the public in that, just like most of the public, they rarely arrest anyone, they don't investigate crime and they avoid getting into confrontation if at all possible.

1829

The police should always direct their actions strictly towards their functions and never appear to usurp the powers of the judiciary.

2021

The police should always direct their actions strictly towards their functions of gathering data for the Home Office rather than troubling the judiciary with tiresome and complicated criminal prosecutions.

1829

The test of police efficiency is the absence of crime and disorder, not the visible evidence of police action in dealing with it.

2021

The test of police efficiency is an 'excellent' rating for data-quality compliance and is achieved through compulsory unconscious bias training for all managers and selling off as many police stations as possible.

CHAPTER 25

DO I THINK THAT THE JOB IS ACTUALLY FUCKED?

S o, finally, the $64,000 question: do I personally think the job is *actually* fucked?

On balance, I don't think that the job is fucked. Not just yet anyway. Rather, I think it's certain parts of 21st-century British society that are fucked. The police are out there twenty-four hours a day, trying their best to fix a lot of things in society that are broken. But this has become completely impossible because so many barriers have been put in their way. They've been badly let down by some terrible leaders who have put their own selfish career ambitions before the best interests of the organisation or the public and by politicians on both sides of the political divide – particularly those since 2010.

What has happened to British policing is a cautionary tale about what happens to a public-sector organisation responsible for dealing with the lives of real people in the real world when politicians with no understanding of what they are messing around with are given free rein. During my time in the service, the police suffered at the hands of a generation of 'professional politicians' from both sides, who had very little experience of life outside the Westminster bubble where personal competence and integrity were (and sadly still are) in very short supply. It was a triumph of expediency over individual and collective integrity and accountability.

It is like the organisation has been in a terrible car crash, which has caused multiple injuries, and it requires a long convalescence and many years of reconstructive surgery. At this moment in time, the victim has been cut out of the wreckage and is being tended to by paramedics, but there's a very long way to go yet. I sincerely hope that the British police can turn things around and return to being the best service in the world.

Boris Johnson's promise to recruit an additional 20,000 cops over the next three years, despite the fact that there are 30,000 who are due to retire, could temporarily make things worse. This is going to swamp the organisation with very inexperienced officers who, for their first two years, will be a bit clueless and who will be trained and mentored by officers with very little service who are only slightly less clueless. This is not a great combination, and unfortunately it will probably result in some pretty major screw-ups and miscarriages of justice. When my generation of police officers joined, we were tutored by officers who were long in service and super-experienced, and they were generally very good at passing on their knowledge.

It's always amazed me that the police service makes almost no effort at all to retain experienced officers who decide to resign or, for that matter, try to capture and pass on the knowledge and learning of the most experienced officers to those who need that knowledge. I'm very fortunate now that I can work with a range of hi-tech commercial innovators to build technical solutions to help law enforcement. However, for every one of me there are many thousands of experienced officers who leave the service and have no means of putting anything back into policing to help inexperienced officers. Whilst most retired officers have no desire to be rolling around in the gutter fighting drug-dealers any more, many of them would like to be able to put *something* back into policing. I think we need to find ways to help them do that, without tying them up in red tape.

Another big concern for me in this development is corruption. Mercifully, the British police force is relatively free of corruption, and those officers who are corrupt get found out, investigat ed and kicked out quite quickly. However, when there is pressure to recruit large numbers of officers very quickly to meet government targets, corners will inevitably be cut and standards will be lowered. Police leaders and HR departments will deny that this is the case, of course, but it is inevitable.

We have known for years that organised crime groups and terrorist organisations are constantly trying to covertly infiltrate the police. They will identify young, ostensibly 'clean' associates, who have no criminal record, that are loyal to them. Then, they will deliberately try to plant these people into the police to act as their eyes and ears, to pass on intelligence and assist them. This obviously poses a massive risk to the organisation. The UK forces need to be incredibly careful that the pressure to recruit in order to hit targets does not open the door to future criminals in uniform.

Another very unhelpful legacy of the muddled and misguided Conservative 'reforms' of policing was the insistence that every new police constable has to obtain a degree either before joining or as part of the training. A university degree does not in any way equip new officers for the realities of operational policing. I was a graduate when I joined and I actually think it was more of an impediment than a help. I over-intellectualised things and it took me much longer to tune into the world of criminals and the dysfunctional characters that the police routinely deal with than my colleagues who had more general life experience before they joined. Many of the very best police officers that I worked with over the years were not graduates and having a degree would not have made them any better at doing what is an intensely practical job that requires loads of common sense and life experience. Expecting non-graduate officers to study for a degree whilst training is also a massive waste of time and money that would be better spent keeping the public safe.

I started writing this book six months before a global pandemic changed the world. At the time, things were looking up for policing. Theresa May had started a new life confined to the back benches of the House of Commons and Boris Johnson had pledged to recruit 20,000 officers to replace those lost over the previous ten years. There were also encouraging signs of significant investment across the public sector generally and everyone was hopeful that policing had turned a corner. But, of course, those hopes have now been dashed. Covid-19 has ensured that Britain will enter another period of financial restraint, and the government is once again talking the language of austerity.

The policing minister Kit Malthouse set out some priorities for policing outcomes for 2021/22 on 17 December 2020, which included the following:

1. Recruit 6,000 officers towards the 20,000 target.
2. Make £120 million of efficiency savings.
3. Collect more and better data.

This simply underlines how out of touch the Home Office are with policing and the needs of the public. There was no talk of catching criminals or improving the response to new crime types that involve technology.

The government want to recruit 6,000 officers, but if they were honest they'd admit that at least 10,000 officers need to be recruited just to replace those leaving in 2021 *in addition to* the extra 6,000. 'Efficiency savings' should simply be read as more police stations being closed and sold off. And data? Seriously? The Home Office loves a bit of data. It has become the benchmark for police efficiency. Not criminals arrested and prosecuted. Not preventing people from becoming victims of crime. Not knives and guns being taken off the streets or kids rescued from County Lines gangs. We need data. More data.

Public confidence and trust in policing has fallen off slightly in the past few years, but I would argue that this is because of a relentlessly negative narrative from politicians and the media. However, despite this, it still remains very high, which gives me much hope.

Every year, Ipsos MORI survey a representative cross-section of British adults and ask the same question: 'How much do you trust the following professions to tell the truth?' This survey has been repeated in much the same format every year since 1983, and the results completely contradict the standard narrative made by journalists and politicians about the police. If only

15 per cent of the public trust politicians, only 23 per cent trust journalists, whereas 71 per cent trust the police, why is the police service painted so negatively in the media? Interestingly, trust in policing has improved more or less continuously since around 2008. Yet, if you listened to the dominant media narrative of negativity, you would think that no one trusts the police.

However, having said that, the horrific murder of Sarah Everard in March 2021 by serving Met officer Wayne Couzens sent shockwaves through policing and the public. This was an abhorrent murder for so many reasons. However, the most shocking aspect of Sarah's death was the fact that the person who had conceived, planned and meticulously prepared for her abduction, rape and murder was a police officer. Her killer was someone who had taken a solemn oath to protect the public and he had turned out to be nothing but a predatory and murderous sexual deviant in uniform.

Every decent police officer in the UK, past and present, was appalled by Sarah's murder, and many of us just couldn't understand how it was that Couzens had slipped through the net and become a serving officer in the Met. Even more worryingly, he had been given a gun as a diplomatic protection officer and had been the subject of a complaint of indecent exposure prior to the murder. Clearly, something had gone badly wrong with the vetting process in recruiting Couzens.

Following Sarah's murder, the fallout for the Met was unbelievably painful. However, things went from bad to worse after a vigil was held in Sarah's memory on Clapham Common. The force was widely criticised for the way officers responded to the gathering when trying to enforce Covid-19 restrictions on the public gathering. A later review of the handling of the vigil concluded that the event was hijacked by a small but vociferous group of activists who were determined to draw the police into a confrontation. During the review, one female police officer stated:

> During the incident, I distinctly remember multiple women coming up to me … wishing I was raped, with one female saying words to the effect of: 'I hope you get raped, so you know what it's like.' Another woman also said words to the effect of: 'I hope you get murdered and that your face is all over the news once you've been murdered.'

The media coverage of the event focused only on the flashpoint involving these activists and showed nothing of the many hours of sympathetic, supportive engagement with the thousands of people who had come to pay their respects to Sarah before the trouble started. I believe that the Met should have discreetly withdrawn from the vigil and let the event go ahead because what resulted was a situation that was impossible for the police to deal with. It was inevitable that trying to impose vague and unenforceable Covid-19 regulations would lead to a public back-lash for the force. However, I cannot criticise the senior officer who ultimately made the call on that night because I wasn't there. Like so many other positions that the police find them-selves in, it was a lose–lose situation.

It has been another dreadful year for UK policing and for the Met in particular. The impact of all of the things that I have described in this book has been compounded by a global pandemic during which the police have been required to enforce constantly changing regulations with confusing and ambiguous guidance from central government. Police officers were given no special status in terms of vaccine prioritisation despite the fact that many of them were being exposed to Covid-19 twenty-four hours a day. The requirement for many officers and staff to self-isolate after coming into contact with someone who tested positive for the virus then put even more pressure on resources that were already stretched to breaking point. This put the service on another collision course with the government and, in July 2021, the Police Federation declared it had no confidence in Home Secretary Priti Patel after an announcement that there would be a pay freeze for police officers in 2022. Further insult added to injury.

The Clapham Common vigil incident, and before that the 'Kill the Bill' disorder in Bristol as well as anti-lockdown and anti-vaccination protests, illustrated how it has now become almost impossible for the police to engage in any meaningful way with political activists and protest groups. In many ways, these incidents reflect a more widespread contemporary culture in which certain ideas have become weaponised by a small minority to create as much conflict and division in society as possible.

In so much public discourse it has become almost impossible for anyone to have a calm, rational debate about certain issues because a minority of vociferous people see everything as being based on a set of binary choices. If anyone dares to disagree with their views on gender, sexuality, economics, politics or anything else they're shouted down, cancelled, bullied on social media and likened to fascists. These new authoritarians, with their humourless sense of moral superiority and faux outrage, are stifling debate. For them, no one will ever be ideologically pure enough or sufficiently committed to the cause of social justice. They don't see the irony that this sort of extreme intolerance logically ends in tyranny.

On the other side of the political divide, we see the worst sort of right-wing populism, bigotry and intolerance where outsiders and migrants are likened to vermin. This faction doesn't care that Britain is one of the most diverse nations on earth and that without migrants our country would be infinitely worse off. We have a proud history of welcoming refugees and persecuted minorities. Without migrants, we would lose hundreds of thousands of highly qualified professionals, and the truth is that most of those who are British and unemployed would refuse to do the jobs done by migrants.

But here's the thing. Neither side speaks for the majority because most people don't think or behave like this. The majority of people in Britain are reasonable, sensible and law-abiding. I truly believe that this is the case. My thirty years of policing have not left me bitter or cynical about human nature; quite the opposite. I have an overwhelming belief and trust in the essential goodness of the majority of people in Britain, but the reality is that they're silent too much of the time and they've got to stop being silent. By not speaking up they're allowing the unreasonable people who shout the loudest to shape government policy and destroy some of our greatest institutions.

Everyone's trying to navigate their own reality and everyone's reality is unique to them, which is why binary belief systems are so dangerous. It's quite possible, and arguably more psychologically healthy, to be 'a bit right-wing' on some issues and 'a bit left-wing' on others. Many of the people I worked with in Special Branch had some very strong views that might have been perceived to be quite left-wing or anti-establishment, but the thing that bound us all together was a strong belief in the democratic process.

Police officers have to navigate, understand and deal with everyone's reality – and it's rarely a happy reality for them in that moment when they call the police. No one ever rings the police to tell them about something really brilliant that has just happened to them. Continually dealing with everyone's pain and trauma is hard, and it can feel thankless. This is probably why so many police officers marry fellow members of the emergency services, because they are one of the few groups of people who also 'get it'. Like police officers, they see the very best and the very worst of humanity, and sometimes in the same person, in a single day.

Comfortable, middle-class, Western lifestyles have created generations of opinion formers who have never suffered trauma or encountered first-hand the reality that life can be incredibly hard, difficult and unfair. These so-called chattering classes have been too quick to judge the actions of police officers and other public servants who routinely have to deal with ambiguity, chaos and violence.

I have been quite critical about the upper echelons of policing over the past ten to fifteen years. I don't believe that any of these police leaders are bad people. Most of them are very decent people and many of them are also extremely competent. However, they have displayed a depressing enthusiasm for trying to appease a vociferous minority of critics who are frankly never going to be happy about the police and should just be politely ignored.

There have also been some truly exceptional leaders in policing in the past thirty years. Sir Peter Imbert, Sir John Stevens and Dame Cressida Dick are examples of Met commissioners who have been respected and loved by pretty much everyone who ever worked for them. As the current commissioner of the Met, Cressida Dick is an inspirational leader, but she has had the political odds very much stacked against her. She has a fantastic mind and has shown herself to be at the top of her game in every role that she has performed at every rank. She also manages to be a thoroughly nice person and has an impressive ability to remember all sorts of people that she met only briefly many years before. She has occasionally received criticism for appearing to be weak on some contentious issues but, in reality, she's been managing an impossibly difficult situation. We definitely need more leaders like Cressida Dick, and we definitely need to stop listening to some of the dreadful police leaders who helped to get us into this mess.

But overall, more than anything, the British police service now needs a new, clearer mission. The force needs to move forward in a way that ensures that the hard, painful lessons from the past are not forgotten but, at the same time, the focus is on tackling the issues that are really important to the average, law-abiding person in the street.

In turn, lawyers, politicians and the media need to lay off the police and stop blaming them every time something goes wrong. Things go wrong in life. They always have and they always will.

Hanging some poor copper out to dry doesn't help anyone. It just demoralises the people who are out there trying to do their best in difficult circumstances.

A report published by Police Oracle in December 2020 showed that in the eight years between 2011 and 2019, a total of 169 police officers committed suicide. This is double the rate of suicide in the general population. This depressing statistic is the result of a number of factors that collectively conspire to make so many police officers kill themselves.

Firstly, encountering human trauma and dealing with complete arseholes every day and then having to try to adjust back to normal life at home with family and friends can be very stressful. Then, there is the impact of working horribly anti-social hours and having rest days and holidays cancelled at short notice. This has a massive impact on families and social lives, as well as screwing up the human body clock. I lost count of the number of significant family and social events that I missed as a result of working in the police: Christmases, school sports days, nativity plays, birthday parties and celebrations. I can also remember many times when I nearly crashed my car driving home after night duty when I momentarily fell asleep at the wheel. Finally, I think that many of the things that I have described in this book have a cumulatively serious impact on the mental health of officers: unsupportive and out-of-touch senior managers, a culture of blame, a hostile political environment and a hostile media.

Exposure to human trauma is obviously unavoidable in the police, and the UK will always have its fair share of arseholes. Equally, there will always be a requirement for 24/7 shift work in the emergency services. However, there is a lot that *can* be done about the quality of senior managers, the support offered to operational police officers and challenging clueless politicians. The media could also adopt a less hostile approach to police reporting.

I was unbelievably fortunate to spend thirty years of my life working with some inspirational, clever, brave and funny people who did some amazing things. Right now, at this very moment, there is a police officer somewhere in the UK who is walking into a situation with no idea whatsoever of what they are going to see or what they are going to have to deal with. But deal with it they must because they know that no one else is going to.

Everyone needs to remember that police officers are just ordinary people doing an extraordinary, frequently chaotic and often dangerous job. They have been treated pretty badly over many years and they deserve so much more support than they have received.

Most importantly, however, as a member of the public you have a fundamental human right to feel safe. Police officers are the only people who get paid to keep you safe day and night, seven days a week. They're doing that for you, and you deserve so much better.

APPENDIX

THE UK POLICE SERVICE – HOW DOES IT WORK?

POLICE RANKS

I think it's worth explaining the rank structure of the UK police service. What follows is a basic guide for the different policing positions and where they fit in the hierarchy of the UK police service.

POLICE CONSTABLE

This is the entry point for the overwhelming majority of people in the service. I say majority because there is now a 'direct entry process' that allows a small number of people to enter directly at either inspector or superintendent rank.

The police constable rank comprises about 80 per cent of the officers in the service nationally, and many PCs will stay at this rank their entire service, moving around laterally to do a variety of roles in a variety of departments. Those with a hankering and aptitude to investigate crime will become detective constables, and it is not unusual for someone to move to and fro between uniformed and detective roles, particularly if they're successful in promotion processes and move up the ranks. Uniformed PCs and sergeants wear epaulettes with their shoulder number printed in silver lettering. In the Met, my collar number was 233, and when I transferred to the West Midlands they gave me a new shoulder number of 0341, which took me a while to adjust to. In the Met, PCs also have their local divisional two-letter call sign above the number. So, in my case, as I worked in Clapham, I was LM 233.

SERGEANT

This is the first rung on the supervisory ladder in the police service and in my view the most crucial supervisory rank. A good sergeant is worth their weight in gold. The best ones have complete integrity: they lead by example, drive performance, motivate staff, create an enjoyable environment to work in and get the best out of their team. A weak, lazy or bullying sergeant will do the exact opposite. Those who investigate crime have the title detective sergeant. PCs or DCs typically refer to their sergeant as 'Sarge'; however, in London they are also referred to as 'Skipper', which is sometimes shortened to 'Skip'. In some forces, including the West Midlands, where I spent the second half of my thirty-year service, sergeants are often referred to as the 'Stripe', on the basis that they wear the three sergeants' stripes on their shoulder epaulettes.

INSPECTOR

This is the first rank where one could accurately be termed a 'manager' in the police service. They typically lead teams of four or five sergeants and perhaps anything between twenty and fifty constables. They are generally uniformed inspectors or detective inspectors, but there are lots of other niche roles where inspectors may not fall neatly into either of those categories. These roles may involve working with partner agencies, managing violent offenders or sex offenders in the community and lots of other things that the police now do, but which the public are probably unaware of. Male inspectors are addressed as 'Sir' by their staff and female inspectors as 'Ma'am', although typically both sexes are addressed simply as 'Boss'. There are again regional variations – in London, inspectors (and above) are frequently addressed as 'Guvnor', which is often shortened to 'Guv'. In the West Midlands and many northern forces, they tend to refer to inspectors and above as 'Gaffer'. I always knew when I was talking to a fellow ex-Met officer in the West Midlands because they would refer to me as 'Guv', which made me smile. Uniformed inspectors wear epaulettes on their shoulders with two silver pips.

CHIEF INSPECTOR

This is the first rung on the senior management ladder, and chief inspectors or detective chief inspectors will sit as a member of the local or departmental senior leadership team or senior management team. This is widely perceived to be one of the most thankless ranks in the police service as chief inspectors carry a great deal of risk and responsibility but get paid barely more than an inspector. In my first chief inspector role, I managed ten inspectors, about twenty sergeants and about 150 constables and members of police staff. Uniformed chief inspectors wear epaulettes with three silver pips and are addressed in the same way as inspectors by their staff.

SUPERINTENDENT

Superintendents carry a lot of responsibility and frequently this is where the buck stops organisationally. That is not to say that ranks above and below do not carry risk, because they all do, but I would argue this based on the breadth and seriousness of the decisions that superintendents frequently have to make. A typical superintendent will either manage the day-to-day delivery of local operational policing or manage a large central department with responsibility for many members of staff. They operate at both a strategic and an operational level and in addition to the day job they have the authority (provided the necessary legal conditions are met) to make decisions that can have a significant impact on the lives of private citizens. For example, they can authorise someone to be kept in custody beyond the statutory period of twenty-four hours. They can authorise covert surveillance on an individual or an address and they can authorise the acquisition of telecoms data and internet data to progress a criminal investigation. A good superintendent, with the obligatory few grey hairs, will know a hell of a lot and will be able to draw upon the learning from a long career in policing to support their staff and make difficult decisions. Perhaps this is why there appears to have been such a high drop-out rate amongst the new direct-entry superintendents since 2016. Superintendents wear a silver crown emblem on their epaulettes.

CHIEF SUPERINTENDENT

Officers at this rank have overall responsibility either for an individual geographical command unit delivering policing services or a central corporate department. Most of the forty-three forces in England and Wales operate fairly similarly, with obvious differences in size. Some forces are massive, like the Met, West Midlands and Greater Manchester, and some are tiny, like Warwickshire or Durham.

In the West Midlands, we had eight geographical command units, all of which were run by a chief superintendent. We had Birmingham West, Birmingham East, Coventry, Solihull, Wolverhampton, Walsall, Sandwell and Dudley. In addition, we also had chief superintendents responsible for the following departments:

- Response department, which managed all emergency calls 24/7.
- Force operations, which managed firearms, dogs, traffic, public order and searching.
- Investigations department (or CID).
- Public protection unit, which investigated child abuse, domestic abuse and offences against vulnerable adults.
- Force contact, which dealt with all of the incoming 999 and non-emergency calls for service, emails and visits to police stations.
- Force intelligence, which gathered, analysed and disseminated intelligence relating to criminality and supported complex investigations.
- Criminal justice department, which staffed the custody suites (cell blocks) and ensured that the criminal justice system and courts got what they need for prosecutions.
- Complaints, discipline and anti-corruption unit (sometimes referred to as the professional standards department).

Chief superintendents generally tend not to get massively involved in the day-to-day running of their command units, leaving this to their superintendents and chief inspectors. They operate at a more strategic level and spend a lot of time meeting with senior representatives from partner agencies and community representatives (e.g. MPs, local authorities, health and education bodies). They get involved in areas of cross-departmental policy and issues impacting on the wider force. Chief superintendents wear epaulettes with a silver crown emblem and a single silver pip above it.

CHIEF OFFICERS

The most senior officers in the police are collectively referred to as 'chief officers' and the titles are the same everywhere in the UK apart from the Met.

The first rank on the ladder is assistant chief constable, a rank referred to as commander in the Met. They can be recognised by the circular, silver bay leaf wreath on their epaulettes.

Next comes deputy chief constable, referred to as a deputy assistant commissioner in the Met. They can be recognised by the bay leaf wreath with a single silver pip above it on their epaulettes.

Then we have the chief constable rank, the Met equivalent being assistant commissioner. They wear the bay leaf wreath with a silver crown above it.

Finally, in the Met, they have a commissioner, who, because of the size of the Met, is even more senior than a chief constable. The commissioner wears the same emblems on their shoulder as a chief constable but with the addition of a single silver pip.

The chief officers of each force work as a team (or, in some dysfunctional forces, actively against one another) and have either wide-ranging geographic or thematic responsibilities. Typically, in a force, you will have one assistant chief constable responsible for all of the geographic command units, one responsible for crime and public protection and one for everything else. The deputy chief constables tend to oversee the performance of the force in the widest sense as well as professional standards and organisational change or business improvement programmes and the chief constable is ultimately responsible for everything.

POLICE AND CRIME COMMISSIONERS

Police and crime commissioners (PCCs) were an unwelcome gift to the police service from David Cameron when he was Prime Minister. PCCs are elected to the role, which sounds great in theory; however, when it all started in 2012, the electoral turnout was woefully poor, and in some regions it was as low as 10 per cent. In 2016, average voter turnout was still only about 27 per cent, which was hardly a ringing endorsement of the successful candidates. The calibre of many of these PCCs has been poor and they all have different priorities, which brings them into conflict with chief constables, who have a completely different set of priorities mandated by the Home Office.

PCCs usually align themselves with a particular political party. Thus, they inevitably see the world through a short-term political lens rather than prioritising what is best for individual victims of crime, regardless of age, gender, ethnicity or postcode.

You've probably guessed by now that I'm not a massive fan of

PCCs. We were blessed with a great one in West Midlands but sadly they're not all like him.

UK POLICE STRUCTURES

The sorry truth is that if someone were given the task today of devising the most inefficient structure for UK policing, they would be hard-pressed to come up with something worse than what we currently have with the forty-three different forces in England and Wales. There are forty-five if you include Police Scotland and the Police Service of Northern Ireland. Every force does things slightly differently and is funded slightly differently. On top of that, there is a motley collection of PCCs adding to the confusion.

As well as having a costly command team of chief officers for every force, there is also a lot of wasted money and duplication of effort in running forty-three separate finance departments, IT teams, HR departments and all sorts of other functions. These functions could and arguably should be delivered more effectively from a smaller number of regional hubs.

Certain policing activities are delivered regionally, like counter-terrorism and serious and organised crime. The counter-terrorism units and the regional organised crime units are funded and managed differently to the forty-three forces, but they still draw their staff from those forces.

Finally, there are the odds and sods of policing. These are police units that have a particular mandate and generally do not have the full range of policing powers outside those locations or functions. One of these is the British Transport Police, which is funded by the rail network. It is responsible for the safety of trains and stations. There is also the Ministry of Defence Police, which maintains the security of Ministry of Defence establishments. Finally, there is the Civil Nuclear Constabulary, which maintains the safety of nuclear facilities and nuclear materials in transit.

ACKNOWLEDGEMENTS

Thank you to my wife Kay for her constant love and support in everything that I do and for picking me up several times when I was falling down. Thank you to my four beautiful kids, Ellen, Jamie, Eve and Sam, for understanding that many times Dad couldn't be with you because he was busy 'catching the naughty men'. Thank you to my brother Steve for inspiring me to join the police in the first place. Thank you to some amazing police officers who I had the greatest privilege to work with along the way. That list is very, very long but you know who you are. You represent the very best qualities that this country has to offer and even if many people in positions of power or influence don't understand that, I do. Thank you to so many of my lovely friends who encouraged me to write this book, particularly Lou Crane and Val Murray. Finally, thank you to my editor James Lilford for his enthusiasm, professionalism and wisdom.